WILDLAND SENTINEL

A BUR OAK BOOK

Holly Carver, series editor

WILDLAND SENTINEL

FIELD NOTES FROM AN
IOWA CONSERVATION OFFICER

— Erika Billerbeck —

UNIVERSITY OF IOWA PRESS • IOWA CITY

University of Iowa Press, Iowa City 52242
Copyright © 2020 by the University of Iowa Press
www.uipress.uiowa.edu
Printed in the United States of America

Artwork throughout by Erika Billerbeck
Design by April Leidig

Printed on acid-free paper

Library of Congress Cataloging-in-Publication Data
Names: Billerbeck, Erika, 1974– author.
Title: Wildland Sentinel: Field Notes from an Iowa
Conservation Officer / by Erika Billerbeck.
Description: Iowa City: University of Iowa Press, [2020] | Series: A Bur Oak Book |
Identifiers: LCCN 2020006505 (print) | LCCN 2020006506 (ebook) |
ISBN 9781609387143 (paperback) | ISBN 9781609387150 (ebook)
Subjects: LCSH: Billerbeck, Erika, 1974– | Conservationists—Iowa—
Biography. | Wildlife conservation—Iowa.
Classification: LCC QH31.B493 A3 2020 (print) | LCC QH31.B493 (ebook) |
DDC 333.72092 [B]—dc23
LC record available at https://lccn.loc.gov/2020006505
LC ebook record available at https://lccn.loc.gov/2020006506

For Mom and Dad

CONTENTS

AUTHOR'S NOTE

THIS BOOK IS ROOTED in incident reports, notes, body camera footage, and memory. While memories are not infallible, I've done my best to reconstruct the events as well as I am able, at times conferring with colleagues who were involved. Conversations and quotations are written to clarify and enliven the story. Some quotations are verbatim; others are paraphrased.

Law enforcement investigations are all too often fraught with wild goose chases, multiple interviews, and dead ends. To avoid confusing the reader, some stories have been streamlined. In most cases, names and identifying characteristics have been changed to protect the privacy of those involved.

A few stories in this book appeared in a different style or structure in the *Wapsipinicon Almanac* or in *Iowa Outdoors Magazine,* for which I wrote the "Warden's Diary" column for several years.

ACKNOWLEDGMENTS

THIS BOOK WOULD NOT EXIST if not for the critical (sometimes, brutally so) editorial eye of my mom and the steadfast support of my dad, who has always encouraged me to write. Thank you to my husband, Tom, for putting up with the hours I spent staring at the computer screen instead of cleaning the house. And to my children, Andi and Silas. You are the reason I want to come home every day. And you are the reason I wrote this book.

Many thanks to Holly Carver for taking my manuscript to the next level and for giving it a home with the wonderful folks at the University of Iowa Press. A special thank you to Carter Johnson for introducing me to Holly and to Tim Fay and Jody McKee, who took the time to read earlier versions of this book and to offer their critiques and encouragement.

Finally, I want to express gratitude for those who have made this book possible. Without the users of our public lands and waters, and my coworkers and seasonal officers who have walked the thin green line to serve and protect them, I wouldn't have a story to tell. Thank you to the deputies with the Johnson County Sheriff's Department and to the troopers with the Iowa State Patrol who have come to my aid on numerous occasions. To those who inspire me and have always had my six, both physically and mentally—Nick Rocca, Travis Graves, Aric Sloterdyk, Meleah Droll, and Chuck Humeston—thank you.

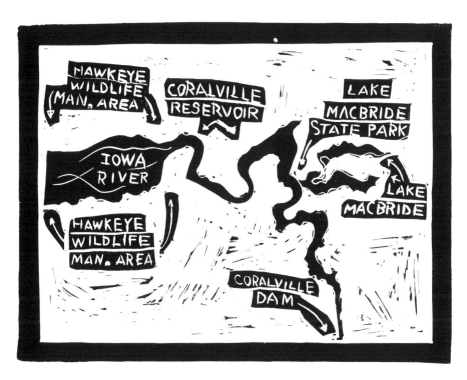

—BEGINNING—

"Competencies required: Knowledge of procedures and objectives of fish and game enforcement and management programs. Knowledge of conservation principles and practices necessary to promote and operate a conservation program. Knowledge of state and federal fish and game laws. Ability to enforce all laws and regulations as required. Ability to operate an automobile. Ability to work outside in all types of weather conditions. Ability to withstand occasional strenuous work. Displays high standards of ethical conduct. Exhibits honesty and integrity. Refrains from theft-related, dishonest or unethical behavior. Works and communicates with internal and external clients and customers to meet their needs in a polite, courteous, and cooperative manner. Committed to quality service. Displays a high level of initiative, effort and commitment towards completing assignments efficiently. Works with minimal supervision. Demonstrates responsible behavior and attention to detail. . . ."

—Iowa Department of Administrative Services,
Human Resources Enterprise, Conservation Officer, Class Code: 05355

O N THE DAY I WAS SWORN IN as a state conservation officer, you could almost drink the sweltering July air. As I stood in a stuffy conference room in the Wallace State Office Building getting a badge pinned to my chest, heat hazed from the cement parking lots in downtown Des Moines. Outside of the city, corn plants had reached heights of over five feet, their breath visible as the leaves rustled with rapid growth. The heavy air pressed down on the rolling Loess Hills of western Iowa and blew across the central plains before tumbling over the eastern bluffs into the eddies of the Mississippi River.

Iowa is not known for vast expanses of wilderness. There are no stunning mountain ranges, white sand beaches, vast tracts of forests, or deep, awe-inspiring canyons. It is a landscape once carved by prehistoric glaciers and more recently transformed by humans and agriculture. Iowa is a deeply altered place. Natural grace is found in smaller bites here—the spaces etched between the petals of pale purple coneflowers dotting the roadsides, cattail mazes along marsh edges, and the silhouettes of solitary oaks, stout and twisted, in a pasture.

My first assignment as an Iowa conservation officer sent me to Webster County in the central part of the state. There, the wind is a relentless presence that bites your face in winter and burns it all summer long. Where there were once vast expanses of prairies and wetland potholes banked by oak savannahs, there are now crop fields extending flatly to the horizon, where they meet the sky's arc in hazy summer heat. Gravel roads stretch out in a grid of almost perfect square-mile segments, hemming in the corn and bean fields in neat, computer-generated rows. One of the few places biological diversity finds a foothold is in the occasional roadside ditch. And even that's a crapshoot. Many ditches are either mowed or are being slowly consumed by extra rows of crops.

I am an Iowa native. I know the need for nuance and a discerning eye when seeking out natural places in some parts of the state. But as a newly badged officer, standing in the bed of my pickup for a better view, I still saw the stark landscape as impossible. I found myself wondering if I would be able to find the natural resources I was sworn to safeguard.

Later, I transferred farther east to Johnson County, an area with more natural and cultural diversity. Tucked between two urban areas, the northern section of my territory encompasses a large wildlife area, two rivers, a sizable federal impoundment, a large university, and an endless supply of headaches. The southern half of the territory is home both to large-scale farming operations, where combines the size of semi-trucks trundle over the fields, and to Amish families, whose horses and buggies kick up dust on dirt roads. My job in this varied territory is a tightrope act in which I feel always on the verge of plunging over one side or the other. When I do fall, I find myself either splashing into the pool of modernity and all its conflicts, where progressive opinions hold sway, or into the land of tradition, where resistance to change is steadfast.

Conservation officers are tasked with protecting the state's natural resources, mainly by way of law enforcement. In Iowa, conservation officers are state peace officers, which means we can enforce any of the laws of the state. Our primary focus is on those laws that could impact the state's wildlife, land, and waters, but although we work for the land, we spend much of our time dealing with people and their problems. In *Nature Noir*, his memoir of fourteen years he spent working in a pair of river canyons slated to be inundated by a dam, law enforcement park ranger Jordan Fisher Smith summarized a conservation officer's duties like this:

> You protect the land from the people, the people from the land, the people from each other, and the people from themselves. It's what you are trained to do without even thinking, a reflexive and unconditional act. If you're lucky, you get assigned to people who seem worth saving and land and waters whose situation is not hopeless. If not, you save them anyway. And maybe in time, saving them will make them worth it.

If places where the condition of natural resources seems most hopeless are the exact places most in need of protection, Iowa would be a good candidate for a bodyguard. About 98 percent of Iowa is privately owned, which places it forty-ninth in the nation for the percentage of publicly held land. In comparison with many states, Iowa's wild places are fragmented, small, and under pressure. Funding for the management of state-owned natural areas comes almost entirely from hunting and fishing licenses and from a special fee that supplies money for maintaining wildlife habitats. At the same time, public areas are used by a wide variety of people, some of whom may not always have the best of intentions or habits and many of whom don't contribute any funds toward the management or upkeep of the areas they use.

As I patrol Iowa's public land, I wonder if someday I'll look back on my work with a sense of fulfillment or if, instead, I'll be left with a feeling that my career was fruitless. I want to know if the hours spent peering through my squad truck's windows, crunching over gravel roads, hiking through brambly weeds, sorting through lies, and following up tips in pursuit of protecting our scarce wild places would have been better spent elsewhere. I wonder if my own ephemeral existence will have made a difference to this natural world and the land that I love like nothing else. If, someday, I discover that my time as a conservation officer was an exercise in futility, at least I will know for certain that it was not for lack of good faith on my part. I maintain a stubborn hope that, despite an uncertain future, my work will not have been in vain and that this beautiful place was worth my time.

I ONCE READ A MEMOIR by a game warden who seemingly emerged from the womb with a badge on his chest and a gun on his hip. Each chapter told a tale from his career as a conservation officer. The stories all had the same, predictable ending—without exception, he solved the case. Every time. Poachers wilted before him, criminals wept, and guilty souls rolled over like submissive dogs at his mere presence in the interview room. He was the eternal paragon—clever, wise, brave, and quick. He didn't screw things up. In one story, the officer went so far as to swim underwater to sneak up on and nab some unsuspecting illegal fishermen. I couldn't re-late. As I read the book in bed each night, I compared my own story to his, and my self-confidence gradually dissolved into a little puddle on the sheets. My story is much less heroic.

While I imagine that many of my colleagues knew from a very young age that they wanted to be conservation officers when they grew up, I didn't even know there was such a thing. Instead, I stumbled along my own life trail, which eventually led me to the field of environmental education. My days as a county naturalist were spent leading outdoor programs aimed at teaching people about the natural world. Eventually, though, due to happenstance, college acquaintances, and a craving for more excitement, I shifted my career trajectory and headed toward conservation law enforcement.

It turned out that my chosen career was lopsided not only in terms of gender equality but in personality traits as well. As an introverted, left-leaning woman with nerdy, anxiety-ridden tendencies, I found myself in a crowd made up of many extroverted, often conservative, and habitually confident men. I didn't fit in.

Given my childhood, it's no wonder that I sometimes found myself sitting in my squad and thinking that my life hadn't really turned out as I had imagined it would. That realization usually occurred during moments when I was tasked with something that seemed totally incongruous with what I had envisioned myself doing when I was a young girl.

One evening, while watching a skunk from the safety of my squad, I experienced the familiar, yet disquieting feeling that I was standing outside my life and observing my childhood self. There I was, a ten-year-old girl sitting cross-legged on my bedroom floor. My blond hair spilled over my shoulders as I madly snipped photographs of wolves, deer, and whales from magazines and pasted them into a notebook I'd titled "Hunting for Pleasure Is Evil." I soaked in my own sense of righteousness. As a kid, I was an animal rights activist in training. Even then I felt the spirit of a cause. I was motivated to change the world, and I knew I'd have to take matters into my own hands.

My home was situated on the edge of the city limits. A small stream emerged from a storm drain near the end of my street and trickled its way around the bend of the bean field behind our house. My friend Heather and I were frequent visitors to the stream. It was our oasis, and we spent many barefoot hours there catching frogs and crawdads. We were intrepid explorers and pioneers in our personal Eden until the faint echo of my mom's shout beckoned me home for supper.

One day we encountered something foreign in the stream—clear evidence of an evil interloper trespassing on our refuge. The objects were metal jaws attached to chains staked into the ground with a piece of metal rebar: traps set to catch "brother" raccoon. I found a stick and quickly jabbed at the pan of the first one. It thwacked shut with a splash. I loosened the stick from the jaw's hold and tripped the second trap. Never had I felt so satisfied and, at the same time, so terrified of my own handiwork. Somehow, that experience set me on the path from the person I was at ten to the person I became—a conservation officer responsible for dealing with a skunk trapped in a ditch.

The complaint had come by way of a late afternoon phone call from a concerned citizen. He reported a skunk whose foot had been stuck deep in a foothold trap for three days, apparently left by a trapper who had neglected to check his sets. The sun was low on the horizon as I drove to the site of the trap. Soft orange light refracted off the snow, rolled over the hills, and settled around me. The warm hues did nothing to lessen the burden of the cold. School had been delayed that morning due to gelled fuel in the school buses. The wind chills had reached thirty below zero, and the bus engines wouldn't turn over. While my kids were snuggling deeper into their beds, savoring the unexpected morning laze, the skunk had been hunkering down against the wind.

As my truck eased along, the tires made popping sounds against the frozen gravel road. Then I spotted it—a black and white ball perched near the top of a steep ditch on the north side of the road. Not wanting to startle the skunk, I watched briefly through my binoculars hoping that it had already succumbed to the frigid temperatures. Maybe the incremental solidifying of blood moving through veins as it slowly froze to death would be preferable to the sharp gut puncture of owl talons. As soon as I glassed it, the animal slowly stood up. It made a weak, unsuccessful effort to pull its foot from the trap then stiffly laid back down, burying its head in its furry chest.

I scrolled through my phone numbers and typed a quick text message to Dan, a trusted trapper who was always willing to answer my inane questions.

Hey Dan. Best way to kill a skunk caught in a foothold without getting sprayed?
Shoot it through the lungs.
Thanks. I'll try.

I glassed the skunk again. It was still curled up and facing away from me. A shot through the lungs would require more luck than skill. I stepped out of my truck into the glacial air. Wind howled down the road as if it were a tunnel, blowing clouds of my frozen breath away. I turned back to my squad and dug through the gearbox in the back seat until I found the .22 pistol—my designated small critter killer. It only took five seconds for my bare hands to lose feeling as I loaded the magazine into the gun. When it clicked into place, I walked to the front of my truck where I deemed it safest to take a shot.

The skunk was still curled into a ball, making a shot to the lungs a particularly difficult proposition. I took a few more steps in the skunk's direction, hoping my movement would encourage the animal to switch positions. It worked. The skunk sensed my presence and slowly stood up. Just as it turned slightly to the side, I took aim and fired.

Whenever I pull the trigger on wildlife, I unconsciously merge with my younger self and a feeling of protest sparks from somewhere deep. I'm prone to anthropomorphizing, and I still cringe at the thought of killing for the sake of it. But I no longer spend much time internally debating when necessity presents itself. My job isn't to stop the hunting and trapping I once so despised when I was young. Rather it's to try to stop those who disrespect and skirt the laws that were designed to protect wildlife and wild places.

The skunk bucked when the bullet punched its body. I climbed back into my truck and waited to silently witness the death. The skunk's legs straightened and flexed as its brain circuits crossed and misfired. The process of transitioning out of this world is never as quick as I want it to be.

I thought about the nature of this particular animal's existence. Skunks are nocturnal and generally don't venture out much in the dead of winter. They spend their days holed up in burrows and come out at night to wander the countryside in search of seeds, dead animals, nuts, or anything else to fill an empty stomach. Hunger would have been driving this animal's foraging instinct during this cold, lean month. I imagined this skunk ambling across the cornfield and into the ditch three nights before, exhaling small puffs of breath on that winter night.

People schooled in science are not supposed to project human feelings onto other species. But I do it anyway. I began to doubt my selfish decision to trade the stink of my clothing for the life of this creature. Surely, I thought, the skunk, having survived three days caught in a trap during a harsh Midwest winter, deserved to be released alive as a reward for persistence if nothing else. I'd heard that the trick to releasing a skunk without getting sprayed was to approach it with a blanket outstretched.

The blanket, presenting a less threatening image than a human, would help the animal to stay calm. The person could then attempt to hypnotize it by speaking with a quiet, calm voice, saying "Don't worry . . . everything will be okay."

When the skunk stopped moving, I grabbed a catchpole from the back of my squad and approached the limp body. Based on the lack of skunky stench, I assumed that I'd somehow managed a successful lung shot. But once I jabbed the body with the pole, the putrid smell wafted around me and caught on the frozen wind. I pried the skunk's foot from the trap and cut the anchor cable.

The trap was properly tagged with the owner's name and address. I took the trap, wrapped it in a plastic bag to stifle the embedded smell, and drove to the trapper's house.

"I don't know how I missed that trap." He shook his head, failing to make eye contact with me. "I'm in the military—I mean, I follow the rules," he insisted.

"I know it can happen," I said, "but I treat everyone the same, and in this situation I always issue a ticket for not checking the traps." I explained that even legal and ethical trappers already have an uphill battle when it comes to convincing the general public that what they do is acceptable. It clearly doesn't help their cause when an animal is left to suffer in plain view for three days.

"I understand, but I just don't break the law," he repeated. I held my tongue, trying to follow the advice of a field training officer who once advised me to either lecture or cite, but to avoid doing both. I'd said enough.

It was dark by the time I pulled into my driveway. Lights shone from the kitchen window where I could see my son sitting at the table reading a book. I walked up to the front door, kicked the snow from my boots, and stepped into the warmth. As I slung my coat over the back of a kitchen chair, a musky odor drifted into the room. My son closed his book, and the dog sauntered over to sniff my pant leg. The heat of the house wrapped around me, and I wondered how many other animals would be spending the upcoming night in a ditch, cold seeping into their bones.

That evening, as I tucked the kids into bed, I saw the timeline of their lives stretching out and branching infinitely like the topographical map of a vast watershed, each decision made during the course of their lives forcing them down one route, leaving others unexplored. Picking and choosing, falling and soaring, all the way to an unpredictable future. I saw them as adults reflecting on their lives and examining how they arrived at this place and time, at a destination they couldn't have ever imagined.

FOLLOWING MY STINT as a county naturalist, I moved to an A-frame house tucked into the piney woods of Wisconsin. There I was hired to be a deputy conservation warden for the Wisconsin Department of Natural Resources. My job would be to assist and learn from the full-time wardens, working just enough to fall short of the benefits package full-time wardens received. Before starting, however, I first had to attend Wisconsin's law enforcement academy. It was there, along with recruit officers from other agencies, like sheriff's departments, city and tribal police departments, and Department of Natural Resources forest rangers, that we learned police basics. It was also during the last weeks of academy training that I started having the dreams that have persisted throughout my career.

At the academy, many days were spent sitting in a classroom. Our brains were clogged with lectures that poured from the instructors in a never-ending flow. Law enforcement training is built on a foundation of repetition—a brick wall laid with procedurals, laws, and scenarios. We studied criminal psychology, community policing, interview and interrogation techniques, and traffic enforcement. We watched videos about domestic abuse, deciphered code language concerning search and seizure, and practiced delivering babies with plastic dolls and fake pelvic models. Our bodies were bruised and beaten during defensive tactics sessions. Our egos were equally damaged and our personal space invaded when forced to practice handcuffing and pat down searches. Unforgiving instructors hid knives, syringes, or red plastic guns in our classmates' crotch zones to teach us that anything less than a thorough pat down is a death wish. The only humiliation worse than frisking the privates of a classmate was missing a weapon hidden in a bra.

But I believe that my dream had its roots on the shooting range. Aside from the moment when my new supervisor handed me a sidearm and sent me on my way to the academy, like a first-grader on her way to school with a new pencil box, attending the police academy was the first time I had ever held a handgun. Like all officers in my department, I was issued a .40 caliber Glock. Although simple in its blocky appearance and clean mechanics, the weapon's heft was intimidating.

In the beginning, we shot at an indoor range. One day, reloading my weapon with bullets from a pile scattered on the back-room counter, I accidentally loaded a .380-caliber bullet into my .40-caliber gun. When I tried to fire, it malfunctioned. My mistake turned into a teaching moment for the entire class, a role no female recruit ever strives to play. The instructor barked, "A smaller bullet will fit into a larger gun, but something bad will happen when you pull the trigger. If you are lucky, like Erika just was, it will malfunction and fail to fire. If you aren't so lucky, it may very well blow the barrel apart in your face. Always load the correct round, people!" My classmates glanced sideways at me, thankful that the spotlight hadn't been on them.

The initial time on the range was spent focusing on shot placement and accuracy. We lay on the floor, our cheeks resting against the inside of our shoulders, our legs splayed out wide behind us. The closer the grouping of holes punched through the paper, the better. I listened for the instructor's tinny commands through my muffs, not wanting to make the mistake of firing at the wrong time. I never again wanted to provide material for a teaching moment.

When I fell into my bed at night, shouted words resounded like an echo reaching through the dark: "Focus on the front sight!" "Squeeze the trigger evenly!" "Don't anticipate!" "Let the shot surprise you!" Sleep eventually overtook me through a haze of head shots and bullseyes.

Later, the focus of our firearms training shifted from accuracy to speed drills. Firearm qualifications require quick shooting, the ability to clear malfunctions, and solid fingering. Under the pressure of the clock, recruits had to focus on the front sight and squeeze the trigger without anticipation while churning out accurate shots before the targets spun away. We double-tapped, triple-tapped, reloaded, reloaded, and reloaded. Two shots to the body, one to the head. The target turned.

Ultimately we underwent video simulation training. The computer program was high tech for the time and, like much of police training, scenario based. The limited background information provided to us during our individual turn was that the simulation focused on a "shoot–don't shoot" decision. We had to imagine that we weren't alone in a classroom with instructors hovering nearby and that the people who would appear on the movie screen in front of us were breathing, sentient beings. We were meant to interact with those people as we would in real life. The gun was wired to a computer and, we were told, could assess the accuracy of our shots at the screen in front of us. Before being shuffled like a herd of nervous cattle into a classroom to await our turns, the firearms instructors strongly encouraged us to not fuck up.

Eventually the instructor opened the door and called my name. He waved me through into the dark room. I felt my classmates' eyes on my back as I left them behind, each of those as yet untested breathing a sigh of relief that their names hadn't been called. "Remember that I want you to act as if this scenario is really happening. Work your way through it. Verbalize to the subject and make your decision," the instructor said. I took a deep breath, offered up a silent prayer for mercy, and stepped into the shooter's box.

A woman appeared on the right side of the screen. She was standing on a sidewalk in front of a clothing store, holding a purse, and looking off to her left as if waiting for a bus to arrive. After a few seconds, a man wearing a plaid flannel shirt entered from the left side of the screen. He strolled casually down the sidewalk toward the woman. The man's stringy black hair touched the top of his collar, and I noticed that he was carrying something black in his right hand. Before I had a chance to fully process the scene, he began running toward the woman. In a split second he hooked his left arm around the woman's neck, pulled her back into his chest, and held the muzzle of a revolver to her right temple. The man began screaming at me. "Back off! Back off or I'll kill her!"

I drew my gun and yelled, "Police! Don't move!" My voice cracked with its sudden volume. My immediate immersion into the scene surprised me; my commands were sharp and loud. "Drop the gun! Now!" The man made no move to comply, his forearm firmly gripping the terrified woman's neck. Adrenaline flooded my every cell as I shot him. A red X flashed on the man's right rib cage below his armpit. A hit.

"Exercise complete" flashed on the screen, and I began to breathe again. From beginning to end, the scenario had lasted only seconds, but I was sweating, and my heart was pounding. Based on the instructor's nod in my direction as I left the room, it appeared that my decision to shoot had been the correct one, although I wondered how that could be. I was still adjusting to the fact that my new career just might put me in situations where life and death could be measured in a matter of inches and by my ability to focus on the front sight.

That night I had the dream for the first time. I'm running through the woods. Thorns and brush scratch at my arms, and mosquitoes hover in clouds as I frantically scramble for a place to hide. Sweat trickles down my neck. My duty belt, heavy on my hips, makes running awkward and pathetically slow. I trip on exposed roots and land heavily, face down on the ground. Gasping for breath, I roll onto my back and watch the tips of the towering pines sway in the wind. I sense that he's catching up to me, and I'm desperate to find a hiding place. But it's too late. He is weaving through the trees, coming in my direction. I hear his boots pounding the pine-needle-covered ground vibrating under me. I roll onto my left side, my ear sinks into the dirt, and I awkwardly draw my gun. I point it at him and manage a hoarse whisper. "Police! Don't move!" Front sight . . . breathe . . . but I can't breathe . . . the front sight is gone. And when I try to squeeze the trigger, the pull is too hard, and the trigger won't budge. I squeeze harder and harder, but the trigger pull seems to weigh a hundred pounds. Craning my hand to the right, I clench the gun's grip hard in my fist and make one last attempt to move the trigger. Finally, the gun fires. The shot is far to the right, and bullets spray wildly from my inability to make a smooth trigger pull. Finally, he stands over me, looking down. The muzzle of his gun blots out the treetops as I stare into it. I shake my head back and forth in an attempt to wake up. I know I have to wake up.

I hear myself uttering a strangled yell and rouse myself from the dream, covered in a sheen of sweat. My heart beats wildly.

The next time the dream occurred, I was conducting a building search. For some reason I'm clearing the building without a team. I'm all alone, with nobody gripping the shirt on my back. Nobody's got my six. The space is an abandoned warehouse. It's a place littered with debris and crawling with mice. Homeless squatters peer at me from the dingy rooms as I pass through them. I clear each dark corner as my ragged breath echoes through my ears and fills my headspace with white noise. I sense that someone is behind me. There's nowhere to take cover. Before shaking myself from sleep, all I can hear is my breath, and all I can see are murky shadows and the glint of a muzzle.

The time after that, I dream that I'm in my truck. The steering wheel is convulsing as I try to keep the tires on the road. Potholes jar my squad like a wild bronco trying to buck me from its back. I'm zigzagging over the gravel roads of a wildlife area, trees bending over the roof and branches scraping against the doors with a high-pitched squeal. I keep checking the rearview mirror and see that the headlights are coming closer. I push harder on the gas pedal, but it's no use. The headlights are chasing down my bumper. And then it's too late. He has caught up to me.

Again, I'm sprinting through a tallgrass prairie, my ankles twisting on the uneven ground. I'm trying to find my way through a maze of cattails along the edge of the marsh. My feet break through pools of ice, slowing me down. I'm looking for cover on a frozen tundra, only to be left totally exposed. Each time, the trigger pull is heavy, and my shots veer to the right of the target. Each time, my panic escalates, running up my throat like a cinching knot. He always catches up to me in the end. Every time I find myself staring into the black muzzle.

Versions of my dream have followed me like a black cat stalking its pathetic prey. I've tried bobbing and weaving and sprinting into hidden corners to lose my predator in the shadows. But all my efforts to trick the cat have been in vain. The dream followed me after I graduated from the law enforcement academy. It chased me into the woods and lakes of Wisconsin. And, after I left Wisconsin for a full-time position with the Iowa Department of Natural Resources, I continued to be ambushed in my sleep. Even today, I have to shake myself awake some nights, sit up straight in bed, and drag myself to the bathroom to splash water on my face. Only when I'm fully awake will the prowling black cat disappear and leave me to rest.

—THE OFFICERS—

"It is the mission of the Law Enforcement Bureau to protect the State's natural resources, to provide public safety and to educate and serve the public. We enhance, promote, and protect the natural resources of this state through public relations, education, and law enforcement, thus ensuring for future generations the rights, privileges and benefits we now enjoy."

—Iowa Department of Natural Resources Law Enforcement Bureau,
Policies and Procedures Manual

MY SON, SILAS, is a seventy-year-old man in the body of a ten-year-old boy. Much like me, he is an introspective worrier. Once the sun dips below the horizon and the sky turns to ink, he lies in bed waiting for his eyelids to grow heavy with exhaustion. It is then that troubling ideas start to invade his thoughts.

"Mom, why do you have to have such a dangerous job?" he asked one night as I lay next to him in his bed, snuggled against his squirming body under a comforter covered with comic book superheroes. Silas had forgotten to take off his glasses before getting into bed, making it difficult for me to see his green eyes in the dim room behind his perpetually smudged lenses. This wasn't the first time he'd asked me this question. And it wasn't the first time I didn't know how to answer it. The job of a conservation officer can be dangerous, so I didn't think I should dismiss his concerns entirely. Silas knew, at least vaguely, what the job entailed. I'd spoken to his class about my job when he was in second grade, he'd overheard multiple phone conversations about work, and he has seen me rush out the door to respond to emergencies. Every day he watches me zip into my bulletproof vest.

We lay there in silence for a moment while I tried to figure out what to say. Finally, I asked, "Why do you think it's dangerous?"

"Well, you deal with criminals, and I know criminals are dangerous," he said. "And you drive a lot, and driving can be dangerous. You get home late at night sometimes and I don't know where you are. I worry about you when you go to work."

Not wanting his worry to spiral out of control, as it tends to do, I said, "You know, it's good that the only thing on my agenda for tomorrow is to write a report."

"That could be dangerous too," he said.

I waited a beat, and a smile began to form at the corners of Silas's mouth. "Oh, yeah?" I laughed. "How is that dangerous?"

"You could hit your head on your desk and get knocked out. Or you could electrocute yourself when you plug in your computer," he said, dissolving into giggles.

When I left Silas's room that night I thought more about the answer to his question. Why *did* I have to have such a dangerous job? Why wasn't I doing something else with my life? What in the world was I thinking when I entered a profession that required carrying twenty-five pounds of duty belts and body armor, was overrun with men, required hours of stressful training exercises, often left me alone with hunters miles from my nearest backup, and would necessitate spending most of my time alone in a truck patrolling gravel roads?

I don't have a solid answer. Most lives don't roll out in straight lines, and mine is no exception. The only reasonable explanation is that I love the outdoors. But even that conclusion falls flat. Many career paths are available to people with a love of nature, most of which don't involve coming face-to-face with the uglier side of humanity. I suppose that, as a group, individuals' reasons for choosing this career are as varied as the officers themselves. For some, it's an outgrowth of a passion for hunting and fishing; for others, it is grounded in a desire to serve the public and the natural world; and still others are inspired to follow in their fathers' footsteps.

Despite the fact that we are all standing on the same green line, working the same beat toward a communal purpose, some philosophical division remains among our ranks. The Iowa Conservation Commission was formed in 1917. From the commission's conception until the 1980s, when it combined with other divisions to become the Iowa Department of Natural Resources, or DNR, the law enforcement bureau was split.

Prior to the merger, water patrol officers fell under the water section of the Land and Waters Division. Their role, as spelled out in the 1964 edition of the Iowa State Conservation Commission report, was to "provide a water safety program, to protect the state's interest in all the state-owned water areas, and [to] preserve these water areas for the recreational-educational use by the public." In other words, water patrol officers stuck to the water. They weren't involved in poaching cases.

Fish and game conservation officers, on the other hand, fell under the conservation officer section of the Fish and Game Division. The 1964 report stated that

> fish and game conservation officers are on duty twenty-four hours a day. The officers drove a total of one and three-quarters of a million miles during the past year. The officers are called out repeatedly at night to investigate illegal hunting and fishing activities, [to] pick up car-killed deer and to attend various public functions. In addition to the officers' law enforcement activities, they are responsible for local public relations and education work, field surveys and census for the season and bag limit recommendations, the hunter safety program, preliminary investigations of pollution caused fish kills, fish and game management practice recommendations on privately owned lands, license sales and the overall activities of the commission in their respective territories.

In other words, fish and game conservation officers had nothing to do with boating enforcement.

By the time these separate divisions were unified, the officers from each section were firmly rooted in their own respective job duties and possessed a unique sense of identity and pride. Somehow those divisions from our past have been carried forward in time, implanted in officers' subconscious like latent genes harbored inside cells. A sort of invisible Mason-Dixon line of identity, foggy and in flux, spans the state from the Missouri River to the Mississippi. On one side lie those who identify as game wardens. They are the vintage edition of the fish and game conservation officer who focused on hunting and fishing enforcement. Many of these traditional game wardens balk at the advent of technological advances such as in-car computerized mapping that discloses their GPS locations in real time. For them, the intrusion of additional duties like ATV and boating enforcement is like a nagging and chronic pain they just can't shake. On the other side of the line, conservation officers tend to see themselves as a more modern version of the officer from the days of the Fish and Game Division's integration with the Land and Waters Division. These officers take a broader view of their duties, and they often embrace high-tech advances like body cameras or electronic citation filing.

While my gender gives me a stiff nudge over the line into the conservation officer camp, I can't begrudge others a doctrine that may be different from my own. The past is our foundation, and it is strong. If nomenclature alone could suture our rift, maybe "conservation warden" would be a curative choice.

In any case, the officers who have made the biggest impact on my life are the women and men from both sides of the line who have been willing to acknowledge not only their own strengths but their weaknesses as well. They are people who think not only of themselves but also of that which they have sworn to protect and serve. These officers recognize that whether they think of themselves as game wardens or as conservation officers, their differing philosophies should not put them at odds with each other. They recognize that we are all on the same team, striving for the same greater purpose.

My guess is that most of my colleagues today could, in essence, agree on an answer to my son's nagging question—Why do you do what you do? Game wardens, wildlife officers, fish and game officers, conservation wardens, and conservation officers around the globe might concur when I say that there is something indescribable about walking the thin green line, that being—on a good day—a voice for those who can only quack, grunt, swim, and sway in the breeze is the only thing they can imagine doing with their lives.

EVERY LAW ENFORCEMENT OFFICER holds a place on what I think of as a magnetic spectrum, an imaginary bell curve. One has little control over where one sits on it. Some officers, located at the far end, possess an extremely strong polarizing force. They are known as the shit magnets.

A complicated equation determines one's location on the magnetic curve. Factors include such variables as territory assignment, doggedness, genetic mutation, and cosmic accident to the power of three. The only way a shift on the magnetic continuum can occur during the course of a career is by changing one of those factors. Even then, of course, one can do little to change the essential, esoteric nature of one's being. Whether you find yourself on the uphill slope of the shit magnet bell or the downhill, it doesn't take long to figure out your lot. The bigger question is whether being a shit magnet is a blessing or a curse.

I learned early in my career that I was the polar opposite of a shit magnet. At my distant end of the spectrum, life was dull. Months would pass in a blur of tedium. Driving, hoping, searching, watching, and driving some more. While shit magnet officers are always close at hand when something exciting or unusual occurs, I'm the one stuck behind a slow-moving tractor six miles away. I arrive just as everyone else is leaving. While magnets struggle to keep up with accumulating case incident reports, some days I struggle simply to find a hunter to check. Magnets have a thrilling new story to tell every time you talk to them. I recycle the same old tale until eyes glaze over.

Different strategies can be employed to counter such weak magnetic pulls, lest the poor soul languish too long in the depths of boredom. I've tried them all, with varying success. Strategically placing myself in the vicinity of a shit magnet in an effort to poach off his magnetism works sometimes. The only snag is that my oppositional magnetism can strangely overpower the shit magnet's pull. When that happens, it may become necessary to remove myself from her company entirely just long enough for the magnet to drum up some business. Only then will I step back in for my share of the action. It's a perverse and maddening loop.

Jace Travers, the park ranger for Lake Macbride State Park, is familiar with my embarrassing condition and is usually willing to help me out. Jace is always wading in shit up to his knees. He transferred to Lake Macbride, in my territory, after a busy five years assigned to Lake Manawa State Park. The move put his young family closer to home, grandparents, and good schools. To imagine Jace doing anything other than law enforcement work is impossible. His entire being is made for the career.

The first thing I noticed about Jace was his voice. It came from somewhere behind his ribcage, strained its way out through his vocal cords, and pinched his voice like he was perched on the edge of a perpetual case of laryngitis. His right ear sported the tell-tale signs of a cauliflower ear, revealing his history as a wrestler. But even absent that, his confidence and tenacity were evidence enough of his fortitude. I suspect that, unlike me, Jace had a bodily need for the occasional adrenaline dump. The more stressful and challenging the situation, the more he reveled in it. Jace's ability to parse the delicate balance between protecting the land within the borders of the park and playing referee to the people who use it make him the ideal protector of Iowa's park system and its visitors.

State parks are especially important to Iowa's landscape. With so little public land available, citizens flock to the parks to commune with a bit of green space. To many, the parks are oases in the midst of a rural monoculture. Many users acquire a sense of ownership for their favorite park.

Iowa state parks don't charge entrance fees, they are open year-round, and they are located throughout the state within easy driving distance of most residents. Each park is surprisingly unique. Across the state one can find trails meandering through forests, gaping caves that drip and echo, lakes with sailboats bobbing and turning with the wind, campgrounds where families spend the night under the stars, and beaches for basking in the mid-summer sun. State parks are traditionally places where time bends toward a simpler era, when honest fun was found outdoors, and problems were forgotten at the entrance gates.

To the rangers tasked with maintaining public safety in Iowa's parks, however, the view is often far less utopian. Today things aren't always so simple. Along with camping gear and picnic baskets, visitors transport societal issues and personal baggage with them into the park. At times, the special features of any given park work to bring these issues and problems to the surface. When this happens, the park ranger must sort through it all—to restore social and natural order as much as possible. For a ranger like Jace Travers, that's just part of the fun. He roots through his park's flaws like a treasure hunter digging through a chest of jewels, each problem intriguing in its own right.

Located within the city limits of Council Bluffs on Iowa's border with Omaha, Lake Manawa State Park was known as a crime-ridden place. At the time Jace was stationed there, rangers worked closely with the Council Bluffs Police Department and Iowa State Patrol when local trouble, gangs, and drug-use infiltrated the boundaries of the park and took up residence in the campground.

Not unlike an urban police department, the rangers at Manawa often arrested the same people over and over—people like Timothy "Blade" Thompson, who kept the rangers busy responding to calls to a housing development within the park boundaries. Blade lived in a run-down house with his mom. His temper was fierce and his moral sensibilities lacking. One day, Jace assisted police officers in dragging Blade, his fists flying, off the inert body of his own mother. When officers arrived, Blade was straddling her stomach, pummeling her with a series of wild haymakers. By the time Blade finished beating her for failing to provide his friend with a blow job upon his request, she was lying unconscious and bloodied on the living room floor. In Blade's view of proper family dynamics, it was his mom's duty to do as she was told.

By virtue of the territory alone, Jace was automatically inducted into the league of shit magnets. It wasn't uncommon for phone conversations to be abruptly cut off with a Manawa ranger announcing something like, "Hey, I gotta go. There's a naked person walking up the road toward my truck." Sometimes there was no explanation at all, just a sudden end to the call followed hours later with a recounting of some bizarre incident. Encountering that naked person running down the road high on life or drugs, getting into a foot chase and tackling a wanted person, or happening upon a violent fist fight likely wouldn't have been the most interesting part of any given night shift.

"Did I ever tell you about the time a couple set each other on fire in the campground?" Jace asked me one day, his eyes taking on a faraway look he got whenever he basked in the memory of his glory days.

"Nope. I think I'd remember that one," I said.

"This guy and his wife were both drunk and arguing at their campsite. They started squirting lighter fluid at each other." Jace grinned with the recollection. "They managed to start each other on fire, but the flames kept going out. When the fire didn't work, one tried stabbing the other with a fork. The best part was that we didn't even have to clean up the campsite. While we were transporting the two to jail someone else came along and stole the tent and everything."

"Sounds like a magical place. Just where I'd want to go on a family vacation."

"Yeah, I had to carry around a wad of registration money because almost every time a decent family would come in to camp they'd end up deciding not to stay the night and would ask for their money back."

"So what did you do?"

"I'd just tell them that I didn't blame them, and I'd give them their money back."

One afternoon while patrolling at Manawa, Jace turned into the boat ramp parking lot to find a white car, its trunk partially open, driving in continuous circles. A small child clung to the roof of the car like a miniature body surfer riding a wild wave. As soon as the driver noticed Jace approaching in his squad, emergency lights flashing, she slammed on the brakes, sending the child sliding through the sunroof and planting him headfirst onto the dashboard. Shortly after the car stopped, another small child emerged from the trunk and climbed into the back seat of the car.

"Ma'am, the reason I'm stopping you is due to the fact that you're driving around with your kids in the trunk and on the roof," Jace explained, as if it was neither unusual nor surprising. "I'll need to see your driver's license, registration, and insurance."

The woman rifled through the glove box in search of the documents. "I had no idea that they were on the roof or in the trunk."

Jace turned around, rolled his eyes, and walked back to his squad to write out charges.

"I'm issuing you a citation for reckless driving," Jace said when he returned to the woman's car, citation in hand. "Just curious. Where did you think your kids were if they weren't on the roof or in the trunk?"

"Look," the woman snapped, "this was my weekend to see my kids. I just wanted to have something fun to do with them." Jace cocked his head, nodded slowly, and handed her the paperwork. After making sure the driver was sober and the kids were unhurt and buckled in, Jace sent her on her way.

It wasn't until a few weeks later that Jace received a court subpoena. The woman was fighting the reckless driving charge. Always one to enjoy raising his right hand and testifying on the stand, Jace particularly enjoyed court that day. For him, there wasn't much of anything more satisfying than a quick guilty verdict handed down from a tired and scowling judge who'd no doubt seen worse come from within the boundaries of Manawa State Park.

When Jace transferred to Lake Macbride, he worried that his new park wouldn't deliver his required regular dose of adrenaline. He didn't want to live out the rest of his career cleaning bathrooms, patrolling aimlessly, writing citations for dogs off leash, and pining for his past life. But it didn't take long to find out that, while his current assignment would probably never fully meet the high standards set by Manawa, Lake Macbride had charms of its own. Jace learned that it wasn't just the park itself that had provided him with endless hours of entertainment, it was his personal degree of magnetism that did the trick. No park, not even Lake Macbride, would ever be the quaint place it pretended to be as long as he was around.

Lake Macbride State Park, at just 2,180 acres, is Iowa's largest, which speaks to the lack of public land in the state. It is home to two camp-grounds, a beach, a boat rental operation, a concession stand, a lodge, several hiking trails, boat ramps, and picnic areas. The two arms of Lake Macbride run perpendicular to the Coralville Lake, with the waters of the lake spilling into the reservoir as either a trickle in dry months or a gushing waterfall in wet ones. The outline of the lake itself forms the shape of an alligator's mouth, open and ready to gobble up the small town of Solon that lies to its east.

On the surface, Macbride induces a sense of Norman-Rockwellesque nostalgia. Driving into the north side of the park during the fall is like entering a wooded wonderland. Shafts of sunlight through the autumn canopy light the forest floor with glowing patches of creamy yellows, or-anges, and reds. Deer, accustomed to the presence of people, lazily munch on brush along the roadways and rarely spook from picnic areas. Early summer mornings drip with humidity as fog hovers among the oak trees, casting an air of storybook enchantment on the park while masking its flaws in a blanket of mist.

One cannot know a place intimately unless charged with its care. Oc-casional visitors to parks see only the superficial: nature set aside to awe and beguile. But rangers are forced to dig further into the sublayers, where troubles lurk and problems fester. At best, the ranger remembers that, despite the park's imperfections and its users' foibles, the place is inher-ently worth conserving. At worst, the one place they dreamed of working becomes nothing more than the place they most want to escape. Luckily, most rangers I have worked with have always remained stewards at heart.

THE MOVING VAN hadn't even arrived with his furniture when Jace took the first call at his new location: a car accident. A pair of college students had raced along one of the park's curvy roads in an apparent attempt to mimic a car commercial. Exceeding the posted limit of fifteen miles per hour by approximately four times that, the car had no chance of staying on the pavement. It screamed off a sharp curve and rattled through some underbrush before slamming head-on into the base of a giant oak tree, wrapping it in crumpled metal.

When Jace arrived at the accident scene, he quickly triaged the occupants. The passenger's face was gushing blood, droplets spewing from his mouth as he screamed for help. The driver was busy trying to free himself from the grip of the crushed dashboard.

Sirens wailed in the distance, letting Jace know that an ambulance was getting close. He moved from the driver's to the passenger's side, where the young man was still pleading for help. As soon as Jace approached the side window, the passenger's mangled arm reached through the broken glass. Blood dripping from his fingers, the man grabbed Jace's forearm, begging for help.

Jace, a germaphobe, had unfortunately chosen a career filled with exposure to bodily fluids. He always had a giant bottle of hand sanitizer at the ready and never failed to glove up when there was a chance he would be touching someone. Unfortunately, the gloves didn't extend the length of his forearm. The sight of blood running from the passenger's hand and trickling down Jace's own skin made him recoil. Fighting the manic urge to pummel the victim's bloody hand with his baton until he let go, Jace managed to speak calmly with the passenger until the ambulance arrived. It wasn't until the jaws of life had pried the doors off the car that Jace could see the passenger's intestines spilling onto the floor through a hole in his lower abdomen.

As the medics worked on the passenger, Jace noticed that the driver had managed to free himself from the wreck and was outside the car, pacing up and down the road with a noticeable limp.

"Hey, you okay?" Jace asked the driver.

"Yeah. I'm fine," he replied.

Jace looked down and noticed blood dripping from the man's pant leg onto the pavement. "What about your leg? It looks like it's bleeding."

The driver bent down and pulled his pant leg up, revealing the lower half of his right leg. His shinbone poked through the skin like a shard of glass.

"Nope. Not fine," Jace said. "You're going to the hospital, too."

After the ambulance left and while the tow truck crew worked at pulling the buckled mess of metal from the woods, Jace scrubbed his forearm with hand sanitizer. He assumed the worst of prognoses for the passenger. After all, innards aren't supposed to be on the outside. But, surprisingly, the passenger pulled through. Following several weeks and multiple surgeries, he was released from the hospital. By then, the driver, his leg snugly wrapped in a cast, had quietly slipped back to his home country of China, likely thinking that was his only chance of avoiding a charge of vehicular manslaughter.

The oak tree still stands strong along the road's banked turn. Its topmost branches sway and its leaves whisper on windy days. Its bark is scarred and mending at the base. Whenever Jace takes the curve, he remembers his welcome to Lake Macbride, then reaches down and pumps a dose of hand sanitizer into his palm before rubbing it over his forearms. Preventative measures are better than nothing.

I'M TOLD OF A TIME when conservation officers were issued a badge, a revolver, and a handful of bullets and bestowed with a priestly blessing from the chief of law enforcement before being set loose to maintain law and order. Training was, at best, minimal and vague. Wardens patrolled in personally owned sedans to tackle the poaching problems in their territories, educate young hunters in the ways of the outdoors, and get stuck in the mud due to the lack of four-wheel drive. Stories from that time are rife with excitement and shenanigans. Not only was it the heyday for poachers, with spotlighting for deer and raccoons at its zenith, but sometimes the wardens were up to no good as well. As a whole, the group had a reputation as policy-bucking freethinkers, prone to alcohol and practical jokes. Unlocked squad cars were an invitation for gifts of dead fish or live snakes. Beer was conspicuously consumed during lunch breaks, and the rules of search and seizure were viewed more as suggestions than as law.

When I was hired, the last of these free-wheeling officers were headed to retirement. But even with the old-timers gone, when I was plunked down into my assigned territory, I found myself surrounded by officers I considered to be legends in their own right. Among them was clever Lloyd Holter, an obsessive fan of the Iowa Hawkeyes, and ever sarcastic. Lloyd played electric guitar, had a degree in journalism, and was a beautiful writer. He was my neighboring officer and would often call to ask if I wanted to meet for beans, by which he meant lunch. He sported a tattoo on his shoulder, had survived cancer, and sometimes expressed frustration over the absurdity of the state government he worked for. After retirement, Lloyd grew his hair long and didn't waste time pining for his previous employment.

Sam Stone was a blond-haired practical joker. When I think of Sam, I picture wide smiles and hear laughter. Before I was hired, I'd ridden along during season openers with Sam's partner, Rick Stephen. Rick hummed odd tunes to himself as we tooled the gravel roads looking for hunters to check. He was a devout Catholic with approximately one million children, each of whom he and his wife home-schooled. I always assumed that the reason Rick jumped at the chance to attend any overnight training program was to give himself a mini-vacation away from his crowded house.

Don Bradford was a bulldog. The first time I met him was while riding along with Rick during pheasant opener. We stopped for lunch and met up with Don, Rick, and Lloyd. Don had three tiny baby shoes hanging from the rearview mirror of his squad. At the time, I'd assumed he'd become a grandfather to triplets. Only later did I learn that he wasn't a grandfather. After marrying a younger woman, he became father to three baby girls. These men, all in mid to late career by the time I was hired, didn't hesitate to let me into their group. I was honored, humbled, and thoroughly entertained by their presence during my first years.

The process today is much more complicated than loading six bullets and swearing on the Bible to serve and protect. One of the most stressful parts of the procedure for a new officer is field training. Each newly hired recruit is assigned a series of field training officers throughout the state. FTOs evaluate performance on a daily basis, making the entire experience an endless source of stress and anxiety for the recruit at the receiving end of criticism, only some of which is constructive.

The recruit spends a couple weeks with each FTO. In the beginning, the recruit watches the FTO at work and, by the end of field training, the FTO shadows the recruit, watching silently and scoring her progress. By the time the recruit figures out how one FTO likes things done, she is shuffled on to the next one. She must then start from scratch, trying to please a new FTO who, more often than not, does things quite differently.

It was during my field training phase that I first felt like a real conservation officer.

IT WAS PHEASANT OPENER in late October, when the walnut leaves turn a dusty shade of yellow and the temperature subtly drops lower every evening. I was in the midst of my third round of field training, and I was excited to be in the north central region of the state, an area thick with pheasants. My most pressing concern was getting through each day without making an ass of myself. FTO Don Bradford wasn't part of the generation known for drinking during lunch breaks and disregarding policies, but he was old enough to intimidate me. It wasn't his stature that made me fear him: I stood a good three inches taller (though I wasn't about to point that out to him). Despite his height, Don was a commanding presence. He was scrappy, his fuse was short, and he was eternally confident in the perfection of his own opinion. I learned that it was best not to argue the finer points.

We spent opening morning patrolling a grid of gravel roads, stopping occasionally to check the bag limits and licenses of orange-clad hunters. In general, pheasant hunters are an easygoing crowd. Compared to a gun deer opener, when otherwise seemingly normal folks temporarily lose their collective minds in fits of buck fever, most pheasant hunters are simply happy to be out working the dogs and enjoying the weather.

Just as I sat back in the passenger seat of the squad and began to enjoy the Zen-like experience of an easy season opener, Don shattered my meditation. "Keep in mind that pheasants aren't the only things getting shot today. Sometimes guys will take advantage of an opener to go out and poach something else. They assume we'll be focusing on pheasant hunters on a day like today, so they'll head to the marsh or the woods. Sometimes they'll sneak into refuges, too."

Almost as soon as the words left Don's mouth, his cell phone rang. On the other end was a local hunter calling to report someone shooting geese inside a waterfowl refuge. "He's on the island in the middle of the marsh," the caller said. Don cursed under his breath. "He doesn't look like your typical hunter," he went on. "The guy's wearing a red plaid shirt. He's an old dude with long gray hair."

Don sighed. "Alright. I gotta get a boat, then we'll be on our way."

Don and I exchanged glances, and the squad surged as he pressed the gas pedal down a little harder. Fifteen minutes later, we pulled into the parking lot at the wildlife unit. We quickly found the johnboat, covered in dust and parked inside a gloomy wooden shed. Don shook the gas tank to be sure it was full, then we hooked onto the trailer and headed to the marsh.

When we arrived, we found the marsh parking lot empty but for a dilapidated heap of an RV parked at the far end. It was stitched together with rust and looked like it had spent the previous ten years in the junkyard.

"Oh, shit," Don said, "it has Arizona plates. I know this guy—George O'Dell. He's got relatives around here and comes back to hunt every year."

I scanned the water and caught sight of a man standing on the edge of a small island in the middle of the marsh. He was wearing a red plaid shirt. "There he is," I said, pointing the man out to Don.

O'Dell was standing on the northernmost point of the island overlooking a spread of duck decoys bobbing in the water. He held a shotgun, while his dog, an overweight black lab, paced the shoreline before shoulder-diving to the ground and rolling in the mud.

Don opened his truck door and jumped outside. "I guess we better get out there."

He heaved himself into the still trailered boat and waited for me to realize I was supposed to back the boat into the water. I took the hint and climbed into the truck to back it down the ramp. After parking the truck, I joined Don in the boat, and we pushed off from shore, turning in the direction of the island. The going was slow. Mud from the bottom of the shallow marsh churned just below the surface, bubbling like a witches' brew as the prop struggled to push the boat forward.

As we approached the shoreline, Don shouted, "Any luck today?"

"Not yet," O'Dell answered. "Been a few flying over, but I haven't taken a shot."

"Yeah, well, it would be hard to do without a gun," Don said as he climbed out of our boat. Don nodded toward a tree thirty feet away, where the gun O'Dell had been holding earlier was now propped against the trunk. O'Dell's dog came over and nosed Don's crotch, which prompted a sharp clip of his knee into the dog's chest. With a whimper the dog slunk back to O'Dell.

O'Dell shrugged. "I saw you coming, so I unloaded it. I'm a safe hunter, ya know. I always teach my kids to be safe hunters, too."

"I'm sure you do," Don said flatly. "We need to take a look at your hunting license."

As O'Dell dug in his pockets searching for a license, I got out of the boat and walked away to have a look around the island. Small willow trees, rushes, and thorny bushes pocked the upper shoreline before merging into a thicker stand of willows. I pushed my way through the willows and emerged on the other side of the spit, which had been hidden from our view from the parking lot. A second set of decoys floated in the water twenty feet from shore. I paced the water's edge, searching for something of greater importance. I wanted above all to win the approval of my gruff FTO, and my time was running short to make an impression. Don's voice carried through the willows as he argued with O'Dell about something. As my eyes drifted over the muddy sand I noticed small, dark-red droplets peppering the ground. Blood.

"Your boat doesn't have any registration on it," Don was saying when I returned to my FTO's side. "If it's in the water, it's got to be registered." His voice was getting louder, teetering on the knife-edge of yelling. I'd witnessed Don's temper before and pitied the person on the receiving end of it.

"I don't need it. I'm from Arizona—we don't need registration in Arizona."

The corners of Don's eyes visibly twitched and his jaw clenched. "I'm here to tell you, you need registration on that boat. Now start packing up your stuff. You can't have your boat on Iowa water without a registration."

As O'Dell began gathering his things, I pulled Don aside. "I found another set of decoys and some blood over on the other side of these willows." I nodded toward the trees.

"Okay. We'll look into it. I checked his gun. It was unloaded but it wasn't plugged—big surprise." The charges were beginning to add up. O'Dell, having given up picking up his decoys, was sitting in a lawn chair watching his dog wrestle with a stick.

"So, if we look around this island for a while, are we going to find any dead Canada geese?" Don asked.

"No," O'Dell said.

"Are we going to find anything we shouldn't find?"

"No."

"Then get off the chair and start picking up your shit," Don ordered, clearly annoyed. "We're going to have a look around."

I led Don through the willows and showed him the decoys and blood. "Let's look around here and see if we can't find a goose," Don said, heading away up the shoreline.

By default, I walked in the opposite direction, scanning the ground and nearby brush. As I bent over to take a closer look at another blood spot in the sand, my eyes were drawn to the branches of a small bush nearby. Gray blood-speckled feathers poked out from the bottom of the bush. I reached into the thorns and pulled a Canada goose from the greenery.

I whistled to catch Don's attention. Like the Statue of Liberty raising her torch, I triumphantly held up the goose for my FTO to see. Don nodded his approval. A slow grin spread broadly across his face as he held aloft a shotgun he'd found stashed behind another tree. It was loaded and had been lying flat in the sand.

We pushed our way back through the willows to find that O'Dell had still made little progress in picking up his supplies. A darker shade of crimson flushed over Don's face when he saw O'Dell seated on the ground, petting his dog like a petulant toddler. "What's with the decoys on the other side?" Don questioned, pointing at the trail through the willows.

"I was over there earlier this morning, but the wind switched directions, so I came over here."

"Are you absolutely sure you didn't shoot anything today?"

"Well, come to think of it, I did shoot a white-front, but the dog wouldn't retrieve it."

"Was the white-front in a flock or by itself?"

"It was a loner."

Don's patience suddenly ran dry. "Look," he said tersely, "we found the dead Canada that you stashed in the bushes, and we've got your other shotgun. So get your stuff into your boat and meet us at the boat ramp. Now."

"I'm too old to paddle into this wind," O'Dell protested.

"Then paddle to the other shore, and WALK to the parking lot," Don directed enunciating each word slowly, with increasing pitch. "Since you're from out of state, you're going to have to post bond in town for killing that goose in a refuge."

"I'm broke. I don't have no money to post bond with, and I'm not asking anyone for money," he whined.

I could almost see smoke curling out of Don's ears as he snapped, "Well, then I guess you'll be going to jail. Pack up and meet us at the boat ramp. I'm not going to tell you again."

We packed the goose and guns into our boat and began slogging our way back across the water. The extra weight was all it took to ground our boat into the muddy bottom of the marsh. The motor growled and complained as it strained to do its job. Finally, the deep chocolate ribbon spitting out from the prop disappeared, and the boat came to a stop.

As I was fairly certain that my daily evaluation score rested on my ability to keep my FTO dry, I quickly volunteered to get out and push.

"No. Just stay there." Don grudgingly lifted his foot over the edge of the boat and dipped his boot into the water. As soon as his full weight pushed onto the marsh bottom, he sank two feet deeper into the muck. The rotten stench of marsh mud seeped out of the water with each squelching step. Don leaned into the back of the boat, straining as he pushed, while I made the best progress I could with a paddle.

Eventually, back on dry ground, we unloaded our gear, the dead goose, and the guns. Don climbed into the truck and instructed me to get started on the paperwork. As I struggled through the required seizure forms, Don sipped from his coffee cup and coached me on the process of posting bond for nonresidents. As I copied down the guns' serial numbers and O'Dell's driver's license information, Don intently worked on cleaning the caked mud from the creases of his fingers, muttering about the "dumbass" we had to deal with on what was supposed to be an uneventful pheasant opener.

I finished up the paperwork and realized that it seemed to be taking too long for O'Dell to make it back to the ramp. I glanced in the rearview mirror to check on his progress. "Um, I don't think he is planning on coming back to shore."

"Huh?" Don was absorbed in the task of scraping away at his mud-encrusted fingernails.

"Well, he's sitting in a lawn chair reading a book."

"WHAT?" Don exploded through clenched teeth. He turned around, craning his neck to look out the back window of the truck. "He's doing WHAT?"

I cringed as I repeated, "Looks like he's reading a book."

Don leapt out of the truck and stormed to the end of the boat ramp like the Tasmanian Devil in his tornado rampage.

"HEY! You get over here!" he screamed as if O'Dell were a disobedient dog.

O'Dell placidly looked up from his reading and casually called back with a mockingly pleasant tone, "If you want me, you're going to have to come and get me."

"If I have to come and get you, you'll be wearing handcuffs and I'll be hauling your ass to jail. So I recommend that you get over here, RIGHT NOW!"

"I figure you were going to do that anyway." O'Dell shrugged his shoulders. "So come and get me if you want me."

Don stomped back to the truck and snatched his phone from the dash. "I'm calling Link," he said, wanting more help than I could offer in dealing with the situation. My FTO clearly didn't think I was ready for the task of forcefully removing O'Dell from the marsh. Craig Link, the warden from the neighboring county, was an experienced officer and outweighed me by a good hundred pounds.

Approximately twenty minutes later Link arrived, followed by a sheriff's deputy. The three of them unloaded the boat again and set out for the slow slog to the island, while I was left on the boat ramp to monitor the action through my binoculars.

I watched as they pulled up on shore and began speaking to O'Dell, Don's arms gesticulating madly like a coach arguing with an umpire. The interaction quickly moved from verbal commands to a short scuffle that ended with O'Dell in handcuffs.

"Oh, shit," I whispered to myself as I watched the officers fill the boat with O'Dell's decoys. By the time O'Dell and his dog sat down for the ride, the weight of its cargo forced all three officers to push the boat as O'Dell and his dog rode like royalty to the boat ramp.

When they arrived on shore, I tied the dog to the RV and supplied it with food and water. The deputy transported O'Dell to jail, where he fulfilled his promise of failing to post bond.

Over the next several days, O'Dell made a nuisance of himself. The jailer was at wit's end as O'Dell continued to refuse to post bond or to make any phone calls in an effort to get someone to bail him out. On more than one occasion O'Dell faked a heart attack, winning him a personalized field trip to the hospital by worn-out jail staff. There, he frustrated the nurses charged with his care. After every trip the doctors informed the jailers of what they already knew. Nothing was physically wrong with O'Dell. He was lying.

Eventually, after realizing that O'Dell was treating the county lockup like the Ritz-Carlton, the judge cut him loose. O'Dell refused to pay his fines, and his hunting privileges were suspended for three years.

A year later, finally free of training, I was on patrol in my own territory when my phone rang.

"It's Don. Guess who I just caught hunting?"

"No way," I said.

"Yep. I just dropped him off at the jail. Man, were those jailers pissed! He refused to post bond again."

The following morning O'Dell sat before the county judge and attempted to spin more lies. The judge kindly reminded O'Dell that he was the same judge who had listened to his lies the first time around. He invited O'Dell to either pay his fines or rot behind bars for as long as it took for him to pay up. O'Dell, shrinking under the judge's frosty gaze, finally reached for his wallet and pried open its creaky hinges.

LARS DUNCAN cut an imposing figure. Standing over six feet five inches from the soles of his hiking boots to the tips of his flat-top hairline, Lars was a solid mass of a conservation officer. I never saw Lars without the signature mustache that spanned the breadth of his upper lip and not a pinch more. When I first transferred into Johnson County, I kept my distance from Lars, unsure exactly what to make of him. But as the years went by, it became apparent that Lars was the proverbial giant teddy bear. He was empathetic, direct, and always had a story to tell.

"Are you ready for this one, young lady?" Lars asked over a Subway sandwich one weekend during deer season. He always referred to me as "young lady" even as my gray hairs sprouted in greater numbers. And he always began his stories by asking me whether I was ready for it, the answer to which was generally irrelevant. Aside from Lars's ability to continually lecture me about his retirement savings plans and to quiz me unabashedly about my own finances, I could always count on Lars to come up with unlikely stories. They came by virtue of his territory. Lying in a county north of mine, Lars's assigned territory was full of interesting characters who often travelled south, contaminating my territory like invasive species. His was a land bound for perpetual trouble, immune to the cleaning-up effect that hard work could have on more rural counties.

"I'm ready." I took a bite of my tuna salad and waited for the tale.

"Remember that guy I told you about a few years ago? Bob?" he asked.

"You're going to have to be more specific. Aren't they all named Bob up there?"

"He's that old guy who drives that crappy green pickup. We sat on him one night just south of the park because I had complaints about him shining deer in his field right after sunset," Lars said, jogging my memory.

"Oh, yeah, I remember him."

Bob was a short, balding man in his late sixties. Lars and I had parked our trucks one night up on a hill behind a silo and watched Bob in his pickup crawl the surrounding roads at a snail's pace. He scanned the fields as if he was on the prowl for deer, but we weren't able to catch him casting a light or taking a shot. Lars had told me that night that it would only be a matter of time before we caught Bob. And I believed him. Lars was nothing if not doggedly persistent.

"Well, his wife turned him in," Lars said, dropping the bombshell and watching for my reaction.

"For what?" I asked incredulously.

"Killing a deer over bait." Baiting deer is against the law in Iowa, but its illegality doesn't stop some people from scattering corn, dumping piles of apples, or putting down a mineral block to entice deer close to their favorite hunting spot.

"Wow, that's bold. Are they still married?" I asked. Ex-wives often made great informants, but a current wife would be a noteworthy anomaly.

"Nope." Lars paused for effect. "She died two weeks after she turned him in."

Lars went on to tell the story.

"Linda, Bob's wife, called me one day a few weeks ago and told me she had something to show me," Lars began. "I couldn't believe it when she said who she was. I've been trying to catch Bob for a few years, so she was the last person I expected to call. She told me that Bob goes to town for coffee every morning at 8:00, so she wanted me to show up at their house at 8:15. So I got there right at 8:15 just like she said." Lars paused for a bite of his sandwich. "Linda looked sick when she answered the door. Her face was gaunt, shadows under her eyes. She told me she had cancer. The doctor apparently said that she only had a month or two to live. Anyway, so she leads me up to the attic of their house. When we get up there, she walks over to this big cardboard box in the corner, reaches into it, and pulls out a shotgun."

"Holy crap, she pulled a shotgun on you?"

"No," Lars chuckled at my question. "It was Bob's gun. She'd hidden it in there. Anyway, she gave it to me to unload." Lars mimicked the pumping action of unloading a shotgun. "I racked it, and two shells popped out. Then I asked her if Bob knew that she'd taken his gun, but she said she had no idea—apparently they'd stopped speaking after he killed her deer."

"What do you mean, 'her deer'?" I asked.

"It was basically her pet deer. She'd been feeding it every day for the last year. Said it was her favorite one. But are you ready for this?" A smile crept over his face as Lars lingered, waiting for my regular response.

"Yeah."

"She even had it named. She called it Sweety."

"Oh, boy, that's not good," I said.

"Nope, it's not. His wife is dying of cancer, and he stands on the front porch and pops Sweety right in front of her. Who does that?"

"Apparently Bob does that," I replied, my opinion of humankind sliding even further south.

"So then, we go outside, and Linda shows me the deer. It's hanging right there from the tree in the backyard. And there's a typical baiting site—you know, a giant bare spot where the deer had been eating the corn.

"By this point, Linda's in tears. She's telling me all about her diagnosis and how feeding Sweety was basically the only thing she looked forward to every day. Said she'd sit there for hours and watch that deer."

"Geez, who does that?" I said, repeating Lars's question.

"Apparently Bob does that," Lars grinned, repeating my answer. "I'm sorry," he shook his head. "It's not funny at all. The worst part is that she felt like the whole thing was her fault, because the deer were so used to seeing her that Sweety probably didn't think twice about Bob standing on the porch."

"So, what happened when you talked to Bob then? Did you tell him that Linda turned him in?"

"I don't think I really had to. He knew how upset she was. He just didn't care enough to not kill her deer," Lars said.

His story was interrupted by a herd of high schoolers entering the restaurant. They were chattering and laughing, seemingly blind to life's cruelties. I finished my sandwich in silence.

"But you know what, young lady?" Lars asked as the high school kids settled into a corner booth.

"What?"

"We'll catch him again. He won't stop." Lars's persistently positive outlook was almost catching.

"I'm sure you're right. I just hope I'm there next time," I said.

"You'll be there. I'm sure you'll be there."

Lars and I stood up from the booth and returned to the winter temperatures in the restaurant parking lot. As Lars climbed into his truck, he asked, "Well, ready to go look for deer hunters, young lady?"

"I suppose I don't really have a choice," I said. Cold air blew small piles of snow into streaks across the cement as I put my truck in gear and drove north.

— SOME WERE WOMEN —

"After the season had been underway for a few weeks and some of the men had taken advantage of being permitted to accompany up or downstream, they came to realize that their better halves were not so dumb after all, especially when it came to making a graceful cast and being rewarded with a beautiful trout, or perhaps coming in with a creel holding the limit. It did happen many times. In spite of comments received the first season proved to be a success; perhaps not financially, but by the interest, enthusiasm, and cooperation shown by women participants."

—William Teague, *The Hartford Courant* (1934)

O N A WINDSWEPT RAINY DAY in April 1933, Edith Stoehr cast a fly into the swollen Branford River. It wasn't an easy cast. The trouty spot she was aiming for was bordered by low-hanging tree limbs, the bane of every fly-fisher. And then there was the pressure. The contest judges' brows furrowed as they scrutinized Edith's fishing technique and the accuracy of the fly's placement. For Edith and the other contestants, the stakes were high. Whichever woman proved herself in this competition of casting distance, accuracy, fishing knowledge, and "personality" would receive the special assignment of the first female game warden in Connecticut.

Despite the weather and the talented rivalry, Edith won the day and the badge. As deputy warden, she was assigned to a territory that consisted of a section of the Branford River open exclusively to women and, later, to a women-only hunting area.

Based on newspaper reports at the time, Edith apparently thrived in her duties as a deputy warden. In addition to policing her territory for lawbreakers, she also spent considerable time teaching women how to fish and hunt. She stocked the river with fish and the grasslands with game birds and assisted her male counterparts in special assignments outside her area. Edith was a sworn officer, carried a gun, and had powers of arrest, which she occasionally used to arrest male violators. Edith was an accomplished angler, an experienced dog handler, and a crackerjack shot. In short, Edith was pretty badass.

On a shelf in my office sits a dust-covered three-ring binder filled with my research about Edith Stoehr's life and career. Among other things, the binder contains lists of Stoehr's job duties, newspaper articles detailing her first pursuit, typewritten letters from radio stations in New York requesting interviews with her, departmental performance evaluations, requests from Edith for pay increases, copies of photographs of her in uniform, and her obituary from the *New York Times,* marking her death on March 6, 1946, at age forty.

The newspaper clippings tell an interesting story of Edith's life as a game warden. But I'm even more intrigued by the stories left untold, the stories she took to her grave at such a young age. If only I could sit down with her ghost and ask all the questions that nag me when I try to read between the lines of the archived newsprint and the bureaucratic paperwork. What was it like to be the only woman in such a man's world? Was her experience at all like mine? Did she feel the isolation I've felt? Did she see herself as some kind of an ugly bug under a hand lens, her every move examined, critiqued, and subtly ridiculed? Were there times when she wanted to quit? Did she encounter any of the more blatant sexism that would have been commonplace during that time? Would her stories reflect those of almost all the women I know who have tried or are now trying desperately to scratch and claw their way down the brambled path she began to clear more than eighty years ago?

Since the day Edith won the fly-fishing contest, some progress has been made, but it has been slow. My own department's homogeneous statistics beg for more diversity in terms of gender, ethnicity, and race. Iowa is divided into ninety-nine counties. As I write this, the DNR employs seventy-six conservation officers, including supervisory staff. Most officers are assigned one or two counties. In addition, some officers must also cover the yawning territory vacancies that, in the name of cost savings, have plagued our department for years. We are white. And with the exception of only six of us (just seven percent), we are male.

Fish and game law enforcement has historically been a place crowded with men. While it's admittedly a tough time for anyone working in law enforcement, females face additional challenges. Women constantly struggle to fit in and to prove to colleagues, the public, and ourselves that we belong.

Nobody warned me that the hardest part about being a female conservation officer wasn't going to be fulfilling the job duties but, rather, finding my way through a labyrinth of self-doubt. The creeping growth of nagging insecurity throughout my career was like moss smothering a dead tree, its advance so slow that I wasn't aware of it until, ten years after my initial assignment, decomposition had set in. My looks have never inspired catcalls or inappropriate come-ons. But most problems women encounter in the workplace don't relate to one's place on a scale of perceived femininity.

They relate to a combination of gender perception and narrow thinking. Almost every woman I've spoken with who wears a badge feels at one time or another that she's under the microscope. She must constantly try to prove her worth in a land of low-level chatter telling her that she was only hired because she's female, that she was the token woman in a field of much more qualified men. And deep down, almost every female officer believes it's true, because there's a good chance that it is. She may very well have been hired because they "needed" to hire a female.

When it comes to hunting and fishing, the image still reigns of the old-fashioned game warden (always male) lurking in the woods to spy on hunters and hanging out at coffee shops shooting the shit with local sportsmen. This good-old-boy system has always resisted change. But each year brings a bit more hope: the appointment of female supervisors, the acknowledgment of same-sex partners during award ceremonies, the intelligent and motivated young women who work as seasonal patrol officers, and the growing acceptance of the fact that women have a vital role to play in the field.

Last year I attended a women's leadership training session with female officers from a variety of state law enforcement agencies. We discussed the challenges we've faced in our careers, and we tried to come up with strategies to overcome such difficulties. But mostly we told stories, commiserating over our collective circumstance. And we laughed. We laughed, and we felt included. And in the back of the room, seated in the last row, I saw Edith Stoehr, dressed in full uniform, proud and resilient. She was smiling.

WHEN I WAS TWENTY-FOUR YEARS OLD, I asked the hairdresser to cut off my hair. When she asked, "How much do you want me to take off?" I replied, "Most of it."

I'd always been told that I had my grandma's hair. Long, dark blond, and very thick: ponytail headache thick. I was tired of the pain from restraining its girth and tired of the hair in my eyes when I didn't. By the time I emerged from the salon, my hair was an inch long.

Pixie cuts like mine are meant for people who resemble pixies: short, dainty, and light. My six-foot-tall frame doesn't shout dainty. And neither does the fact that people expect to see my uniform on a man. That's what conservation officers are supposed to be, after all.

I used to get distressed when someone called me sir. I'd call up my friends on the phone and say, "I just got called sir. Again. I'm going to grow my hair back out." But that wasn't going to happen. I'd grown to love the comfort and ease of my buzzcut.

Most of the time when someone called me sir I'd wait for the awkward moment when the fisherman I was checking gave me a second look, turned red, shifted uncomfortably, and said, "Oh, sorry. Um . . . um . . . I just saw the gun. . . . You want to see my license?"

Over the years, to satisfy my own curiosity, I conducted a very unscientific study of the kinds of people who don't make the correction from "sir" to "ma'am." The evidence overwhelmingly showed that the person who didn't figure it out was likely to be drunk.

One summer, I was called to the scene of a boat accident where one of the boat drivers was suspected of operating his vessel while intoxicated, a serious misdemeanor and a jailable offense. I arrived at the boat ramp to find one boat anchored on the beach with a gaping gouge in the fiberglass hull extending four feet along its length. Thankfully, the middle-aged couple who were on the boat when it was T-boned were uninjured, although, understandably, they were shaken up. The woman had been absorbed in a book when she looked up to see the belly of a twenty-four-foot Baja ten yards away and bearing down. Her husband, who was driving their boat, tried to get out of the way, but he was unable to avoid the collision.

"Where is the driver of the Baja?" I asked the state trooper, who was sitting in his squad car at the boat ramp. He pointed to the Baja, which was pulled up on the edge of a nearby beach.

The trooper got out of his car, put on his Smokey hat, and tilted his head toward a college-aged guy sitting on the parking-lot curb. "His name is Chris." Chris sat hunched on the curb, his head buried in his hands.

I walked over, introduced myself, and told Chris that I wanted to administer a few tests to make sure he was sober enough to drive his boat back to the marina.

"You need tests for that? Can't you tell I'm drunk, sir?" he asked. I smiled and glanced over at the trooper, hoping he hadn't heard the gender snafu. He didn't seem to have noticed.

For the next ten minutes, Chris struggled through the regimen of field sobriety tests.

The first was the Horizontal Gaze Nystagmus test.

"Watch the tip of my finger with your eyes only. Don't move your head. Do you understand?"

"Yes, sir," he answered. I flinched at the "sir," once again hoping the trooper hadn't heard. Chris's eyes jumped around like ping-pong balls, a positive indicator of alcohol impairment.

I read the instructions for the Walk and Turn test and asked, "Do you understand?"

"Yes, sir." I cringed yet again.

The test posed a significant challenge for Chris.

Finally, I read the instructions for the One Leg Stand test. "Do you understand?" I said, attempting to forcefully lift my naturally low voice into a slightly higher octave.

"Yes, sir." Son of a bitch.

For the first fifteen seconds of the test, Chris stood on one foot and hopped around wildly, like a preschooler demonstrating a newfound skill. I finally stopped the test early when, instead of jumping, he began to lean so far to the right that I thought he was going to faceplant into the cement.

Chris was most definitely drunk.

The trooper drove Chris to the police station, where he would be faced with the decision of whether or not to provide us with a breath sample to be tested for alcohol content. I followed the trooper to the station. The ride lasted at least twenty minutes. As the trooper pulled up to the station, Chris was on the verge of leaving a puddle in the back seat of the squad car. The trooper and I helped him out of the car and steadied his elbows as he moaned like a sick cat, pressing his knees together. He waddled inside.

We buzzed our way through the security doors and eventually reached the OWI processing room. Chris instantly made a beeline for the attached bathroom, the trooper fast on his heels to chaperone him. I sat down at the desk and began to fill out paperwork.

Chris must have gotten himself into position in front of the john before realizing that, with handcuffs on, he had no way of aiming properly. As I tried to focus on the paperwork, I could overhear Chris asking the trooper for some help.

"I'm nice. But I'm not that nice," the trooper replied before I heard the click of the handcuffs being removed. Chris proceeded to relieve himself for the next several minutes. It was the longest piss I'd audibly witnessed from a drunk.

Finally, Chris and the trooper emerged from the bathroom. I asked Chris whether he would consent to the breath test.

"Sir, are you going to, like, take my breath from me then?" Chris asked.

"Uh, what do you mean, take your breath?"

"I mean, are you going to, like, suck out my breath?"

"No. You have to blow. You know, like when you blow up a balloon?" I spoke slowly and demonstrated the act of blowing into the mouthpiece.

"Okay, so you won't, like, take it from me then." He breathed a sigh of relief.

"No," I said.

Chris marked the box labeled "Consent" on the form and proceeded with the test. The result popped up on the screen a few minutes later: .237, almost three times the legal limit.

Next I asked Chris a series of questions. They started with simple ones like, "What is your occupation?" and "What did you have for breakfast?" Then the questions became more specific and incriminating: "Were you in control of the vessel?" and "How much alcohol did you drink?"

Chris was having trouble concentrating. He pushed a pencil around on the desk, a millionth of an inch to the right, then a millionth of an inch to the left. He crouched down low, so his eyes were level with the desktop as he peered at the pencil, like Tiger Woods lining up a putt. Then he resumed the pencil pushing routine until I interrupted it with my last question, "Were you involved in an accident today?"

"No, sir," he answered confidently.

I assumed he must have misunderstood the question. "I mean today. Were you involved in a boating accident today?"

Chris stared at the ceiling as though the answer might be hovering somewhere near the light fixture. He kept staring. I followed his gaze upward to where a fly was making its way from one end of the room's ceiling to the other in a slow-motion crawl. "Chris," I said sharply, trying to refocus his attention, "were you involved in an accident today?"

He snapped out of the fly trance and looked back at me. "Nooooo, siiirrr! No accident for me, sir."

I glanced up at the trooper who was having trouble hiding his grin. "Well, then, I think we're done here."

After booking Chris into jail, the trooper and I were walking back to our vehicles when he suddenly burst out laughing.

"What's so funny?" I asked.

"He called you sir the entire time!" the trooper said. "You should really put that into your report. If he can't even get that right, he was obviously bombed."

I smiled. "Well, thank you very much, sir."

I'D ALWAYS BEEN OPPOSED to hiring seasonal patrol officers younger than twenty-one. Too many lacked the maturity to deal with the chaos that a summer on the reservoir could deliver. There were court-ready reports to be written, bodies to be recovered, intoxicated people to manage, citations to be issued, and thousands of dollars' worth of patrol boats to avoid crashing. It all seemed too demanding a challenge for someone lacking a fully developed frontal lobe who couldn't yet legally drink.

Gloria Dayton proved me wrong. She came to my patrol station as a seasonal officer at nineteen, having finished her first year of college majoring in politics. She was bright and personable, with hair almost as short as mine. In the first month of Gloria's employment, I arrested a drunk boater who intentionally shoved dirt and grass into his mouth in a strange attempt at beating the breath test. The whole way to jail he heaved insults in my direction, among other things making fun of my hair and calling me bald. From that moment on, Gloria and I named ourselves the Badass Bald Girls.

One evening while patrolling the Coralville Reservoir, county deputies were dispatched to Bobber's Bar and Grill, situated on the reservoir, for an intoxicated suicidal woman. We were close, so Gloria and I pulled our patrol boat up to the docks at Bobber's and found the reporting party sitting in a black pickup truck in the boat ramp parking lot. He pointed toward the water. "She walked over the hill there with a bottle of vodka. I asked if she was going to hurt herself, and she told me that she wouldn't promise me anything. She's had a rough year—her husband died a few months ago."

"Okay, what's her name?" I asked.

"Her name's Kim. She's had quite a bit to drink."

Gloria and I walked to the edge of the parking lot where it dropped away and then stepped over the edge to the rocky shoreline below. Seated on a large rock, Kim was hunched over, talking loudly into a cell phone lying on a rock next to her. I could hear the conversation over speakerphone as the man on the other end of the line was trying fiercely to convince Kim that her life was worth living. "Don't you want to see your grandkids someday?" he asked.

"I don't even care anymore," she cried. "I don't care about anything."

As the man continued talking with Kim, Gloria and I picked our way down the rocks until we were standing next to her. Kim's face was wet with tears, she was barefoot, and blood trickled down her leg from a cut on her knee. A broken vodka bottle was shattered on the rocks at her feet.

"Kim?" I said, trying to gain her attention. She ignored my presence completely and kept talking on the phone. Gloria stood by and listened for several minutes in an attempt to discern something of the situation.

Based on the phone conversation, I concluded that the man was her ex-husband, whom she'd abandoned years ago. She'd taken their children with her, leaving him devastated and heartbroken. Kim had moved on and remarried, but her second husband had recently died. Now she wanted to end it all.

After a few minutes, two sheriff's deputies arrived. The younger of the two, Deputy Derrick Rice, climbed down the rocks and stood with us.

"Kim?" he said. "Can we call him back in a little bit? I'd like to talk to you."

"I don't have a fucking thing to say to you," she barked. "Who asked you to come here anyway? Just get the hell away from me."

"We can't do that, Kim. Some people are concerned about you," he said.

"Nobody gives a damn about me. I'm just trying to sit here with my husband. And don't you dare fucking touch my husband."

I suddenly realized that the small wooden box sitting on the rocks amid the shards of vodka bottle was an urn.

"We're not going to touch your husband," he assured her. "We just want to help you."

"Well, I don't need your help, so you can just leave."

"We can't do that," he repeated. The back and forth continued for several minutes with Rice trying to help and Kim refusing it, ordering us all to leave.

"Can we at least just help you get back up to the parking lot? I don't want you to trip and end up in the water," Rice said.

"I'm not going anywhere with you. But if you'll get my sandals, I'll leave when I'm ready. I'm just trying to sit here with my husband. This was his favorite place, and I never took the time to come here with him when he was alive. And then he fucking died on me. I watched him die," she wailed.

"Where are your sandals?" Gloria asked. "I'll get them for you."

Kim pointed to the top of the hill, and Gloria set off to search for them. While Gloria looked for the sandals, Kim went on with her story. She told us about her two sons. One was grown and on his own. The other would soon be joining the military. "They don't want anything to do with me either," Kim said. "The younger one told me he wishes I was dead. By the way, not that it's any of your business, but I stopped taking my meds. I hate the way they made me feel. Then my husband died five months ago. I've been drunk ever since."

"Which medications were you on?" I asked.

Kim told us that she took medications because she was bipolar and had split personality disorder and PTSD.

"I was raped by my dad and by my uncle. So that's why I hate men. The only one I trusted died at fifty-seven," Kim said, nodding in the direction of her husband's ashes.

"I'm sorry to hear that," Deputy Rice said. "Why don't we move to the parking lot, and we can talk there."

"I TOLD you I'm not going ANYWHERE with you!" she shouted. "Weren't you listening when I said that I don't like men? I don't trust men, and if you try to touch me, you'll regret it!"

"I don't want to touch you. I just want you to move to the parking lot where it's safer."

"Get the FUCK away from me," Kim seethed. "If you so much as lay a finger on me I'll fight. I'll get violent, and it won't be pretty!"

Gloria returned with Kim's sandals after finding them stashed among the rocks near the top of the hill. "I heard you say that your son is joining the military," Gloria said, changing the subject. "That's something you should be proud of."

Kim took a deep breath, visibly relaxing at the distracting change of subject. "Thank you. I am proud—just scared to death."

"It sounds to me like you've done a lot right with your kids. I mean one of them has a job and is on his own, and the other is going to serve.

You can't ask much more from a mother than to get her kids standing on their own two feet, right?" Gloria continued. "You were strong to make it through all that you did. You're still here."

"Yeah. But now I'm paying the price. My husband is gone, and my boys don't want anything to do with me. The only person that cared about me in the world is in that fucking box." Kim pointed at the wooden box at her feet. "Can I have a smoke?"

Deputy Rice told Kim she could smoke once we moved to the top of the ramp. Kim exploded in a rage over the suggestion that she leave and again threatened violence if the deputy touched her. "It's nothing against you. I just don't trust men, and I don't like them touching me. So just back off. You are only here because some dumbass person wouldn't mind their own business. I ain't gonna talk to you. I'll only talk to them." Kim nodded her head in the direction where Gloria and I were standing. "I trust them—they're women."

"If he waits up in the parking lot while you smoke one more cigarette, will you walk up to the parking lot with us?" I asked.

"Yeah, I'll go with you," Kim answered. Rice shrugged and climbed back up the rocks to the parking lot.

"My name is Erika," I said. "And this is Gloria." Kim shook our hands.

"I want you to know that we aren't here just because we were called here. I truly care about people, and it bothers me to see you like this," Gloria said. "You're strong. I know you can get through this. Look at all you've gone through already."

Kim smirked. "How old are you anyway?"

"You got me there," Gloria smiled. "Maybe I'm too young to understand everything, but the one thing I know is that you're strong."

Gloria, Kim, and I continued to talk about her life for the next hour. Kim told us that this was her first visit to the reservoir. She explained that she'd come to see it because her late husband had always talked about growing up in the area. She wished she had come to visit it while he was still alive.

"What was your husband's name?" I asked.

"Robert," she said, breaking into another round of tears. "His name was Robert Miller."

When her tears began to dry, I pointed out over the water. "Look at that sunset." It was especially brilliant that night. Oranges mixed with pink through a series of brush-stroked clouds reflected on the water's surface.

"I bet one of the reasons Robert loved this place so much was for the sunsets. It's one of the best places to watch the sun go down."

Kim nodded and cried, her face buried in her open palms. "I'm just sorry I didn't come here when he was still alive."

"I get that. But I also think he knows you're here now," I said.

"I hope so." Tears streamed down Kim's cheeks.

"I suppose we better walk to the parking lot before they send more officers," I suggested.

"What can we carry for you?" Gloria asked.

"I'm taking my husband. You can carry the other stuff."

I picked up her phone and cigarette lighter from the ground and helped Kim to her feet. She was unsteady and swayed dangerously. I put my hand in the center of her back. "I got you. Let's get up this hill." As we climbed, Gloria distracted Kim with a discussion about the outdoors. She quizzed Kim about which tree was her favorite. By the time we reached the parking lot, Kim was smiling. Unfortunately, it didn't last.

The waiting deputies were becoming restless. The list of uncompleted calls continued to grow on their computer screens, and they needed to close out this one.

"I'm gonna be real with you here, Kim," Rice said. "We only have two choices tonight. I can take you to the hospital, where I think you need to be, or I can take you to jail for public intox. I prefer the hospital."

"I'm going home," Kim said through clenched teeth.

After another few minutes of unsuccessful negotiations, Rice grabbed Kim's right arm, and his partner grabbed her left. Kim struggled, screaming and fighting as she had promised to do. "Let go of me! Stop touching me!" she wailed like an injured animal. Her eyes were wild and glinted with reflections from the lights in the parking lot. The music from the live band at the bar pounded through the air, muffling her screeching cries.

"We don't want to hurt you, Kim. Please just sit in the car. All you need to do is sit in the car," the older deputy said calmly. But Kim continued to fight. She threw her weight against the officers as they struggled to maintain hold of her flailing arms.

I stepped in. "Kim, if they let go of you, will you sit in the car? Will you do it for me and Gloria? We're right here." Kim nodded madly. She panted with exertion and leaned against the side of the back seat, on the verge of sitting down.

"Just let her go for a second," I said. When the deputies let go of her arms, Kim sank farther back into the seat of the squad car.

"Give me my husband!" she screamed. "Give me my husband!"

Gloria took the urn from where it sat on the hood of the squad car and handed it to me.

"Here's Robert," I said, holding the box out to her. Kim snatched the urn from my hands, clutched it to her chest, and cowered back against the car's interior. "Kim. You are going to be okay. Everything's going to be okay. Just put your legs inside the car so you don't get hurt." She hesitated, then complied.

As soon as the deputy closed the door, Kim began screaming in earnest like an animal being tortured. Her fists pounded against the windows of the squad car as she wailed to be freed.

Gloria and I returned to our boat waiting at the docks. As we climbed over the gunwale and settled into the seat, Gloria said, "I wish it wouldn't have happened like that. I feel like it didn't have to be that way."

"Maybe not. But no matter what, I don't think she would have been willing to go anywhere but home without putting up a fight. I agree, though. It might have been better if nobody had touched her. But at least we made it a little easier for her because she definitely responded better to us as women than she did to the deputies. I'm glad that we were able to help her—at least a little bit."

We slipped out onto the open, empty lake. The bass from the band beat a deep rhythm across the rippling water and into the distance. We motored in the direction of the crescent moon, its reflection a bright sliver on the water. And on toward home.

THE FIRST TIME I HEARD the term "rolling the cob" was while attending the state's annual meeting during my field training phase. Conservation officers from across the state were gathered around tables in a conference room lined with taxidermy, all specimens of Iowa wildlife. Some officers sipped on coffee and propped their chins up on fists in an attempt to stay awake. Some were fighting vicious hangovers spawned during the previous night's alcohol-fueled storytelling sessions. And others struggled to stay upright after a night of insomnia from being forced to lie in the bunk beds of state park cabins listening to the chainsaw snoring of their comrades.

I'd listened to the other officers, sometimes under the influence of various spirits, share what it was like in the good old days when the job was fun, when the public respected game wardens, and, within the department, the brass had the backs of the field officers. During the evening's informal gatherings, old guys stood around the keg and shook their heads in dismay at the changes they'd experienced over the years. They groused about low morale and how things just weren't like they used to be. They couldn't wait for retirement.

In the conference room, the chief of the law enforcement bureau took his place at the front. His ample belly strained against his shirt as he spoke into the microphone with a southern Iowa drawl. It was the last speech of the three-day meeting, his final call to arms. The chief wanted to inspire us to rise above the stress, the drudgery of never-ending paperwork, the pencil-pushing busywork that distracted us from our real purpose, and he wanted to help us forget about the budgetary woes dogging our department. Speaking in his nasal drone, he hoped to rekindle our enthusiasm for working in the field of wildlife law enforcement. He said, "You guys gotta remember that the best skill you can possess in this job is the ability to roll the cob."

The chief's pep talk was meant to remind us how interesting, vital, and challenging our chosen profession was supposed to be. He wanted to send us on our way with a sense of hope, with the spark of enthusiasm necessary for making good cases. But I could see from the cynical look in the eyes of the older officers that the pep talk held little sway. For them, it came from someone with too much brass weighing down his collar.

I was still new and didn't yet need the chief's rallying cry. I merely wanted to understand what he was talking about. Looking around the room, I wondered if I was the only one who didn't know what "rolling the cob" meant. The bobbing heads and glazed-over eyes did nothing to enlighten me.

"I'm here to tell ya, ya gotta take the time to talk to people. We're different from other cops," the chief continued. "Don't be afraid to stand around, to take your time and chat with people. Rolling the cob means you gotta take the time to stand out in a cornfield and talk with the landowners, talk with the hunters, and listen to the farmers. Don't just do a quick license check and hurry to get out of there. Go talk with the old boys in the coffee shops. Hang out in the bait shops. Be available to folks. You gotta stay there rolling the cob until you grind the kernels right off." He rolled an imaginary corn cob back and forth under his foot. "If you aren't willing to take the time with these people, they won't trust you, and if they don't trust you, ya'll won't get any good information. And I'm here to tell ya, if ya don't get good information, you will not be successful in this career."

I left the meeting feeling overwhelmed and unprepared. I feared that I wasn't cut out to be a cob roller. As a lifelong teetotaler, a non-coffee-drinking young woman, and an introvert, I already felt like an outcast. I didn't know how to fit into this group of people and how, with my discomfort with small talk, I'd ever succeed. The chief's pep talk left me in doubt about my career before it had even really begun. But I knew that I had to try, even if it meant carving out my own path and developing my own style of rolling the cob.

As the years progressed, my cob-rolling skills marginally improved, but the near constant feeling that I was outside my comfort zone kept me in a state of anxiety. My life had never been short on anxiety. It wasn't until I was in my forties that I was diagnosed with generalized anxiety disorder. The diagnosis explained a lot. It provided me with a reason for a lifetime of walking around with my shoulders dangling from my earlobes, tense from the ever-present stress of feeling inadequate. While I had a natural curiosity about other people's lives and could converse about many things, I wasn't a natural bullshitter when it came to the banter of hunters and anglers. My interest waned even more when someone dug into his pocket or swiped through his phone for a photograph of the last deer he killed, its tongue lolling and blood pooling under its body. I would nod encouragingly while my thoughts strayed to other things I'd rather be doing. If I were ever going to feel successful as a conservation officer, I knew that I needed a menu of coping skills. I needed something other than the ability to perfectly roll the cob.

Some days I managed to make it through my daily battle with anxiety by placing myself at the center of a novel. I morphed into the main character of the book: a strong, fearless, female detective. A hero. I acted my way through the days, internally talking through my moves and decisions like a third-person narrator. Pretending to be someone capable of rolling the cob was surprisingly helpful. But when I couldn't manage that level of fakery, I turned to Mackenzie Watson for a little help.

Mackenzie was an attractive twenty-something. Her long dark hair, dimples, and svelte body screamed "All American Girl." But she had a naughty streak, too. There were occasional booze cruises down gravel roads, late night visits to cowboy bars, a dangerous attraction to bad boys, and her favorite wardrobe of impossibly tight jeans and camo-print tank tops. A hot pink decal reading "Silly boys, trucks are for girls" graced the back window of her jacked truck as she whipped donuts in the deepest mudholes she could find. Mackenzie listened to country music, and she wasn't averse to sitting in a deer stand on a cold fall morning. But Mackenzie had one major flaw—which, ironically, made her my greatest asset—she was a terrible judge of character. Her roster of online friends included a long list of criminals, from poachers to drug dealers and thieves to sex offenders. In essence, she was everything I could never be. Mackenzie was my alter ego in the form of a fabricated Facebook persona I created—an avatar game warden dressed like a redneck cliché. She was my technological cob roller and my secret weapon.

When a boat theft notification appeared in my email inbox one summer day, I knew Mackenzie would be the right girl for the job. I was sitting with Ben Harper, a college student working as a seasonal water patrol officer, in my air-conditioned truck in a boat ramp parking lot. It was mid-July, and the air was steamy and thick. We needed a break from the intense heat and had decided to make an ice cream run before heading back out in the patrol boat. I had just logged on to my computer preparing for the drive to town when the email appeared on my screen. "This looks interesting. There's a stolen boat out of Cedar Rapids." I pointed to the picture attached to the email.

Ben leaned over to look at the photo. The boat was a Lowe flat-bottom johnboat tricked out with all the latest equipment, including side-scan sonar, a trolling motor, custom rod holders, and an Evinrude E-Tec motor. According to the email, it had been parked in a rental storage lot facility when it was swiped in the early morning hours by two men driving a gray Ford F-150. Only one name was listed under possible suspects: Underwood.

"That's a pretty distinct looking boat," Ben said. "You wouldn't think it would be too hard to track down."

"You wouldn't think, unless it's already been cut up into pieces, scrapped, and sold." I opened Mackenzie's Facebook account and typed in the name Underwood. "Just for fun, let's see if we can narrow it down by looking at a few profiles. Then I'll call Mark. Looks like this notification came from him, so I bet he has more information about this. They must have a reason for listing Underwood as a suspect."

Mark Vidra was the park ranger at a state park on the outskirts of Cedar Rapids. Every weekend, until the wee morning hours, Mark's voice piped over the radio. He was often out of breath and requesting backup as he wrestled one wanted, drunk, or combative person after another to the ground. It was a rough park, at times, and seemed to have the effect of a high-pitched dog whistle, beckoning all the miscreants within a fifty-mile radius to its borders.

I clicked through the list of Underwoods lining up on my computer screen and compared profile pictures, posts, and friends lists. Several of the Underwood profiles showed mutual friends with Mackenzie, which by itself was a good indicator of criminal behavior. Based on our observations and a bit of intuition, we narrowed our selection down to three guys: Manny, Jack, and Tony Underwood. Each was located in the Cedar Rapids metro area, where the theft had taken place, and each had at least one mutual friend with Mackenzie. And for whatever it was worth, each also had the face of a thief from a Hollywood film.

I called Mark, and his voice coming through my squad's Bluetooth speaker confirmed our speculations. "We think it was either Manny Underwood or his brother Jack." I looked over at Ben, who grinned at the news. "There are Underwoods all over up here and none of them are any good," Mark went on. "Manny and his wife camp here quite a bit. They have a shitty old Starcraft camper. Neither of them is ever sober. Manny doesn't have a valid driver's license, but I haven't been able to catch him behind the wheel. He does have a gray F-150 like the one in the storage-yard security camera footage, but the video is so crappy it's hard to make out the license plate or any faces. The police department got an anonymous tip that the Underwoods had a hand in the theft, but they didn't have enough probable cause for a search warrant."

"Did they break into the storage yard, then?" I asked.

"Actually, they used a code to get in. Each customer has a different code, but they weren't able to determine which code was used at the time the F-150 entered the lot. The security system isn't any more help than the cameras," Mark replied.

"Has anyone spoken to the owner of the storage facility to get a list of his customers? Maybe one of them will have a connection to an Underwood."

"A detective from the police department met with the owner, but I don't know if he asked for a list or not. It sounds like stuff gets stolen from that yard all the time, and they never have much luck catching anyone. The detective left with a bigger stack of theft cases than he came with. They really just need a better security system."

"Alright. Well, I'm going to try friending these guys with Mackenzie's Facebook page and see if they bite. Maybe we'll get lucky." I clicked "Request Friend" on each profile as I hung up with Mark.

"Now we just wait a little while and see what happens," I told Jack. "It usually doesn't take too long for Mackenzie to work her magic."

We returned to the boat ramp parking lot and finished our ice cream cones before grudgingly leaving the comfort of the air-conditioned truck to step back into the stifling mid-afternoon air. Heat hung over the earth like a cloud, sunlight glinting as the waves rippled to shore. I tipped my sunglasses from the top of my head back down over my eyes, donned a life jacket over my sweaty uniform shirt, and headed back to our waiting boat, which was bobbing at the dock like a patient horse. If we were lucky, the remaining hours would pass quickly. Relief from the heat would only come once the relentless sun dipped below the horizon, allowing the world to breathe again.

Later that evening, as we were trailering the patrol boat back to the office, my computer dinged, indicating a Facebook notification. My friend request to Manny Underwood had been accepted. I pulled into a parking lot and opened Mackenzie's inbox. A message from Manny appeared: "Hey—do I know you?" Given her literal nonexistence, every once in a while Mackenzie's friend requests would spur this line of questioning. Luckily, it rarely stopped the person from accepting the request. I answered, using Mackenzie's standard response:

Don't you remember me? ;)
You look really familiar. I just can't remember how we met.
I'm sure it was you that I met at a party about a year ago. It's ok if you don't
    remember me . . . but I definitely remember you ;)
Oh yeah. Lol. I remember you now. What you doing tonite?
Hangin with my girlfriends. U?
I'm with my cousin. Want to see you. Where u at? Can I stop by?

Ben and I looked at each other, shocked at Manny's boldness. It wasn't good. Mackenzie needed to keep Manny interested in talking to her while avoiding actually meeting up.

Prolly not tonight—I don't know what we're gonna do yet. We might just hang
out here for a while. Maybe tomorrow. Who's your cousin?

My cousins Tony. Where u at? We can just swing by—I really want to see you.
I'll stay outside if you want.

I don't know Tony. Prolly can't meet u tonight. But trust me—I'm worth the
wait ;)

"So Tony is his cousin!" I said. "I bet that he and Tony stole that boat."

Can u send me a pic? I wanna see how u look 2nite.

Nah. I look like crap tonight.

Come on. I bet u look hot. Just one pic.

"He's a little pushy, isn't he? But I don't want to lose him yet." I pulled
a screenshot image of a girl's face from the vast selection on the internet
and sent it to him.

Nice. U look great. Can I please come and c u. We can wait outside your house
so your friends cant see us.

"What a tool," Ben said. "I can't believe guys do this. Don't answer for a
little while. Let's leave him hanging and see what he does."

Almost immediately Manny sent another message.

We won't stay long. Just want to grab you up quick.

"Grab me up?" I was offended on Mackenzie's behalf. "What does that
even mean?"

"I don't know. But I don't think he is going to give up anytime soon. You
probably better shut him down."

Sorry—not tonight. I'm heading to Ellis Park tomorrow to catfish. Do you fish?
Maybe I'll see you there.

What time you going there?

Not sure. Prolly afternoon sometime. Have a nice night! ;)

Suddenly my computer began ringing with an incoming video call. It
was Manny, desperately trying to get Mackenzie's attention. I ignored the
call and continued driving. The computer rang again.

Ben shook his head. "You better log her off Facebook. He's gonna keep
calling."

Before Manny had a chance to call again, I quickly logged off.

"Well, I guess we'll swing through Ellis Park tomorrow afternoon. Maybe he'll be dumb enough to show up in a stolen boat," I said.

"Oh, he'll be there. It's just a matter of whether we're there at the right time."

While I drove back to the office, Ben checked in with his dad, the chief of police in a nearby town. Ben's dad told us that his department had pending theft charges against Jack Underwood but that the county attorney wouldn't file the charge until they'd attempted to question him. If we found Jack, we were supposed to let him know so Trent, one of his officers, could meet up with Jack and question him.

Apparently, Jack, a heavy-set man with tattoo sleeves down both arms and sporting a half-shaved head, had a fondness for antiques. After lifting a bunch of vintage items from a local antique mall in Ben's small town, he not only tried to sell them on Craigslist but he also displayed them in the front window of his tattoo parlor in Cedar Rapids. It didn't take long for word to get back to the dealers that their goods were being hawked in a seedy tattoo parlor by the man with the strange hair who had been seen in their antique store the previous weekend. Cedar Rapids police were also looking to lay additional theft charges on Jack. Everyone wanted to talk to him, but nobody knew where he was holed up.

Late the next morning, Ben and I drove to Ellis Park. It was another hot day, and the boat ramp onto the Cedar River was packed with trailers. I pulled my truck onto an adjacent park road while Ben glassed the boat ramp parking lot with binoculars.

"You're not gonna believe this." Ben leaned toward the windshield, staring through the binoculars.

"He's here, isn't he?"

"Yep. I think so," Ben said, handing me the binoculars. "He's got the same goofy hair."

Jack Underwood was standing in the back of a trailered boat, bent over the uncovered outboard motor, cables and wires clenched in his fist. He occasionally reached to retrieve a pair of pliers from a toolbox propped open next to him. The boat was a faded shade of yellow, no longer the bright and festive color it may have been in its youth. Portions of the hull appeared to have been spray-painted black, causing the vessel to resemble a squashed bumble bee. No registration numbers were displayed on the boat's sides, giving us reason to stop it should we see it on the water. The boat trailer was connected to a beat-up black Dodge Ram pickup.

"That's not the boat we're looking for, but it still might be stolen." I entered the truck's license plate information into my computer. "Looks like the truck is registered to Tony," I said. "And Jack can't drive. His license is barred."

Just then, a gray Ford F-150 pulled into the lot and parked next to Jack. Manny and Tony got out of the truck, grabbed a red gas can out of the back, and walked over to Jack, who was still standing in the back of the boat.

"Looks like all three of them came out to meet Mackenzie today," I said.

"Yeah. That's a little creepy. Why do they need three guys just to meet her?" Ben's eyes were glued to the binoculars.

"I don't know, but I bet they weren't planning on taking her out for a fancy dinner," I said.

Manny and Tony climbed into the boat. After working on the motor for several more minutes, Jack got out of the boat and into the black Dodge. He drove it around the parking lot and backed the trailer down the ramp. When it became obvious that they were indeed heading out onto the water, Ben and I devised a plan. We called my other seasonal officer and asked him to retrieve a patrol boat and take it to the ramp downstream. Then we contacted Ben's dad. He sent Trent, the investigating police officer on the antiques theft case, to meet us in the parking lot.

The Underwood clan launched their yellow and black disaster into the choppy waters of the river. Manny cranked on the starter several times before the motor turned over with an unhealthy-sounding clank and rumble. He reached back, removed the motor cover again, made an adjustment with a screwdriver, and replaced the cover. As he did, lettering on the motor cover reading "Evinrude" became clearly visible.

"That might be the stolen motor," Ben said as he squinted through binoculars.

"It sure looks like it." I pulled up the photo of the stolen boat and motor on my computer. From a distance, the motors looked identical, except where the E-Tec logo should have been, a skull and crossbones decal hid any logo that might have been there. "That's probably why they were messing with the motor for so long in the parking lot. They were trying to hook up the cables of the new motor to the throttle on their crappy boat."

With some difficulty, Manny backed the boat off the trailer. Once the boat was in the water, Jack parked the truck, walked down to the dock, and jumped on the boat with the other two men. The boat sputtered, lurched, and finally growled its way out of sight upstream.

"C352, C189," my seasonal officer's voice chirped over the radio.

"Go ahead."

"C220 and I are here with the boat in the water. Let me know when you want us to swing over there and pick you up." I considered C220, Jace Travers, the shit magnet park ranger in my county, as close to a working partner as I would ever get. He always had my back, especially if possible excitement lay ahead.

"Alright. As soon as the police officer gets here we'll be good to go," I told him.

When Trent arrived and stepped out of his undercover vehicle, it was like watching a Sasquatch emerge from a phone booth. He was built like a six-foot, seven-inch brick wall. Any worries I had about confronting three convicted felons quickly faded when it became clear that with this ex-Marine Bigfoot on our side, we were likely to survive any physical altercation.

I explained our plan to Trent: The DNR officers would pick me up in the patrol boat while he waited with Ben back at the ramp, out of sight. We'd stop the boat for the lack of registration decals and inform the Underwoods that they'd have to leave the water until the boat was properly registered. Once we were all safely back on land, we'd move forward with the stolen motor investigation.

The DNR patrol boat pulled up to the dock, and I climbed aboard. I briefed Jace and my seasonal officer and prepped my body camera before we set off upstream. This stretch of river, though rife with problems, wasn't regularly patrolled. It was outside my county, and officers were stretched thin across the state. Boaters gawked at our patrol boat as we passed. The wind cut through the cabin as we changed course with the bend of the river. The chop smacked against the bow, spraying our faces with a mist of dirty river water.

I pointed to a boat that was beached along the shoreline upstream. "I think that might be them." The yellow and black boat was nosed up on the sand, and the three men were inside. As we moved closer, I noticed that the motor cover was off, and Jack was once again bent over it.

"Looks like a boat in distress to me." Jace voiced our probable cause out loud for the sake of the body camera. "We'd better do a welfare check just to make sure they're alright."

"The boat doesn't have registration, so we have a reason to talk to them anyway," I added.

Armed with reasonable suspicion for initiating contact, we approached the boat.

Manny and Tony were sitting in the back, each with a cigarette hanging from a corner of his mouth. Manny's gut hung over the waistline of his swimming trunks. His tattooed right arm was covered with a tangle of blurred barbed wire strands running from shoulder to wrist as though his arm had gotten tangled in a fence. Black stubble sprouted across his wide face and crept down his neck to where it met the dark hair and tattoos on his chest. Tony, on the other hand, was wiry. The shape of his skull was visible through the skin of his gaunt face, and his arms were pockmarked with the scabs of a meth user. Shirtless, he wore blue jeans that had an obvious hole near the crotch. When Tony noticed us approaching, he removed the cigarette and a cloud of smoke poured from his mouth.

"You guys alright?" I asked. Jack turned away from his motor to look at me. As he turned, the shaved side of his head glistened with sweat and the hair from the other side flopped over his right eye. A rainbow pattern of colors snaked up Jack's arm, over his shoulder, and up his neck before petering out behind his left ear. His neck was wrapped with a necklace tattoo reading "Menace to Society" in a gothic font.

"Yes, officer. We're fine. Thanks, though." Jack hiked up his sagging trunks.

"Looked like you were having some motor trouble, so we wanted to make sure you were okay," I said.

Jack patted the top of the motor with his oil-covered hand. "I was just about to start her back up. Just had to make an adjustment. She's running a little rough."

"Okay, well, go ahead and start her up and meet me in the channel. I need to talk to you for a second." Jack shot Manny a quick look. A microexpression of concern crossed his face. "Will do, officer." Manny waved at me with a forced ingratiating smile plastered across his face.

We backed away and watched from the channel as Jack replaced the motor cover, then started it with a rattle and a burst of black smoke. As their boat puttered out to the center of the river, we drew up on the driver's side.

"I just have some questions about your registration," I said, after Jack shut off the racing motor. The interior of the boat was littered with beer cans and tools. Strands of wire and pieces of cut cable were strewn along the back of the boat near the motor.

"What do you mean?" Jack asked.

"You don't have one. A registration, I mean. At least it isn't on the side of your boat. Do you have any paperwork for it?"

"Oh. I have the registration. It's back in my truck. I just bought this boat." Jack's rigid smile was rock solid.

"Okay. No big deal. If it's in your truck, we'll just follow you back to the ramp and take a quick peek at it. You just can't be out on the water without current registration is all," I said, trying to play the part of a harmless game warden. "While we have you here, though, we also need to check your safety equipment. Do you have a life jacket for each person?"

"Um," Jack hesitated. "I think those are in the truck too. We were moving our stuff from one boat to the other. So they're probably still in the truck."

"Alright. It's not a problem. We'll take a look at them back at the ramp, too."

"Like right now?" Jack's smile was beginning to fade as irritation set in.

"Yeah. We'll follow you to the ramp. It shouldn't be a problem, since we're still close." I waved Jack forward, indicating that he could take the lead back to the ramp. Jack started the boat and throttled downstream. I radioed Ben and Trent to let them know we were on the way, then we followed the yellow boat. Jack's ear was glued to his cell phone for the entire trip back to the ramp. He appeared to be having a frantic conversation with someone. The boat carrying the three men failed to slow down as it approached the dock.

"What the hell is he doing?" I said with alarm as Jack steered toward the dock. "He isn't slowing down!"

Seconds later, the boat slammed into the wooden dock at cruising speed. There was a loud crack on impact as the boat nearly vaulted onto the surface of the dock. When it came to a shuddering stop, Jack cut the engine. The sound of the boat crashing against the dock caught the attention of everyone at the boat ramp. Onlookers watched as we pulled up along the opposite side of the dock.

I hopped out of the patrol boat onto the dock. "Why didn't you slow down?" I asked Jack, who was still seated at the wheel.

"I still don't have the throttle adjusted right. I just put the motor on this morning." Jack reached for the cigarette hanging from his mouth and tapped the ashes onto the floor of his boat.

"Oh, really?"

"Yeah. Believe it or not, someone tried to steal this motor last night. It was parked in my yard, and when I came out this morning all the cables were cut. I guess they must have decided not to steal it." Jack's cheeks puckered as he took a long drag from his smoke.

"Interesting," I mused. "What's your name?"

"Brenden Underwood," he lied.

"Okay, Brenden. Go ahead and grab the registration and life jackets from your truck."

Jack climbed onto the dock and walked toward the black Dodge Ram. I gestured to Ben and Trent standing behind the gray truck. They stepped out from behind the F-150 and joined me at the dock.

While Jack rummaged through the Dodge, I updated them. "So, Jack says his name is Brenden and that someone tried to steal his motor last night," I whispered.

"He's obviously mixing himself up with his younger brother whose name is also Brenden," Trent stated dryly.

Jack emerged from the truck a couple minutes later holding a piece of paper. His eyes doubled in size when he noticed the giant standing beside me wearing a black ballistic vest with POLICE stamped in bold white letters across the chest.

Jack was incredulous. "You called the cops because my boat's missing its numbers?"

"Actually, Jack, I *am* the cops," I clarified. "And your name's not Brenden."

"Yes, it is," he insisted.

"Jack, every cop in this parking lot knows who you are." Another squad car pulled into the lot. "Do you have any ID with you?"

"Fuck you." Jack's smile was replaced with a sneer. I rolled my eyes, told Jack to wait where he was with the other officers, and motioned for Trent to follow me.

When we were out of earshot of Jack I said, "This definitely looks like the stolen motor. And we watched him driving while he backed the boat into the water."

Trent nodded. "Okay. We got him for driving while barred then. We can impound the boat to give us time to sort everything out. Where are Manny and Tony?"

I turned around and looked toward the dock where I'd last seen them.

They weren't in the boat. I scanned the parking lot and noticed two figures walking away from the boat ramp and along the park entrance road. I jogged after them.

"Hey, I need you guys to stick around here for a minute," I said when I caught up.

Manny shrugged his shoulders. "Why? We didn't do anything."

"Well, why would you leave then?" I asked.

"Because there are cops everywhere," Manny complained. "Whatever he did, we don't have anything to do with it."

"This will just take a couple minutes. Come on back over to the ramp. I need to take down some of your information."

The three of us walked back to the ramp where Trent was standing with Jack.

"Can you remind me what the driver's name is?"

"It's Jack," he answered. "Jack Underwood. He's my brother."

"Whose boat is it?"

"It's Jack's."

"Where did he get it?"

"He bought it off his buddy Dave. I don't know his last name."

"How about the motor?"

"I don't know." Lies spilled from his lips like a waterfall.

"What were you guys doing out here today anyway?" I asked.

"We were supposed to meet a friend later. Now she'll probably think we forgot all about her."

I thought of Mackenzie and cringed. "I need you two to sit down on the curb until I tell you that you can leave." I pointed to the sidewalk and told the seasonal officers to keep an eye on them. Trent walked over and handed me the sheet of paper Jack had retrieved from his truck. It was a boat registration from the state of Ohio that had expired thirty years earlier.

"Manny positively identified him as Jack," I said.

"That's a shock," Trent said wryly.

I pulled my handcuffs out of their pouch on my duty belt and turned toward Underwood. "Hey, Jack, turn around and put your hands behind your back for me. You're under arrest for driving while barred and interference with official acts."

"What? Why?" Jack whined.

"Because you're not valid to drive, and we saw you drive. And then you told us your name was Brenden when your name is actually Jack. And don't bother arguing—your brother just identified you." At the mention of his brother, Jack turned his head and glared at Manny, who was sitting on the curb sucking on another cigarette. Trent took Jack's upper arm in his huge hand, completely covering the tattoo of a dagger piercing the head of a tiger, and turned him around so I could put him in handcuffs.

As we loaded him into a police squad for the ride to jail, Jack unleashed a barrage of cuss words like a foul-mouthed four-year-old pitching a fit. Manny and Tony became considerably less helpful once Jack was in handcuffs and refused to answer any more questions concerning the boat and motor. They left the park on foot, not daring to drive without a valid license in a parking lot full of cops.

Later, as we were leaving the parking lot to head for home, my computer beeped with an incoming Facebook message.

Hey girl. Where u at? I couldn't find u. Still want 2 meet up w/ u.

"You've got to be kidding me! He doesn't give up," I said.

"That's creepy," Ben said, just as my computer started to ring. Manny was attempting another video call. "His brother just got hauled off to jail and right away he's busy creeping on Mackenzie. He's already texting her before we even get out of the parking lot? You'd think he would have other things on his mind."

"I was fishing but I just left. Caught my dinner! Maybe I'll c u some other time," Mackenzie replied.

"Where r u now?" Manny wrote.

"Just get off Facebook," Ben said. "If you don't, he'll be up all night calling your computer."

"Gotta go to work 2nite. See ya," I wrote for Mackenzie, then logged off before Manny could reply.

At the impound lot the following day we searched the yellow boat. The serial numbers on the Evinrude motor camouflaged by skull and bones stickers matched those of the motor from the boat stolen from the storage yard. The owner of the stolen boat stopped by the impound lot, scrutinized the contents of the yellow boat, and told us that in addition to the motor, he also recognized the batteries, fish finder, and trolling motor. The stolen boat itself, however, was still missing.

A search warrant on Jack's phone revealed a staggering amount of porn, text messages concerning drug deliveries, and compromising photos of Jack with a prostitute.

As Jack sat in the courtroom watching his theft charges pile up like snow during a blizzard, he slowly sank back into his chair. The court found the motor to be inextricably linked to the stolen boat and, even without the boat in hand, Jack was found guilty of stealing both. His barred driving and interference charges, along with the antique thefts and additional charges from other agencies, only compounded his growing problems. Manny landed the final blow by snitching on Jack in exchange for a light sentence of probation for his part in the theft of the boat. Jack would spend the next five years in prison.

I try to remain optimistic. I maintain hope that at least some of the people I've dealt with have learned from their poor decisions. But Jack left me feeling very discouraged. I felt as though no amount of time behind bars would be sufficient to convert Jack's character from that of a criminal to that of an upstanding citizen. He'd have no lightning bolt moment of truth, no hitting rock bottom and climbing back up. When Jack was released from prison, I harbored no doubt that he'd pick up exactly where he left off, living up to the motto tattooed boldly around the base side of his neck: Menace to Society.

I continue to work on my cob-rolling skills. I gaze at scrolling photos of dead deer on cell phone screens and offer congratulations. I commiserate with anglers who tell sad tales of big ones that got away. Sometimes I still rely on my avatar, Mackenzie, to roll the cob for me. When I log onto Facebook and wait for the inevitable ding of the message alert, the incoming stream of messages fills my truck like radioactive waves.

Hey Girl. Wattup 2nite? I really want 2 meet u.

ONE APRIL MORNING, I'd made one last adjustment to my duty belt. It was barely hanging on, and making it any larger would be impossible. Yet my stomach continued to expand. I was at the awkward stage of pregnancy when I wasn't too obviously pregnant but was definitely larger than I had been before. On the passenger seat of my squad I kept a box of saltine crackers that I constantly munched to soothe my persistent queasiness. And I tried not to stray too far from the bathroom, because my bladder reminded me on an hourly basis that I was growing a baby.

I didn't know what the next stage of pregnancy meant for my working life. Whether or not I would be permitted to wear a shoulder holster instead of a duty belt to meet policy requirements wasn't exactly clear. I'd heard rumors that as soon as a duty belt was impossible, I'd be forced to go on light duty. But light duty would only last as long as the brass could come up with something for me to do. Once they ran out of ideas, I'd be forced to take leave. Because I doubted their commitment to finding me desk work, I vowed to search online for a larger duty belt as a precaution, if nothing else.

My truck bounced along the dirt road on the south side of Hawkeye Wildlife Management Area. With each bump, I clenched my teeth as my bladder strained against the onslaught. The road was muddier than I thought it would be. But the conditions made the perfect playground for off-roading trucks, and I hoped to catch one red-handed. Each year the wildlife area and its leased fields sustained substantial damage from grown (and half-grown) men who had never left the Hot Wheels stage of their lives behind.

I navigated the ruts carefully, attempting to choose the best route to avoid hitting the brakes and sliding into the mud. But, finally, a gaping mudhole appeared directly in front of my squad, giving me a split-second decision to make: go through the hole or try to cross the ruts to the better half of the road. I made the wrong decision. As I steered to the left to make a run for the better side, I felt my truck sink deep into the ruts and slowly squelch to a stop. My last-ditch effort to free the truck only made it worse. Black mud sprayed from my spinning tires and coated the windows of my truck with a curtain of sludge.

It was a Sunday, fading toward evening, and my chances of finding a DNR employee to pull me out were slim. The wildlife area employees only worked during the week, and the last thing I wanted to do was announce my predicament over the radio, inviting months of torment from state troopers and conservation officers alike. I started making telephone calls.

After several attempts to reach coworkers went unanswered, I finally got through to Dan Waits, the manager of the Hawkeye Wildlife Management Area. He was at home, comfortably resting on his couch in front of the TV.

"I wish I worked in an office," I said as soon as Dan answered.

"Uh, oh," he said. "What happened?"

"I'm stuck on the south side. And I have to pee. It's close to emergency status." Fortunately, he was understanding.

"Alright, I'll be there in about half an hour."

As I sat in my stranded truck waiting for Dan to come to the rescue, my cell phone rang. "DNR law enforcement, this is Erika," I sighed in frustration.

"Did you say Erika?" The voice on the other end sounded old. "Is this the DNR?"

"Yes, to both," I answered.

"Oh, okay. I was just expecting a man to answer," the caller said. "This is Myra Jennings. I'm just calling to report something my grandson saw this morning. Sorry I didn't call earlier, but he just told me about it a little bit ago," she explained.

"What do you want to report?" I said somewhat distractedly. I wasn't sure I would be able to wait until Dan came to pull the truck out, and I was dreading a bathroom trip to the sparse woods on the side of the road.

Myra went on to describe a fisherman who'd taken more than his share of catfish as her grandson sat fishing next to him. "I just hate to see things like that happen. I grew up in Minnesota, and my dad always taught me the right way to fish."

"Well, that's good. I appreciate your call." Myra described the fisherman and gave me his license plate number. "That's good information. I'll follow up on it."

"You know . . . when you first answered, I was really surprised to hear your voice," she went on. "Growing up, I always wanted to be a game warden."

"Oh, yeah?" I was sure that if she could only see my current predicament, with tires buried to the hubcaps, she'd be glad that she'd avoided the career.

"Well, my dad was quite the sportsman, and he knew the game warden personally. He'd stop by our house sometimes and always had such stories to tell. I always admired the work he did and wanted to have stories like that of my own. But it wasn't meant to be, I guess," Myra sighed.

"Sometimes it's not all it's cracked up to be," I reassured her.

"But at least you got the chance," Myra insisted. "One time I saw an advertisement in the back of one of Dad's magazines. It said, 'Do you want to be a game warden?' Then it gave instructions on how to sign up for a summer camp. It was for kids who were interested in the outdoors, like I was. It looked so fun that I wrote a letter that same day and sent it in to the camp to register. I waited weeks to hear back. Until finally one day I got a letter." Myra's voice dropped. "The letter said, 'Dear Myron,' at the top. I couldn't believe it. They thought I was a boy! Maybe only boys were allowed to attend, I don't know. Or maybe they were only expecting boys to sign up. Well, I was so upset that I tossed that letter right in the trash. I didn't want to go to camp with a bunch of boys. But I should've known better. There were no women game wardens that I knew of. All the women I knew were teachers, nurses, or secretaries. And eventually I became a secretary, too. Don't get me wrong. I mean, my job was okay. But if I could live my life again, I wouldn't have thrown that letter away. I would've at least tried."

Myra told me that she admired me for having the guts to enter the occupation that I had. I tried to imagine wanting something as badly as she had and realizing that, because I was born Erika instead of Erik, the chances of achieving it were slim. While it's true that it's not a cakewalk for women entering the field of conservation law enforcement these days, at least they have the opportunity to try to walk the walk.

As Myra's words washed over me, a flood of guilt spilled into my gut for the times I'd felt scorn for my job. For being stuck in the mud in the middle of nowhere. For wishing I worked in an office. Things weren't always perfect, but at least I had options and hope.

I looked in my rearview mirror to see Dan's truck trundling down the potholed mud road. When he got close, I could make out his smirk through the windshield. I rolled down my window, cracked a smile, and said, "You can wipe that shit-eating grin off your face."

"Did you pee your pants yet?"

"I think you made it just in time. Let's get this truck out of here before anyone sees me."

As soon as Dan had dislodged my truck from the mire, I made a beeline for the nearest gas station. The next day was a scheduled day off, and I intended to use it. It was about time that I started shopping for maternity clothes. And a shoulder holster.

—THE WATER—

"Later, when the report is written and the usefulness of thinking about it is long over, it's hard to forget this omniscient vision you've made of the victim's fated progress toward a bad end you know about, and she doesn't."

—Jordan Fisher Smith, *Nature Noir*

MY MOM HAS NEVER BEEN one for clichés. Her Christmas card last year didn't showcase a jolly rendition of Santa Claus, a sparkling winter landscape, or a posed picture of my smiling parents. Instead, the card was printed on her home computer and depicted a photograph taken by the Cassini spacecraft as it faced outer space from beneath Saturn's icy rings. In the background, beyond Saturn and among the pin-pricked light of distant stars, the planet Earth is visible. During an eclipse of the sun, our planet hangs suspended in deep space shining forth a hopeful, slightly blue-tinged light.

July 19, 2013, the day the Cassini captured the image, was named "The Day the Earth Smiled." Carolyn Porco, a planetary scientist and imaging team leader for Cassini, conceived the idea for the image. She said, "I hope, at the appropriate time, regardless of where or on which side of the planet you are, that you stop what you're doing, go outside, gather together with friends and family, contemplate the utter isolation of our world in the never-ending blackness of space, relish its lush, life-sustaining beauty, appreciate the rarity it is among the Sun's planets, and marvel at your own existence and that of all life on planet Earth."

When I look at the Christmas card, now stuck to our refrigerator with a T. rex–shaped magnet, I can't help but feel ownership for that speck of blue hanging in the dark sky. It is our place. I imagine zooming in on Earth, as though turning the objective lens of a microscope, bringing me closer and closer to the place where I stand. Moving from planet, to hemisphere, across oceans, rivers, and lakes, until I touch down on this place called Iowa. I look all around this tiny portion of the planet where I spend so many days of my tiny life, and I am filled with wonder.

Looking even more closely, I see the ancient oak tree in our backyard, leaning slightly uphill and scarred on its backside. It stands like a sentry over the creek as it cuts south, marking our property's boundary line.

Turkey Creek, where my daughter and son have spent childhood hours splashing, coating themselves in thick layers of mud, and searching for 300-million-year-old fossils, widens as it trickles farther along to join the Coralville Reservoir.

Just downstream from our property, I could climb through the open slit of rocky shore we call the cave and step out onto the bank of the reservoir. There, near the dam where the Iowa River stalls temporarily before it resumes its flow to the Mississippi, I could climb aboard my waiting patrol boat. Rocking across the busy waves and weaving upstream around boats and water-skiers, I could remember the pleasure this water has given to some and the pain it has wreaked on others—life and death swirl together in its sediment-thick swells. Moving north, I could see a waterfall on my right marking the point where Lake Macbride spills into the reservoir. I could scale the berm between the two bodies of water to watch the masts of sailboats as they turn in the wind and the wet lines zinged from fishing reels as they are cast into the quiet coves of the lake.

Back in my patrol boat, I could continue my journey on the reservoir by heading farther north, cruising past Sandy Beach all the way to the I-380 bridge. This bridge, which crosses the Iowa River, marks the official line between the reservoir and the river as it quietly meanders through the maze of the Hawkeye Wildlife Management Area.

These are my watery places, tinged blue like Earth blinking back at Saturn.

THE IOWA RIVER HAS BECOME part of my subconscious. Its borderlands twist and flow through my psyche like a snake pushing across current. The headwaters of the river originate in the north central part of the state. From there, the stream turns and trickles its way southeast to where its two forks meet, boosting in strength before rolling on farther to where it pours over an old hydroelectric dam in Iowa Falls. The river then cuts through the village of Steamboat Rock, moves past the meatpacking plant in Marshalltown and through the Amana Colonies before entering the western edge of my territory at the Hawkeye Wildlife Management Area. Known to locals simply as "Hawkeye," the wildlife management area is a floodplain that owes its existence to the Coralville Dam that lies downstream.

Construction on the dam began in 1949 as part of an effort by the US Army Corps of Engineers to mitigate flooding risks downstream caused by the convergence of the Iowa, Cedar, and Mississippi Rivers. By the time construction was completed in 1958, the hundred-foot-high dam encompassed a watershed of more than three thousand square miles. The federal impoundment can range anywhere from twenty-three miles to around forty-one miles in length, depending on the water level. If flooding is expected downstream, water can be held back behind the dam, raising the level like bathwater filling a tub. The spillway serves as the tub overflow drain, sucking water down through a tube and sending it gushing its way back into the Iowa River channel to wind its way south to the Mississippi River and on to the Gulf of Mexico.

It's in that bathtub, the Coralville Reservoir, that I spend my summers, bobbing on its waves aboard a patrol boat. Summertime marks the end of my solitary work, as temporary seasonal officers are brought on to help patrol the expanse of waterways.

The Res is long and narrow, hemmed in by rocky ledges and sandy shores on alternating sides as the channel bends. On most weekends, portions of the reservoir are a superhighway of speed boats, pontoons, and whining Jet Skis, all in a hurry to get from one spot to another. The seasonals and I spend hours patrolling the length of the lake, keeping an eye out for potential problems. They are never in short supply.

Summer is decidedly the busiest season in my territory, and the Res is at the top of my list of concerns. People seem to crawl out of the cracks intent on exposing their craziness at any given opportunity. Afternoons, especially, are a blur of abysmal behavior. Under the spell of weed, high schoolers with apparent death wishes fling their bodies from cliffs into uncharted waters below. Boaters with only a vague awareness of boating laws race haphazardly around, buzzing through traffic and jumping wakes. Friends, family members, and complete strangers, fueled by cheap beer, beat one another to bloody pulps. I stay busy as long as I can stay awake. And when I do finally close my eyes for the night, my bed rocks and the room spins with a white-water chop.

One Friday night the seasonal officers and I were called to rescue a man who was swimming near the intake of the dam. The area is buoyed to warn boaters of the danger of getting too close to the eddying drain. Debris, unable to sift through the gates, piles up around the intake like a swirling log stew. Unfortunately, warning buoys carry little meaning to someone who is under the influence. By the time we arrived, another boater had already encountered the Speedo-clad swimmer and had accompanied him back to shore. He was dripping wet and raging mad.

The sun was setting, and beachgoers were packing up for the day as I walked across the sand to talk to him. The swimmer, a white man in his mid-thirties, was lean and muscular, and his wet hair stuck up wildly in all directions. He immediately started assailing me, "They were throwing pizza boxes at me!"

"That was a life-preserver," I clarified, having already spoken briefly with the concerned boaters.

"I told them to take their goddamn pizza box and shove it up their ass! They were chasing me with their boat, so I swam to the rocks and got out of the water. It freaked them out! My Speedo freaked them out! I can't even see right now. I mean, I can tell that your shirt is brown, but that's about it. I can't see anything else. And I'm not a faggot."

Something was clearly not right with this incoherent swimmer. I kept my voice steady as I attempted to calm him down and assess what drug might be coursing through his system. "You aren't making much sense right now. Why can't you see? Are you blind?"

"I'm not legally blind, but I'm really close. All I can really see is color. But I am color-blind too. And I'm also legally deaf." His frantic tone was beginning to relax.

"But you can hear me now, right?" I asked.

"I can hear you. I'm just legally deaf is all."

"How much have you had to drink today?"

"I would tell you the truth if I knew, but it might be three or four. I think it was probably like two or three. I was playing disc golf with two friends, but I don't really know them. They were nice guys. Alex and Adam. I don't know them, but I can vouch for them. They weren't belligerent. So please, if you are going to take someone to jail. . . ." He was babbling and then suddenly burst into tears.

His emotions bounced back and forth, and I realized it was going to be a challenge to make any sense of his ramblings. "Did you have anything besides alcohol today?"

"No, ma'am. I'm a truck driver. But I'm not a faggot, I'm not any of those things people called me! If you were stuck on the side of the road, and I was a trucker and threw my chain in your face, would you be very happy? I moved to Iowa because I heard the people were nice and they wouldn't hassle anyone!"

"What's your name?"

"Josh Richards," he choked through sobs.

"Okay, go ahead and blow in this straw Josh," I instructed, holding my preliminary breath tester to his mouth. Josh blew into the straw and a moment later .115 flashed on the screen. He was drunk, but his behavior seemed worse than a .115. "Are you sure you haven't had anything besides alcohol?"

"No, ma'am. I'm a trucker, so they test me for drugs. Can I get my glasses? They're somewhere over there." He pointed at the expanse of beach. "I can't see anything without my glasses."

"Are they on a towel or something?"

"No, ma'am. I didn't bring a towel. I just came here to swim."

"So . . . they're just laying somewhere in the sand? It's dark out, you're blind, and you put your glasses in the middle of a beach?" I was losing my patience.

Ignoring my question, Josh interjected, "Did you hear that? I just heard someone say, 'Josh you're an idiot.'"

"I have no idea what you're talking about."

While I tried to sort through Josh's story, the seasonal officers took statements from the boaters who had made the 911 call. According to the boaters, they had seen Josh approaching the intake and were worried that he was going to continue swimming toward the drain. They asked if he needed a life jacket. He told them that he would only take a life jacket if they gave him a beer with it. Instead, they tossed him a life preserver, because they were worried he would be pulled under. Josh then suddenly went on the attack, accusing them of picking on gay people. He continued cursing and berating his rescuers as they cautiously followed him slowly back to shore.

"Josh, what it comes down to is, you are intoxicated, and you're in public. I don't know what else you have going on here in terms of your mental state, but I'm going to place you under arrest for public intoxication, so you need to turn around and put your hands behind your back." I held onto his wrists and began to handcuff him. "I'm going to take you down to the jail so you can sober up there. Do you have any clothes or anything in your car that you want us to get for you?"

"My snake."

"Excuse me?"

"My snake is in the car."

"What snake?"

"My snake, Sheba. She's a python. She's waiting for me in my car. Are you going to take care of her?"

"Your python is in the car?" I repeated. "It's in the car right now?" Josh looked at me like I was an idiot.

"Uh, yeah," he muttered, clearly annoyed at my ignorance. "She likes to wait for me under the driver's seat. My shoes are in the car too. I need my shoes."

"Where's your car parked?"

"It's a green Subaru Outback parked over there by the playground." He pointed toward the back of the lot next to a play structure.

Brandon, one of the seasonal officers, flashed me look of fear. He was built like a boulder, with arms the circumference of bowling balls, but I'd heard him squeal at the presence of a bumblebee. I thought that it might be worth hearing again.

"Hey, Brandon, let's go find Josh's car and get his shoes."

Brandon looked at me like I'd lost my mind. "Nah, that's okay," he said, "Go ahead. I'll wait here with Josh."

"Zach will stay here with Josh," I gave Zach, the other seasonal officer, a quick wink. "I might need your help finding his shoes."

I headed toward the parking lot with Brandon slowly trailing behind me like a man sentenced to the gallows. I found Josh's car and peered through the back-seat window, trying to catch a glimpse of the snake under the driver's seat. I couldn't see it under the seat, so I pulled my head away from the window and attempted to get a look from a different angle. It was then that I noticed Sheba, not under the seat, but curled up on top of the driver's headrest, her tail draped over the back of the seat like a rope. The splotched pattern along her body shimmered as she shifted positions. Sheba was a ball python, about five feet long and the diameter of a Coke can.

Brandon cautiously approached the car.

"I don't know what he's talking about. I don't see a snake in here," I said. "This guy must be completely out of it." Brandon visibly relaxed in response to my reassuring words. His tight shoulders eased in relief.

"Will you grab his shoes? They're on the back seat. I'm going to go get Josh into my squad," I said, as I headed back to the beach where Josh and Zach were waiting.

I was halfway across the parking lot when I heard Brandon's shriek. It was unnaturally high pitched and carried crisply through the muggy night air. Brandon's voice howled like a lone coyote lost in the blackness, like a seasonal water patrol officer regretting his choice of a summer job.

IN 2007, THE SNOW began to fall in early December. The ground was already frozen solid, its frostline deep below the surface. Every flake of snow and spit of frozen rain was held in cold storage in cracks and crevices on top of the earth. It continued falling through the months of December, January, and February, transforming the landscape into a tundra. Each storm added onto the previous ones, forming layers like sedimentary rock.

March brought a reprieve from the precipitation and raised hopes that we would pull out of the relentless onslaught. But the cold remained, locking the frozen ground like a safe, the soil saturated with rock-solid ice. Quite simply, the land could not drain itself dry. April came, bringing with it strong storms and torrential rains compounded by the melting of the icy mantle. Uneasy jokes about the crazy Iowa weather and the possibility of flooding peppered conversations with an undertone of concern. It needed to stop soon. But it didn't stop. And by the time the third storm finished dumping its load, streams, rivers, and creeks were topping their banks and spilling onto the surrounding land.

The rains kept coming in May, dropping five to ten inches of rain in places. News reports consisted almost entirely of weather updates. Farmers wondered if fields would ever be fit to plant. Everyone wondered if we would ever be out from under the water. Some chuckled, only half in jest, about constructing an ark.

By the time June arrived, the situation was bleak. Once dry basements were now leaking like sieves and thousands of sump pumps gurgled nonstop in a futile attempt to keep up with the steady seepage. Both rivers in my territory, the Iowa and the Cedar, were swollen past their banks, inundating acres of farmland and turning the Iowa landscape into a lake-scape. Six-foot-high sandbag levees surrounded homes and businesses. And the water continued to rise.

Each morning, driving to work across the Coralville Dam, I checked the water level as it crept closer to the lip of the emergency spillway. Black turkey vultures sat like hunchbacked sentries in the fog along the dam's rocky face, damp wings outspread in a fruitless attempt to dry their feathers. The vultures' stoic eyes stared into the distance, ambivalent about anything other than their next meal.

I made my way south to the emergency operations communication center for a daily briefing. Emergency response personnel filled the tiered seats in the conference room, the TV silently and perpetually tuned to the Weather Channel. The emergency management coordinator ran the meeting like an auctioneer, spitting out information and asking for feedback. His voice was clipped and loud. "How many sandbags does the university need? What is the timeline for the completion of the Hesco barriers along Dubuque Street?" The Midwest representative of the National Weather Service outlined projections for the next twenty-four hours. The manager of the dam complex was playing God with the gates, concerned about the current release downstream. The flood scientists reported on what their computer models told them, and then told us what was expected to go underwater next. Attention turned to our department when the coordinator asked, "How many boats and assisting officers can you have in the county by next week? Can you assist the water treatment plant?" The pumps at the plant were slowly disappearing under the expanding tide of the river.

Attempts were made to mitigate possible problems before they happened. Rescue boats were amassed, and evacuations were ordered. But the biggest problem of all was out of our hands. Nothing could stop the rain from falling. And once the water began to flow over the emergency spillway, nobody would be able to tame the wild river.

The magic number was 712. This number echoed throughout the room, bouncing from one person to another like a wild game of volleyball. The top of the emergency spillway lies at 712 feet above sea level. The reservoir was at 711.5 and rising.

We sat in the conference room and tried to put on convincing faces of fear. Each of us regularly repeated the expected and appropriate mantra, "I hope it stays under 712." But unless you or your family lived downstream, or unless you held a position of authority inside the firing line of public blame, it's possible that you were secretly longing to see the water continue to rise. The adrenaline buzz was evident in the eyes of those seated around me whose jobs required them to run toward the fire when everyone else was evacuating, to speed with lights and sirens to the man with a gun, and to force disaster's turbulence under control to help those who were begging for it. We knew better than to outright wish for catastrophe. Nobody wanted anyone to get hurt. But the truth is that bearing witness to history and anticipating the ensuing chaos generates its own excitement.

Despite our half-hearted pleas, the rain continued falling into the watersheds of the Iowa and Cedar Rivers. The Cedar River flowing through Cedar Rapids, Iowa's second largest city, had already caused major flooding. Conservation officers swarmed to Cedar Rapids to assist. They patrolled the city streets by boat to help with rescues and security. They shuttled emergency personnel and supplies from one place to another. We watched our struggling neighbors to the north in Linn County and knew it was only a matter of time before the Iowa River unleashed its fury on us.

As the reservoir basin continued to fill, the road across the dam was closed. A steady parade of people arrived at the spillway to watch the water rise. Some parents, tempting fate, actually walked their children along the top of the emergency spillway and dipped their toes into the burgeoning river on the upstream side.

We were placed on twenty-four-hour dam watch. Nights were spent patrolling the dam and monitoring the rising water. We were told that the force of the water might even threaten the integrity of the dam. I only hoped that any flaws in the wall would politely make themselves known ahead of time rather than by collapsing suddenly and carrying me downstream in the middle of the night surfing on a tidal wave.

Bridges were closed as water lapped through the guardrails or when the horizontal pressure of the river against the vertical structures became a cause for concern. With bridges impassable, people became stranded, unable to return home or to get to work. Special transportation was arranged for doctors unable to drive to hospitals.

My patrol boat would no longer fit under Mehaffey Bridge where uprooted trees, logs, and debris mounded up against the bridge pilings like an ambitious beaver's dam. Roads buckled, washed out, and disappeared into giant holes in the earth. And we continued to watch the water rise, creeping its way up the wall of the emergency spillway. We talked incessantly about the seemingly inevitable topping of the spillway and the drama that such a watery breach would bring to our banal lives. Finally, it did.

ABOUT 375 MILLION YEARS AGO what is now Iowa was a tropical sea. Situated near the equator, Iowa was covered in a shallow ocean that teemed with life. Cartilaginous sharks as well as corals, brachiopods, and armored placoderms were abundant. It's hard to imagine such a watery past in Iowa today. As a landlocked state more than a thousand miles from the nearest ocean, Iowa's memory of the sea is nebulous.

The reservoir had topped the emergency spillway for the first time in 1993, following a long period of continuous rains. Water pumped over the cement lip for almost a month, leaving destruction in its path. Slabs of rock weighing several tons were washed downstream. A roadway and campground fell victim to the raging whitewater that snaked backwards into the channel of the Iowa River and, in the process, ripped open a reminder of Iowa's ancient past. The US Army Corps of Engineers christened it the Devonian Fossil Gorge. The rushing flood waters had cleared away soil and silt, creating a giant wound that revealed a succession of limestone beds, and throughout the gorge fossils in the limestone emerged in relief. While the site's exposure of Iowa's tropical past was fascinating, it also forced me to consider what might become of my own bones one day, to wonder if I, too, might become part of a fossil record, to be picked up and puzzled over or merely tossed away without a thought.

In 2008, as I watched the water once again pour over the spillway and rip through the fossil gorge, pulverizing the concrete road into rubble, I wondered what new secrets from the past might be revealed when the water once again slowed to a trickle.

The seasonal officers and I launched our johnboats from a hilly street in a section of the city of Coralville that seemed to be sinking into the river. The view from the boat was apocalyptic. My brain struggled to corroborate what I was seeing—half-submerged restaurants and retail fronts—with my memory of a highway once hugged by dry buildings and prospering businesses. Our mission, handed down by the county's emergency management coordinator, was to work with city officers and firefighters to evacuate residents from several apartment buildings. Water had already engulfed the ground-floor dwellings, but occupants of some of the higher-level units had decided to stay and wait out the deluge. Now, with the power out, the buildings had become dark islands. Evacuation was no longer optional.

As we approached the marooned apartments, moving through streets covered in murky water, our boat's prop ground over car rooftops, bumped over fences, and nicked signposts. Car antennas poked from the water's surface like metallic twigs in a pond as we navigated through parking lots. The water was greasy brown and smelled like ripe swamp and gasoline. Plastic bags, bottles, and cans that had once littered the ground now bobbed on the waves.

We pulled the boat up to an apartment entrance and let police officers and firefighters pry open doorways. They piled inside. As residents filed out, clinging to their children and bags stuffed with clothing, we passed them life jackets and ferried the newly homeless to dry ground. Some came willingly, thankful for the opportunity to leave. Others argued and had to be persuaded by the cops. Wild-eyed dogs were passed out through open apartment windows. Babies, not trusting this new monsoon world, cried and squirmed on our laps as their parents tossed bottles and diapers into the boat.

We carried on our taxi service role until the buildings were emptied. Covered in mud and stinking of floodwater, we trailered the boat and moved on to the next assignment.

The water treatment plant was on the verge of shutting down. Its pumps, spread throughout an outdoor facility that was at one time adjacent to the river, were now immersed in the channel itself. Eddies twisted around submerged structures, turning the surrounding grasslands into a pulsing waterscape.

Water treatment workers required rides to each pump to keep them all operational. Every hour we piloted our small boat on the unsteady trip through the swirling river with a technician on board to check the pumps. The seasonal officers volunteered to stay the night, sleeping in shifts, so that I could return home to my kids. It wasn't a restful night. I lay awake imagining the young officers sucked into a vast whirlpool and being eaten alive by the river.

The next morning, I drove to the plant to check on the seasonals, only to find them gone. I breathed a sigh of relief when the plant supervisor told me that they had just left to get some much-needed respite. He added that everything had gone smoothly the night before. Nobody had been swallowed up by the river.

The floods of 2008 were followed by months of tedious cleaning, rebuilding, and relocating. Water had wreaked havoc across the state, and many places suffered much worse damage than my territory had endured. Flood control measures were implemented for vulnerable areas throughout the state in the hope that the inevitable next crisis would be less traumatic.

During the ensuing months, I watched as the water soaked languidly back into the earth, leaving marshlands full, fields soggy, and mosquito larvae squirming. Rivers slid back into their banks and waterlogged woodland undergrowth slowly began to green again. Those who had silently hoped that the river would top the spillway were sufficiently satisfied. They were now flood veterans. The next time they were called to the conference room for emergency planning, they wouldn't be the ones harboring secret wishes. That would be left to the rookies craving an adrenaline rush and looking with electric anticipation toward the water lapping at the spillway. They will be the ones muttering the disingenuous, monotonous mantra, "I hope it stays under 712."

IT WAS MEMORIAL DAY WEEKEND, the first foray on the water for the three seasonal patrol officers. The entire crew was new to the lake; they were green, inexperienced, and youthful. They hadn't yet been worn thin by bureaucratic headaches, and their patience was not yet frayed by government employment. They were glad to be out of college for the summer, and they were ready for some excitement.

The seasonals had spent the last two weeks in off-site training, so I was giving them a tour of the Coralville Reservoir. As one of the busiest boating weekends of the year, this was a poor time for an orientation session, but it was the first chance I had had to familiarize them with the water where they'd be spending the next three months. They needed to know the shallow areas, the beaches, the known drug-use spots, the campgrounds, the boat ramps, and the problem boaters.

We'd been on the lake only a couple of hours when the call came over the radio. Just as we approached the dam at the southernmost tip of the lake I heard the county dispatcher sending deputies toward Mehaffey Bridge.

Mehaffey Bridge marks the center point of the reservoir. All boat traffic moving between the north and south sections funnels through the no-wake zone under the bridge. I turned up the volume on the radio in an attempt to make out the radio traffic over the wind, the rumble of our patrol-boat motor, and the Jet Skis whining past. The boat radio was notoriously unreliable and often cut out at key moments, turning efforts to decipher transmitted information into something like playing a preschooler's game of telephone. The most I was able to make out of this call pertained to a possible jumper. Since moving to the territory ten years before, I had frequently heard rumors of late-night drunken jumps off Mehaffey Bridge into the reservoir below, but I had yet to actually witness it.

I hit the siren. Poorly positioned under the T-top, its sound wailed with a wavering, high-pitched tone that bounced off the roof and around the cabin, relentlessly piercing our eardrums and effectively cutting off our ability to hear any additional radio traffic. We cruised full throttle, white-knuckling the bars of the console as we skipped and thumped over waves, teetering on the edge of control, weaving through boat traffic.

We pounded around the final bend before the bridge came into view. Several boats were clustered in the area, and a US Army Corps of Engineers park ranger was standing on the adjacent boat ramp. I pulled up close enough to him to yell, "We got a call about a person jumping from the bridge. What do you know?"

"All I know is that a girl's missing somewhere by the bridge," he called out. "I heard she maybe fell from a boat."

"Okay. We'll head for the bridge."

Boats in the no-wake zone on either side of the bridge bobbed in place, as the occupants watched our patrol boat expectantly. As we wove our way through the crowd of vessels, I noticed a small blue runabout on the opposite side of the bridge. A thin man, covered in tattoos, was kneeling on the back platform of the boat next to a pile of towels. The man turned and began frantically waving his arms at us, beckoning us to approach his boat. Other passengers huddled near the front, their bodies hunched forward and heads lowered. As we moved closer to the small boat, it became evident that what at first appeared to be a pile of towels, was actually a person draped in towels. Even from a distance I could see blood soaking through the towel's fabric, turning it from blue to dark purple.

I'd seen blood like that before, and the sight increased my own sense of urgency. Boat propellers can eat through human flesh like a hot knife through butter, leaving a series of sharp curved gashes, slicing open the skin and cutting cleanly through muscle. If the victim is lucky, he comes away with bone-deep gouges. Unlucky ones lose limbs.

I stood near the bow of our boat shouting, "Put pressure on the cuts!" I mimicked the action of applying pressure with my hands. The thin man at the back of the boat didn't follow my instructions. He merely looked at me blankly, so I yelled again. This time he shook his head, slowly moving his index finger horizontally across his neck. I yelled again, unable to figure out why he wasn't following my instructions. He somberly repeated the slicing motion.

As our boat slid alongside the runabout, I caught a glimpse of a bare leg and foot. The victim was a child. A hint of pink swimming suit was visible through the folds of towels. A little girl. "How bad is it?" I asked the thin man. He peeled back a bloodied towel from the body to reveal a young girl, lying on her back. Her right arm rested at her side; the left arm was missing. She was wearing a one-piece, pink swimsuit covered by a bright yellow life jacket. The jacket, dotted with small stars, was spattered with blood. The victim's head, completely detached from her body, rested on her chest. Long, wet hair curled and twisted around the stars of the lifejacket, tracing the path of a wayward comet.

I abruptly turned away. My gut lurched, and bile rose in my throat for an instant before I swallowed it back down. I'd seen dead people before. Some with vicious shotgun slug holes from hunting trips gone bad, others crumpled under the weight of ATVs, and still others, blue-skinned and bloated, pulled from muddy water. My visceral reaction didn't come from the sight of gore. It came from the unnatural tragedy of the scene playing out before me: an innocent twelve-year-old girl had been decapitated, her young life cut short on a sunny Memorial Day weekend. The thumping bass of music pounded from a cove, brightly colored Jet Skis skipped through the water with a high-pitched drone, cars howled across Mehaffey Bridge on their way to picnics at the state park, and my new seasonal officers, stunned at the turn of events, stood trying to maintain their composure. My own kids, three miles away at our home, were eating popsicles and playing in the yard with my husband. My daughter was only slightly younger than the victim. I was overwhelmed by a strong instinct to get off the lake, go home, and hold my kids.

Instead, I turned back around to face the occupants of the blue boat. I felt everyone's eyes on me. Apparently I was in charge of this unthinkable situation. "Get on the phone and get some other officers out here. And tell them we need to get the medical examiner en route," I instructed Cole Parker, one of the seasonals, snapping him into action. As he moved to complete the order, relief played over his face. Cole had a task to complete, somewhere to focus, other than on the unmoving child lying on the back of the boat.

I turned my attention to the group on the blue boat. "What happened?"

A woman seated at the front of the boat met my gaze, a mask of shock haunting her face. With a wavering voice, she said, "Her name is Jenny. She was tubing with my daughter. They fell off the tube, and that boat hit her." She pointed at a large red speedboat floating a short distance away. A middle-aged man wearing a white tank top sat bent over the steering wheel. His hands covered his face. His body was shaking uncontrollably.

We motored over to the red boat. "What happened?"

"I don't know," the driver mumbled distractedly. He was looking at the floor, and I noticed beads of sweat on his shoulders that had begun to run down his arms. His voice quavered. "I just didn't see her."

"Where did it happen?"

The driver pointed toward the buoys. "I was just coming out of the no-wake zone when my daughter screamed at me to stop. She was in the front of the boat. But by then it was too late. I never even saw. I went right over her." His teenage daughter was sitting on a cushion at the front of the boat. Tears streamed down her face, dissolving her mascara into sad black lines.

I scanned the interior of the speedboat, noting the details. Four people were onboard: the driver and three teenage girls. Brightly colored beach towels were strewn across the seats and lay in heaps on the floor. Bags of chips, containers full of fruit, and paper plates covered a small table. The driver must have noticed my gaze sweeping over the back of the boat where a pile of empty beer cans had been pushed into a corner. When he lifted his rheumy eyes to meet mine, he exhaled his breath on my face. It smelled slightly sour with alcohol. He flatly stated, "I'm not answering any more questions."

"You don't need to say anything else. But I do need to check your eyes," I said. I hoped the driver would submit to at least one field sobriety test, but, as in many situations like this, luck is rarely with the officer.

"I'm not doing any tests. And I want my lawyer," he demanded, effectively ending my interview. Nothing drains a case faster than denying someone access to an attorney. I decided it was time to get our own attorney involved as well.

We carefully moved the girl's body onto our boat, sliding her across the stern on a bed of damp towels. A seasonal officer drove the patrol boat slowly back to the boat ramp. His fingers gripped the steering wheel tightly, and his eyes bore straight ahead as though we were navigating a tight tunnel. I sat near the back of the boat next to the body, listening to the waves lap against the sides, watching the eyes of the crowd as they stared back at us during our slow-motion procession.

An ambulance was waiting at the ramp, surrounded by deputies, detectives, park rangers, and a crowd of onlookers. As soon as our boat bumped against the dock, the medics boarded. They removed the girl from the boat and carefully transferred her through the back doors of the ambulance and out of sight. It would be the last time I saw her, but I carry her image with me, vividly, to this day.

With the body in the possession of the medical examiner and the crowd of first responders thinning, I stood at the boat ramp and drew in a deep breath. That was the only moment of peace I was to have before the onslaught of the disorder and inevitable stress of an accident investigation. A search warrant was needed to obtain a blood sample from the driver to determine his level of intoxication. Both boats would need to be inventoried, impounded, assessed for damage, and photographed. Countless interviews, meetings, and witness statements would need to be gathered and pored over. The physics of the accident would have to be puzzled out.

Boat accident scenes are not static affairs. Vehicles involved in a highway crash stop moving once the forces at play run out of inertia, leaving skid marks and debris. Boats, on the other hand, drift. Evidence sinks into the deep where it is covered by mud, eaten by catfish, or washed downstream. Diagramming a boat accident is often laced with frustration and uncertainty.

At an advanced boat accident training course that I took through the National Transportation Safety Board, we learned how to use toy boats to assist with visualization. We imagined our way through a sequence of events like a child playing with toys in a bathtub. The fact that vessels are powered from the rear challenged my understanding of physics on the water. Boats careen on all planes like untethered balloons in a storm. Their motion is affected by changes in speed and direction and by the force of impact. The bow rises into the air as a boat picks up speed, then levels out as it settles onto plane. Upon impact, however, sections of the vessel may be shoved below the waterline before exploding back up like a popping cork. Meanwhile, passengers can be thrown about the cabin or ejected into the water. If they drown, their bodies will float only if they had managed to put on a life jacket prior to the collision. If they didn't, their bodies sink to the water's lower depths, where they hover just above the lake or riverbed. If we are fortunate, we are able to locate the suspended corpses with a boat-mounted side-scan sonar.

Over the course of the next several days, I interviewed and re-interviewed witnesses. I spent hours poring over their chilling photographs and exhaustive stories. It was maddening trying to piece together a sequence of events based on unreliable and differing witness accounts. Stories evolved and memories melted into the black hole of history, making the chain of events a snarled knot.

I tried to maintain a base level of sanity. Little thought is given to first responders and law enforcement personnel who experience grisly scenes and then spend days piecing together the obscure details of horrific accidents. My thoughts during the course of this investigation were like dominoes. One image triggered the next, which triggered the next, until I was back on the boat, sweat dripping down my neck. Until I was looking at a little girl whose head had been retrieved from the water by a thin stranger, his arms covered with tattoos.

In the days following the accident I wasn't hungry. I couldn't sleep. The seasonals and I met with an officer trained in critical incident stress debriefing. I sobbed my frustration in streams. I cried for the little girl's mother, who had to endure this unbearable loss. I cried as I mentally substituted my own children for the victim whenever I closed my eyes. And I cried because the investigation was far from complete. It was a long way from becoming part of the past tense.

Investigations are usually fraught with flaws and human error. In this case, the error was in the lines of the search warrant, hidden among the legalese. The results of the driver's blood draw were inconclusive. The search warrant had been signed by a judge four hours after the accident.

The warrant failed to include a request for two blood draws. If I'd requested two separate samples drawn with some time elapsed between them, crime scene technicians might have able to use the time between the draws to better calculate the rate at which alcohol was being processed and eliminated from the driver's body. Maybe. But as it was, the evidence of alcohol was insufficient to draw a definitive conclusion. And in a case like this, definitive would be the level of certainty required.

Then the results of the reenactment had to be considered. I had to deliberate the physics involved when a long-bowed Baja boat increases its velocity, sending its nose into the air like a dolphin taking a breath. Then, fully satiated, the boat flattens out again as it exits the no-wake zone and cruises nearly parallel to the surface of the water at a set speed. When that transition happens, with that specific type of boat, given the simultaneous unfortunate location of a small body floating in the water, it is possible that even stone-cold sober the driver may not have been able to see the girl he was about to run over. The front of his boat likely broke his line of sight to the water directly in front of his vessel. A deadly blind spot. Possibly. It could have been that way. The uncertainty of my investigation plagued me and kept me awake at night.

The day after the accident, we launched a boat and scanned the lake floor for the victim's missing arm. We looped the scene over and over for hours to no avail. Perhaps the target was too small. Perhaps it had already begun to decompose, transitioning from the limb of a living being to a scavenger's nutrient source. Before long the transition to organic molecules, pushed by the waves and twisted by the currents, would be complete.

One never walks away from a fatal investigation unchanged. In my case, the changes were both good and bad. A good change was that, following the accident, I became a more aggressive presence on the lake—a constant sentinel alert for signs of impaired drivers. A bad change was that I've become a more paranoid mother, verging on enforcing house arrest until the kids are grown. I came away from the investigation with reinforced knowledge that the urge to retch must be instantly replaced with thick skin and mock confidence. I was reminded that stress-induced shaking must be stifled with calculated deep breathing.

The details of this experience left other indelible marks on my subconscious. I can no longer drive over Mehaffey Bridge without looking to the north at the buoy line that marches across the lake, spanning the curvature of the channel. I can still see the static cluster of boats caught in suspended animation. I can still feel my gut filling with dread. It was here that music pounded over the water and Jet Skis whined with abandon as a young girl's arm drifted down through the water and settled into the deep, dark silt. In this place outlined by grey rock and green foliage, part of a once vibrant being began its process of returning to the earth. And I am soberly reminded that, even as a result of the most unnatural and unexpected turn of events, returning to the earth is the most natural and anticipated occurrence shared by all things once living.

WHILE STANDING ON the banks of the Iowa River at two o'clock in the morning, the distant plinking of banjo music is likely one of the last things you will want to hear.

We'd been dispatched around midnight, along with county deputies, to the Greencastle Bridge over the Iowa River at the Hawkeye Wildlife Management Area for a fight between two fishermen. Paul Wilson, a constant troublemaker I'd dealt with on numerous occasions, had gone out fishing near Greencastle Bridge with his dad, Clyde, and Clyde's friend, Jasper Carlson. Apparently, everything had been fine with the trio until they ran out of beer. A fight broke out between Paul and Clyde about who would abandon fishing long enough to drive to town and re-supply them with another case. Push came to shove with Paul's right fist making crushing contact with Clyde's left eye. Jasper dropped the two off on shore to continue their fight, and he returned to the water to fish. After the fistfight, Paul attempted to peel out of the parking lot, but in his drunken stupor he steered his truck right off the road and into a stand of willow trees instead. By the time we arrived, Clyde was sitting in the parking lot with his left eye swelling shut. Clyde pointed us in the direction Paul had gone, and the county deputies, my seasonal patrol officer, Mike Read, and I spent the next hour tracking him down as he attempted to walk home under the cover of darkness.

After sorting out the father-and-son skirmish we reconvened with the deputies back at the boat ramp to finish up the paperwork generated by the incident. I was tired and ready to head for home. It was then that we heard banjo music coming from downstream. The twanging sound of the strings reminded me of the movie *Deliverance*, and I shivered despite the heat. The music, combined with the sputter of an outboard motor, seemed to be getting closer to the bridge. I sighed, knowing that I wouldn't be going home anytime soon.

"Hey, has anyone talked to Jasper?" I asked the deputies. "I haven't even seen him or the boat these guys were fishing from."

"Nope," Carter Benson, a county deputy, replied. "He's probably still out fishing."

"Well, his truck and trailer are still here, so I'm guessing that music is coming from his boat," I said. "He probably helped them run out of beer in the first place."

I squinted downstream and made out the boat as it slowly weaved its way closer to the ramp adjacent to the bridge. The boat didn't have any navigation lights, but the glow from the moon reflecting off the water made visible the tall, slender silhouette of Jasper Carlson, cowboy hat and all. He was standing near the back of the boat as its front tapped the shoreline. One moment Jasper was standing bent over at the waist to adjust the volume on the radio, and the next moment he was careening overboard, arms flailing like a bird's wings. He landed with a splash and a curse in the waist-deep water next to his boat. Mike dashed over to help Jasper clamber onto dry land.

Mike held Jasper's elbow as he stumbled out of the water. He was dripping wet but had somehow managed to keep the ragged straw cowboy hat perched on top of his head at a rakish angle. "You okay?" I asked.

"I'm just fine, Erika. How are you doin' tonight?" Jasper replied calmly as though nothing unusual had happened. I'd met Jasper several times during past hunting seasons. He lived just a quarter of a mile down the road from the boat ramp, and he was generally a congenial guy.

"Where have you been? Sounds like there was quite a bit of action with the Wilson boys tonight," I said.

I accompanied Jasper as he wove his way through the tall grass and stood unsteadily in the parking lot. "Oh yeah. Those dumb shits. Can't even fish without fighting," he said, one word slurring into the next.

"Sounds like you've had a bit to drink, too. How many beers did you have?"

"I've had two, Erika. Just two."

"Alright. If you've only had two, you should have no problem with a few field sobriety tests, right?"

"I'll do whatever you want, Erika. Anything you say," Jasper drawled. "I'm just trying to enjoy my vacation." I turned to Deputy Benson and rolled my eyes. Not many people choose the Hawkeye Wildlife Management Area as their vacation destination. Especially if they live within walking distance of it.

Jasper attempted the field sobriety tests with little success. When Benson held a preliminary breath test straw up to Jasper's mouth and asked for a breath sample, Jasper's mood took a turn for the worse. "I'm not blowing in that thing! You'll arrest me if I blow into it!" Jasper complained. "Can't a guy go fishing without getting harassed? I'm just on fucking vacation here!"

I tried to reason with him. "Jasper, you've been cooperative up to this point, so I hope that doesn't change. I understand you're on vacation, but you still have to be sober when you drive. You don't need to blow into the PBT if you don't want to, but the problem is that you didn't do well on the tests, and you're too drunk to be driving," I said.

"Erika, I'll do whatever you want me to do. What do you WANT me to do?" Jasper said obligingly, as his mood took another swing, this time for the better. "Do you want me to blow, Erika?"

"I don't care what you do, Jasper. It doesn't matter. Either way, you're going to have to go to jail tonight for driving your boat under the influence."

"But I'm on FUCKING VACATION!"

By the time we arrived at jail, Jasper had repeated the phrase, "I'm on fucking vacation!" so many times that it became our mantra for the rest of the summer. Whenever the seasonal officers and I had to deal with a difficult person or were on the receiving end of someone's bad attitude, we could always manage to resurrect a smile by whispering to one another, "I'm on fucking vacation!"

Unlike Jasper, I don't drink. Aside from my generally boring personality, I've seen too much stupidity and consequent suffering from the use of alcohol—especially when it's used in excess. As a rule, I don't find that the results of mixing alcohol with boating inspire humor, but occasionally, I can't help but smile at the actions of the inebriated.

For example, without alcohol, I never would have had the chance to arrest Owen Anderson. Owen was a nineteen-year-old with a habit of making poor life choices. When I met him, he was involved in stealing his father's boat, filling it with friends, and then filling those friends (and himself) with massive amounts of alcohol. By the time I encountered Owen and his friends on the reservoir, the carpeted floor of his boat was littered with beer cans and slippery with an oily slick of vomit from a female passenger who, after having heaved her lunch into her lap, passed out in the stern seat.

We towed the boat and all its intoxicated passengers to the ramp. Once on shore, I attempted to administer a series of field sobriety tests to the boat's driver, Owen. As if trying to prove his profound ability to make consistently poor decisions, Owen responded by reaching down and plucking handfuls of dirt and grass from the ground. In an attempt to beat the breath test, Owen, in a move that somehow made sense to him, proceeded to shove the greenery and soil into his mouth with gusto. If not for the dirt caking the front of his teeth and the grass poking from the corners of his mouth like a cow chewing its cud, one might have thought, based on his enthusiastic chewing, that he was eating handfuls of Skittles.

Owen declined to follow my simple instructions, "Stop eating the grass!" With each handful that he consumed, I lost a little bit more patience. Finally, I burned through my remaining fuse when, without batting an eye, Owen pissed his pants. He soaked the passenger seat of my squad all the way to jail.

Without alcohol, Cole Parker, my former seasonal and later friend and fellow conservation officer, would've been far less entertained after arresting a drunk driver on the Mississippi River. The old man had been operating a small boat, which he constantly referred to as a "dinghy," after having consumed a few too many beers at a riverside bar. Unfortunately for Cole, he couldn't stop mentally (and incorrectly) associating the word dinghy with the word for the male reproductive organ. And unfortunately for Cole, the man really liked to talk about his dinghy. During the long ride to jail, he entertained Cole with numerous tall tales and adventures involving his dinghy. His dinghy this, and his dinghy that. His dinghy was apparently the love of his life and his favorite topic of conversation. By the time they reached town, Cole had almost bitten through his tongue from constantly restraining himself from bursting out laughing at each mention of the word. Dinghy. Dinghy. Dinghy.

Without alcohol, I never would have arrested Beth Nielson. She sat in the bow of my patrol boat as she prepared to attempt a series of field sobriety tests. However, upon learning that one of the tests would involve clapping her hands together, Beth became agitated. She insisted that her breasts were much too large to allow her to successfully accomplish the hand-clapping motion. Beth tried to demonstrate her ailment by taking a deep breath, sitting up tall and pushing her chest out while feigning her inability to clap. The ruse didn't work.

I arrested Neal Washington on an especially busy weekend in July. With the help of alcohol, Neal found the courage (while handcuffed) to repeatedly ask me if I would allow him some time alone with a woman who'd been a passenger on his boat. He insisted that it would only take five minutes and that he hoped his girlfriend wouldn't interrupt them. After denying his request for a pre-jail conjugal visit, I transported Neal to town. When we arrived, a line of cops was already waiting to book their prisoners into jail. Knowing I'd be waiting a while for my turn, I sat in my truck to finish up some paperwork while Gloria Dayton, my seasonal patrol officer, stood outside my squad with Neal, allowing him to stretch his legs.

After a few minutes outside, Gloria rapped her knuckles against my truck window. I rolled it down to see what she wanted. "Can you come out here for a second? We need some help." Gloria's face betrayed a look of embarrassment.

I got out of my truck and walked around to the other side to see what the problem was.

"Sorry," Gloria said. "He asked if he could smoke a cigarette while we waited. I told him that he could if he could get the pack out on his own. Somehow this happened." Gloria tilted her head in Neal's direction as she tried to maintain a semblance of professional composure.

Neal was bent over at the waist, his forehead almost touching his kneecaps. His handcuffed wrists, which had previously been situated behind the small of his back, were now clutched together behind the backs of his knees. Neal's rear end was pointing up into the air as if he were trying to moon the streetlight but had forgotten to pull down his pants. It was evident that Neal was stuck tight, unable to return his hands over the hump of his backside.

"I know this is funny as fuck," Neal said, laughing uncomfortably, as he peered at me upside down from between his knees, "but I'm stuck."

"What in the hell," I said, for lack of anything better to say.

"I was trying to get my cigarettes!"

"Were they in your socks or what?"

"No!" he laughed. "They're in the pocket of my shorts! I don't know how the hell I ended up like this!"

I pulled out my handcuff key and crouched down to unlock his wrists while muttering under my breath, "Can't say I've done this before."

After finally booking Neal into jail without his desired smoke break, Gloria and I returned to my squad. "I was so worried you were going to be mad at me for letting him get into that position. I guess you can't leave me alone for two seconds without something stupid happening!" Gloria said.

"Oh, don't worry about it," I replied. "Something stupid is bound to happen when guys like Neal take a fucking vacation."

WHEN A BOAT CAPSIZES in extremely cold water, two things are true: First, even strong swimmers are much less likely to be capable of keeping their heads above water for very long. Second, if located, the probability of successful resuscitation is higher, even after prolonged submersion.

The second fact is why, when a canoe capsized on the Coralville Reservoir during the frigid first week of January, the response started as a rescue operation. If the young man could be found within an hour of submersion, it would still be possible to save him.

But the first hour turned into the second, and the second ticked on into the third. And as night fell, the hopeful rescue silently transitioned into a body recovery. As a conservation officer, boat accident investigations in my assigned territory are my responsibility. But drownings fall under the jurisdiction of the sheriff's department. So, as the primary focus changed from a rescue operation to a body recovery, responsibility for the investigation shifted too.

That night my supervisor, Paul Meintz, and I stood in the yard of a large lakefront home. The yard, situated at the top of a hill, overlooked the lake. The search area, based on the last known location of the canoe, consisted of the small cove near the home's property line.

Paul and I helped move equipment and assisted rescue personnel as they made their way down the slick slope to the water's edge. Meanwhile, rescue boats looped the icy cove, their searchlights occasionally sweeping the crowd gathered on the hill, illuminating hovering clouds of frozen breath.

As I stood in the snow, I was reminded how crisply sound carries through frozen air and echoes off ice-covered water. Rescue equipment clanked against the metal hulls of the johnboats, hushed voices spoke in bursts of panic, and radios beeped, hissed, and chattered. Random wails from the hillside where the victim's friends were gathered raised the hairs on the back of my neck. The most intrusive noise came from the cadaver dog aboard one of the search boats. I tried to will the howling dog to keep silent in an effort to lend the victim's parents the slightest reprieve from the reminder of their son's condition. But my pleas went unheeded. He barked incessantly, as if delivering a refrain he knew by heart.

As the temperature continued to drop, ice relentlessly formed along the shore. The searchers were forced to chip through the ice with paddles, beating it into gray slush. The heavy plastic of the rescue team's yellow dry-suits audibly crackled with each movement, and cops in down coats shivered. I began to regret how hastily I had thrown on my uniform before racing out of my house to respond to the call. Snow squeaked underfoot, and my toes began to go numb. I curled my tingling fingers inside my gloves to keep them from freezing.

Despite the subzero temperatures, nobody wanted to be the one to call off the search. Stopping was too final. Many of the emergency responders knew the victim. In this small community, everyone knows the star football player. He was an ace student with a broad smile—a boy with a plan and a future. But the decision had to be made, and eventually the search was stopped for the night.

Paul and I made plans with the sheriff's department to aid in the ongoing search at first light the following morning. Our main concern was for the stretch of water between the boat ramp and the cove. Ice would form overnight. If too much accumulated, the search would be impossible. Paul and I planned to retrieve a large metal boat typically used on the Mississippi River to serve as the primary icebreaker.

The following morning, we met the dive team and other search and rescue boats at the ramp. As the first morning glow touched the surface of the lake, it revealed an unpromising view. Five feet from shore, ice had formed, and it spanned the width of the lake.

Paul, Jace Travers, and I backed the metal beast of a boat into the water only to quickly discover that the plug hadn't been inserted. We pulled the boat back out and I used a screwdriver to chip away at the ice-covered plughole with little progress. Finally, Paul sacrificed his thermos of hot coffee. While he dumped the coffee through the hole, I leaned over the back bench seat to get better access for my screwdriver. Folgers-scented steam wafted over my face as I scraped away at the opening. The coffee was only partially successful in melting the ice, but I wedged the frozen plug in as best I could, and we launched the boat.

It was an eerie feeling riding a boat onto a frozen lake. As the boat moved forward, we seemed to be sailing over solid, opaque ground. The deafening rumble and grind of heaving ice told us that the metal hull of our boat was doing its job. Large sheets of frozen lake cracked and slid under the surface in our wake. I briefly imagined being on the deck of an Arctic icebreaker.

Within thirty minutes we had managed to clear a narrow path in the direction of the search area. At first we were uncertain which was the correct cove to clear. The perspective from shore the night before had looked drastically different than the view from the lake in the dawn light. But soon our destination became apparent. Ahead, gathered on a hillside and covered in blankets, a crowd of young people awaited our arrival.

We cut ice into the cove, then turned back to widen the path for the dive team and dragging boats. As our boat made a turn, I noticed gas spurting from the hose near the motor. I quickly grabbed the gas line to stop the bleed. Apparently the hose had frozen to the ice-covered transom, causing it to pull loose from the motor during the turn. For the next half-hour, Jace and I took turns lying on the back of the boat, holding the gas line to force its connection to the motor. We inhaled fumes while Paul drove in circles, turning the lake water to slush.

By the time we headed back to the ramp to repair the hose, ice was already forming across our initial path. The lake had a will of its own, and it seemed as though it wanted nothing more than to clot its wounds, forcing us to abandon the operation. Mother Nature consistently lacks empathy.

We cobbled a fix to our gas line, relaunched the boat, and continued the ice-breaking route. For the next few hours, three boats constantly circled the distance from the boat ramp to the cove in slow motion laps with the sole purpose of stopping ice formation.

Finally, as Paul turned the corner at the edge of the cove, I noticed a subtle hand signal from one of the rescuers aboard a dragging boat. Body recovery teams try to keep their locates quiet. The last thing a grieving family wants to hear is a triumphant shout from a dragging boat. Body hooks can slip the target, and they can hook more than bodies, leading sometimes to false positives. For that reason, a body isn't considered recovered until it is lying securely inside the boat. So, when I noticed the gesture—a slight lift of the hand in the direction of the ramp—I knew the search was over. They had the boy.

It felt wrong to say that we were relieved, or even that we were pleased with the good outcome. Nothing about pulling a seventeen-year-old boy from the frozen depths of a lake seemed like it should be described as good. But if we hadn't found him that day—or even within the next two hours—the lake would have forced an end to the search. And then, the alternative to good would have been unbearable.

Just as the bow of our boat scraped over the riprap at the shoreline, the motor abruptly quit, apparently gelled up from the cold and the leaky line. I climbed onto solid ground and walked to the top of the ramp just as a van pulled into the parking lot.

I don't know why it hadn't occurred to me that the victim's family would come to the ramp. They stepped out of the van and walked to the top of the ramp. In that moment is was hard to understand why they would want to see their son as he was unloaded from the dragging boat. I couldn't stop thinking that they would regret this memory. The circumstances of his death were tragic. His limbs were solid. His skin was blue.

The victim was moved from the boat onto a stretcher. Someone from the rescue crew carefully dried the boy's face with a towel and then wheeled the stretcher to the top of the boat ramp. There, the boy was taken into the arms of his family.

I unconsciously held my breath and turned away, my eyes gazing ahead at a dirty snowbank. Raw grief is personal and palpable. It is weeping, vomiting, and unbalanced embraces. It is immense and organic, and I felt like an intruder.

That night I went home and lay awake thinking the inevitable thoughts that always come when my job lands me the task of a fatality investigation—especially in the case of a young victim. It's the curse of every emergency responder—or maybe it was only the curse of my own imagination. Either way, the thought was an unstoppable train wreck. It swarmed and consumed my mind as soon as I closed my eyes. What if that boy had been my own son? What then?

Only when the unthinkable was thought was it possible to begin to understand why parents so often choose to bear witness to the things you, as an officer, think they shouldn't. Why they expose themselves to ultimately indelible memories. Why they choose to open their eyes and arms to their blue-skinned, frozen child, pulled from submersion under ice.

From the moment my children were born I believed that I was the only person capable of properly caring for them. When my daughter was born, and the nurse took her to the nursery for the night, I waited impatiently for her return to my room. When I dropped my son off at daycare for the first time, I struggled with the idea of passing the torch of responsibility for his well-being to someone else. When they are sick, hurt, sad, or in pain, my instinct is to wrap them up in a hug and make it all go away. My arms are a magic tonic prescribed only for them.

Logically, I know this can't be true. Mothers aren't bequeathed enchanted limbs, healing lips, or any curative powers. But try telling that to a mother. Parenting is a messy, complicated, and arduous business, but it is a business born of a love stronger than anything else.

I don't know how it would feel to leave my son's body to nature's cruel whim or his recovery in the hands of emergency responders. But I am closer to understanding my own true role as an officer charged with investigating fatal incidents.

The goal of a rescue and recovery team isn't about closing a case. It's not about packing up gear, congratulating each other for a job well-done, or writing a seamless report. The goal isn't even about the perfect hook. Recovery teams only have one true mission. It will always be about giving a parent one more opportunity to rescue her child from the depths of uncertainty. To see her beautiful boy. To hold him in her magic arms.

—THE LAND—

481A.6 GAME MANAGEMENT AREA

"The commission may establish a game management area upon any public lands or waters, or with the consent of the owner upon any private lands or waters, when necessary to maintain a biological balance as provided in section 481A.39 or to provide for public hunting, fishing or trapping in conformity with sound wildlife management. . . ."

— *Code of Iowa* (2019)

HAVING AN ASSIGNED TERRITORY, one designated as mine to watch over, is like having an unruly, yet lovable child. Just as I'm familiar with the strengths and the weaknesses of my own progeny's personalities, I know my assigned territory. From county line to county line, each section—marked by roads named alphabetically from west to east and numerically from north to south, starting at one hundred and increasing by tens—has its own set of perfections and failings. I know where a patch of Virginia bluebells fills an entire hillside in the spring and where a pile of deer carcasses will be discarded in the fall. I know where neighbors' disputes will break out during hunting season and where to sit for the best view of a summer sunset.

Private property landowners call me with their share of issues, like trespassing, poaching, and nuisance wildlife. But my heart pounds for the public land under my care. I see places like the Hawkeye Wildlife Management Area and Lake Macbride State Park as my unruly and lovable children.

The Hawkeye Wildlife Management Area is a land of contradictions. It's a place filled with wildness and with human tinkering. There are blazing sunsets silhouetting cattail-lined marshes where geese lock wings and glide against the sky. But around the next corner is a steaming garbage dump hastily pitched in the dead of night. The dichotomy of the place leads me to alternating bouts of love and loathing.

Hawkeye's fourteen thousand acres abut the western edge of my county, where the Iowa River interlaces its fingers into a labyrinth of mudflats, flowing water, and standing pools. The channel weaves a hidden path through the flat plain of water to the federal impoundment downstream. A wildlife unit of four technicians, one of whom is my husband, manage the wetlands, prairies, food plots, timber stands, and leased crop fields that constitute Hawkeye. Their work is an exercise in patience as they periodically and predictably watch a year's worth of sweaty work slowly succumb to the river's rising water. It is the inherent risk of working in a federal flood containment basin. The obliteration of what the wildlife technicians strive to maintain can be undone by the hands of Mother Nature, with the cooperation of the US Army Corps of Engineers when they close the dam gates to hold back the water. But despite the floods, Hawkeye has greater difficulties to face, and those originate with the continual disagreements among its population of users over management plans and practices.

Public land has always been the fraying rope in a multidirectional game of tug-of-war. Interest groups, individuals, and stakeholders on all sides ceaselessly squabble over access, permits, resource extraction, rule changes, protections, grazing rights, special use opportunities, and a piece of the landscape to call their own. Public land is for everybody. But not everybody is good at sharing.

At the federal level, huge and fierce wrestling matches take place over land use for national parks, forests, and wildlife areas. Iowa's percentage of public land is one of the smallest in the nation, but disputes over it can sometimes be just as contentious as the federal face-offs, albeit on a smaller scale. Making matters even trickier, when it comes to our state-owned wildlife management areas, about the only interest groups footing the bill are the hunters and anglers who purchase hunting and fishing licenses. This unequal financial relationship between the land and the people who use it turns the idea of forced, balanced sharing into something resembling a schoolyard smackdown.

Whether over an individual laying personal claim to a small footpath on public hunting ground or over something more controversial, lasting, and large-scale, like grazing rights, questions about equity, long-range land planning, sustainability, and preservation lead to unabated conflict.

But despite the inevitable festering problems, I carry concern for our public land like I would carry an afflicted child: I hold it tight, whisper encouragement, hope for the best, and protect it with all my might.

A NARROW FOOTPATH leads into the woods from a gravel parking lot at the Hawkeye Wildlife Management Area. Though only about fifty feet in length, it is well-maintained. The encroaching brush on either side is neatly trimmed back on a regular basis, and low-hanging branches are snipped to keep the path clear. After dark, solar lamps poking up from the forest floor on either side of the path cast an eerie, yellow glow into the surrounding trees. Each year, a fresh layer of wood chips appears on the path, further establishing the permanence of a short trail where it isn't meant to exist.

The trail from the parking lot ends at a white, knee-high wooden cross jutting up from the ground. A small maple tree grows just west of the cross, urgently pushing its way up, searching for any available sunlight in the dense woods. On the other side of the cross, a plastic box containing a memorial book and a few pens rests on the leaf litter. The box also holds several photographs of the young man who, several years before, chose this location to sit on the damp spring earth, lean against a small tree, put a .40 caliber handgun to his temple, and pull the trigger. The footpath was born shortly thereafter.

One summer evening a few years after the suicide, I found three cars in a new parking lot just off the roadway near the memorial. The original lot, tucked back out of sight from the road, was gated in an effort to deter its use as a hidden party destination. The cars were out of place for the time of year. No hunting seasons were open, and no fishing holes were nearby, leaving few reasons for traffic. I sat in the lot for a while and waited. It was getting dark, and the mosquitoes were starting to come out in force, but still no one returned to the three cars. I ran the license plates through dispatch and peeked into the windows, looking for some clue as to what the owners might be up to, but I found nothing telling.

I climbed over the gate that blocked vehicle access to the old parking lot. The gravel driveway was still used as a service road for wildlife area workers. As I walked over it, the beam of my flashlight bounced rhythmically, its light reaching through the tree trunks on either side. Eventually the shadows of three people came around the corner. I heard a startled shriek.

I announced my presence, "Conservation officer!"

"Oh my god. You scared us!" a young woman gasped.

"The feeling's mutual. What are you guys doing here?"

"We were just visiting Jeff," an older woman said. "He's my nephew. We haven't been here in a while."

At first I didn't understand what the woman was talking about. But then I recalled the name inside the plastic box by the cross. "Okay. Just wanted to see what was going on. It's an unusual spot to be parked at this time of year."

What I failed to mention to the visitors was that their footpath had been a recent topic of conversation among our staff. The use of public land as a permanent memorial placed the land manager in an awkward position. While Jeff certainly wasn't the first to choose Hawkeye as a place to commit suicide, his was the first to be commemorated with such enduring dedication.

The trail had become a source of confusion for other wilderness area users. Hunters asked whether they were allowed to hunt in the woods near the cross. Other visitors asked why the DNR had made the trail at all. In our minds, we assumed there was probably an appropriate time period to allow the family to grieve in this place where their loved one had chosen to die. Maybe there was a suitable time span for the footpath to remain. Perhaps there was also a time when it would be appropriate for the DNR staff to disassemble the pieces of this family's grief scattered on the forest floor and to allow the path to start the process of reverting to its natural state. If we had already acted, plants would, by now, be poking up through the wood chips, dispersing and melding them into the earth. The surrounding branches would have reached across the temporary void of the trail's headspace, filling it up like crosshatching in an ink drawing.

Somehow all our hypothetical deadlines had slipped by like a leaf wending its way on a deceiving current. Now it just seemed too late. Maybe this year, we hoped, the family would stop maintaining the strip of woods where their son, brother, and grandson had leaned against a tree. Maybe this year we would pull the solar lights from the ground and return the plastic box to the family. Maybe, we hoped, they would accept our apologies and understand that their claim on this bit of public land could only ever have been an ephemeral one. But if we don't get it done this time around, maybe we'll do it next year instead. And if not then, maybe the one after that.

WILDLIFE AREAS IN IOWA don't have any designated campgrounds. While the law allows for tent-camping in wildlife areas for no more than ten days at a time, tents must be placed at least one hundred yards distant from any parking lot, road, or building. And since driving off maintained roadways is also prohibited, you'd have to walk that one hundred yards into the wild to set up your tent. For problem campers, one hundred yards might as well have been one hundred miles. They weren't inclined to walk that far, and they sure as hell weren't going to sleep in a tent.

Tiki torches glowed orange against the black sky as my seasonal officer, Nate Moser, and I neared a group of RVs parked along the river on the south side of the wildlife area. The camping spot, once an area of mixed wild grasses, had been mowed down like a golf course fairway. Deep muddy ruts channeled down from the road, ran through the ditch, and ended in a line of five campers parked along the riverbank. Tim McGraw blared from a speaker in the back of a new red Chevy pickup backed up to a group of adults sitting around a bonfire, deep into the Busch Light.

I parked my truck, and Nate and I approached the group from behind the beams of our flashlights. "Mind turning the music down?" I asked as we stepped into the ring of firelight. A husky man with gray stubble I recognized as a hunter from the previous deer season strained as he pulled himself out of his chair, shuffled toward the pickup, and turned down the music.

"How are you all doing tonight?" I asked, playing my best Barney Fife.

"Not too bad. Yourself?" the big man standing beside me answered. The stench of his beer breath hit me in the face.

"I'm okay. But I wanted to chat with you about your arrangement here," I began. "You guys are out here quite a bit, so I know you're aware of some of the problems we get out here."

"Oh yeah. People treat this place like shit. But not us. We grew up here, ya know, so we always pick up all our garbage. You shoulda been here about an hour ago though. Group of about five trucks came through here, hell bent on goin' somewhere. They looked young too—must be a party goin' on down there." He tilted his head to the west.

"I'll have to check that out. When did you guys set up camp?"

"We came out this afternoon around three I'd say. Were gonna camp last night but with the fucking rain we decided to wait until today."

"Yeah, I didn't see you out here yesterday. But I could've sworn when I came through yesterday that this grass was a lot longer."

"Yeah, I had to whack it down a bit," he said. "The ladies don't like walking through the tall grass."

"I can understand that, but the thing is, this place isn't actually a campground. It's a wildlife area, so the tall grass is there on purpose. It's habitat. It's not really meant to be a campsite for big campers like this."

"We've been camping out here for thirty years! Hell, I camped out here when I was just a kid. This place is as much our place as anyone's. In fact, we'd like to see you guys do more to help out the campers," the man's words slurred.

"That's kind of why we have state parks with designated campsites. There are also county parks and Corps of Engineers campgrounds. Lots to choose from around here. Just not a wildlife area."

"But you have to pay for a campsite at those places. I ain't doing that. Not when I can come here for free and not have to listen to a bunch of drunk people set up next to us." By this point, the man's voice had risen to a shout.

"Do you have an ID with you?" I asked.

He glared at me for a second before sticking his hand into his back pocket and pulling out a large black wallet attached to his pants by a silver chain. His fingers fumbled as he attempted to pull the driver's license out of the sleeve. The beer fumes leaking from his pores mixed with the campfire smoke and gave the air a sweet, sickly odor.

When he handed over his license, I was able to put a name to the face that I recognized. George Schroeder was a well-known local. Born and raised near the wildlife area, he never felt compelled to ask for any landowner's permission before traipsing through their woods and fields in pursuit of a buck. But the fear of retribution was enough to deter anyone from reporting him.

"Which camper is yours?" I asked George.

"That one." He pointed to a large fifth-wheel camper. Its AstroTurf-carpeted patio was lit by a string of shotgun shell Christmas lights. A large garbage bag, overflowing with beer cans and liquor bottles, was propped against the camper's steps. The muddy tracks that ran through the ditch led directly to George's camper.

I gestured at the ruts plowed through the mud by his tires. "Looks like you had a hard time getting through the mud."

"If you guys would put more rock down it wouldn't be so bad," he accused.

"Is there a reason you didn't pull down to this spot using the gravel lane?" I asked, referring to the service road that was visible nearby.

"I couldn't back it down here from that far away. Besides, I wanted the camper pointed toward the river, so we had to come in off the road," George said. "It's how we always do it."

"Well, this time you're going to get a citation for it."

"What?" he shouted. "You can't do that!"

"You drove off the roadway. You've been around here often enough to see the signs posted at all the entrances saying that you have to stay on the road," I explained. "Also, you can't go around cutting down the grass wherever you want, but I'm just going to warn you for that. If it happens again, though, we'll have a problem."

"I'll fucking see you in court then," George growled.

I returned to my truck, wrote out a citation and went back to the campsite to explain the ticket to George. He ripped the paper from my hand and stormed back toward the fire where I could hear him loudly complaining to the rest of the group. As George spewed curse words in my direction and called me names much worse than Barney Fife, Nate and I photographed the damage left by the campers. As we finished and began walking back to the truck, George approached us again.

"If you're going to write me a ticket for driving off the road, are you going to write the next group? They're off the road, too, and I bet you'll just let them go. I'll ask them what you did, so you better not fuck up," he threatened.

Given George's putrid booze breath, I warned him, "I haven't even gotten to the next group yet. But I suggest you not drive anywhere unless you want to be arrested for OWI." I doubted, however, that George would walk any farther than fifty feet from the comfort of his camper.

"You don't have to be such a bitch. You just don't want anyone to have any fun." George stalked back to the campfire in a rage.

Flames from the bonfire sparkled through the branches like stars leading us to the next group. George had been right about one thing. These people were way off the road. Tucked back in the trees, eight trucks were backed into the woods, circled like covered wagons. I could make out silhouettes of several people standing around the fire as I pulled my truck up to the edge of the woods and shut off the headlights. A few cars lacking four-wheel drive were parked back along the roadway, their drivers likely worried about getting stuck in the woods.

"They're probably underage," I said.

"Good thing I have my running shoes on," Nate joked. I had yet to see Nate chase anyone, and I doubted he would start tonight.

"Looks to me like there's at least twenty people back in there," I squinted through my binoculars at the group gathered around the fire. "I think I'll let the county know they should start a car this way, just in case."

I radioed dispatch and requested a deputy for backup before hiking to the group. Country music pounded through speakers set up in the back of one of the trucks, and laughter spilled through the dark woods. As we neared the group, I flipped on my flashlight.

"Conservation officer," I announced. Three people standing on the opposite side of the circle turned and sprinted, beating feet through the thicket at a scared rabbit's pace. I radioed the deputy and cautioned them to be on the lookout for the three runners.

"What's up with them?" I asked the rest of the group.

"I dunno," a tall kid wearing Wranglers and a cowboy hat replied. "Guess they didn't want to talk to ya."

"Obviously. Well, I'm going to need to check IDs. You've got lots of booze here, and I'm guessing your friends there had something more interesting than beer?"

The tall boy piped up again. "Nah, they're just shy."

"Yeah. Right." The kids began rummaging through purses and pockets looking for their driver's licenses. Nate wrote down information for those who couldn't come up with any form of identification, all of whom, not surprisingly, were underage.

"Aside from the underage drinking and littering, you have a few other problems," I told them. "You can't have a bonfire out here, and you can't drive your trucks way off the road like this."

A blond girl in a skintight tank top and cropped jeans sitting on the dropped tailgate of a mud-covered pickup complained, "How are we supposed to get back here then?"

"If you want to come back here, you'll have to walk." She stared blankly at me in response. "Like with your feet," I clarified. The girl continued gaping at me, apparently astounded by the suggestion.

"Oh, come on," a lanky boy whined. He sat next to a very pregnant girl who was propped up next to him in the back of the pickup, beer in hand. "My girlfriend is pregnant. You don't expect her to walk all the way back here do you?"

I looked at the skinny boy and could almost see his future billowing up in flames with the smoke from the campfire. Motherly lectures fought to escape my lips, but I managed to mostly contain them. "Actually, yes. If your girlfriend really wants to be out here in the woods at one o'clock in the morning instead of at home in bed, then she needs to walk back here, too. This is a wildlife area—not a party destination."

Pin-pricks of light darted through the trees as the deputy made his way down the potholed dirt road, heading in our direction.

"C352, 52-99," I heard from the radio mike on my shoulder.

"C352, go ahead," I answered.

"We found your three runners," the deputy said, "but now we're stuck."

"What do you mean?"

"They were running through a field on the south side of the road near the boat ramp. We drove in after them. Didn't know it was this soft out here."

"Alright. I've got some paper here, then I'll head your way," I said.

Nate followed the path the runners took through the woods, picking up their dropped marijuana pipes on his way, as I finished writing tickets for underage possession and driving off the roadway. When we arrived at the deputy's squad, we found it buried up to the axles in mud. The three teenage runners were sitting sullenly in the back seat, citations in hand, waiting for their parents to arrive.

As we sat in the field at 3:00 in the morning waiting for a tow truck, I unloaded on the deputies, complaining about issues at the wildlife area. I'd had enough of the problems that came with the place. I was sick of some people's sense of entitlement. I was tired of people using the land any way they saw fit, no matter the destruction they caused. It was time to put a stop to the music-blasting, party-campground atmosphere, the pallet bonfires that left parking lots littered with nails, the piles of beer cans, the dumping grounds for household trash, the bullet-blasted signs, the underage consumption, the permanent campers, the meth-cooking, and the graffiti.

The deputies nodded in agreement. They were sick of it, too—though their frustration probably had less to do with the destruction of the land and more to do with the amount of time they spent responding to and typing up reports about all the calls they took at Hawkeye.

After the tow truck freed the squad car from the mud and the deputies went on to the next call in the queue, I leaned against my truck and looked into the deep dark night surrounding me. It was a new moon, the blackest of black nights. A perfect time to stand in the void and listen to the cicadas and katydids filling the air with their steady chorus. It was the perfect moment to close my eyes and appreciate Hawkeye for what it was. An imperfection.

FOR SOMEONE looking to escape life's responsibilities, Hawkeye Wildlife Management Area provides the perfect black hole she's looking for. The nooks and crannies of Hawkeye are a haven for those seeking to escape from bosses, spouses, children, in-laws, exes, military assignments, the critical eyes of society at large, and, of course, the cops. Folks who want to slip away under the cover of wilderness are drawn to Hawkeye like vultures to a carcass, to the point that the river valley seems to become a conference of misfits.

One summer afternoon, Kate Pearson, a seasonal officer, and I were working our way north toward Hawkeye. We'd just come from a backwoods river access and campground in the southern part of the county where we had checked anglers as they stumbled out of their boats and onto the riverbank in a haze of beer breath and gas fumes.

The sun was past peak and starting its westward drop by the time we pulled out of the river access. Hawkeye would be the last stop for the evening—just a quick run-through to make sure the wildlife area was put to bed properly, so that we too could retire for the evening.

My police radio chattered as Kate and I made our way toward Hawkeye. The main topic highlighted in the radio traffic was a pursuit involving a motorcycle in the northern part of the county. According to the voices chirping on the radio, a blue crotch-rocket-style motorcycle was hell-bent for the county line after fleeing a traffic stop in Linn County, just to the north. Officers from two law enforcement agencies were chasing the bike.

The pursuing officers narrated developments as the motorcycle screamed into Solon, a small town south of the county line. There the driver took a hard right turn west toward the causeway that crosses the south arm of Lake Macbride, crossed the causeway, and sped off in the direction of Mehaffey Bridge. The bridge spans the Coralville Reservoir and is adjacent to the most popular boat ramp accessing it. On hot summer weekends, the road the motorcyclist had taken is one of the busiest in the county as pickups packed with swimsuit-clad crowds trailer boats to and from the boat ramp.

The deputies in pursuit weighed the risks of chasing the bike down the busy road and decided to call it off. Switching off their emergency lights, they pulled over to the side of the road to turn around, leaving the bike to get away. The lack of cops in his rearview mirror, however, didn't stop the motorcyclist from continuing his run. A deputy near Mehaffey Bridge obeyed the order to cease the chase and remained still as the bike streaked past his parked squad at over one hundred miles per hour. The crazed biker threaded the needle through oncoming traffic, over the bridge, and up the hill toward the busy town of North Liberty. Police stood by watching as the motorcycle passed through several stop signs without so much as slowing down before disappearing from sight.

"Just watch," I said to Kate, "he's probably going to end up at Hawkeye." That was my refrain every time I heard of a pursuit underway in the county. But, despite its obvious potential, even I had doubts that the driver of the crotch rocket would take to Hawkeye's potholed roads to keep company with the swarms of mosquitoes that hung like low-hanging storm clouds. Crotch rockets are designed for high speeds, requiring the driver to lean over the body of the bike like a toddler riding a rottweiler. The wildlife area would be a rough ride.

By the time Kate and I reached the road accessing the south side of Hawkeye, the radio traffic had come to an end. The officers had moved on to the next call in the queue. I guessed that the motorcyclist was probably sitting at a bar by then, tipping back a cold one.

As we drove through the S-curves that followed the lay of the river we soon found a fisherman set up along the shore watching his lines for a bite. Ben was a Hawkeye regular. He knew the area better than I did and spent countless summer nights in an endless pursuit of the catfish that lurked in the holes of the Iowa. I could never figure out if Ben had a job or what he did when he wasn't at Hawkeye. I knew that he lived in a garage on the outskirts of a nearby town where his sister concocted terrible smelling stink-bait and his elderly parents used the driveway to camp in their RV. After several years I gave Ben the nickname "You Shoulda" for all the times he started sentences with "You shoulda been here," followed by a dramatic story of some blatant violation that I'd passed up by not being in the right place at the right time. You Shoulda had anointed himself Hawkeye's watchman. As with many of my informants, though, You Shoulda used skills of deflection to direct my attention toward everyone else's crooked ways in the attempt to distract me from his own occasionally questionable behavior.

"Fish biting?" I asked.

"Nah. Not much," he replied. "But you shoulda been here about an hour ago. A fucking crotch rocket came flying through here. I couldn't believe it! And he's still down there." You Shoulda cocked his head, which was covered in a mess of unruly red hair, in the direction the motorcycle had gone. "I was gonna leave here an hour ago, but I wanted to see if he was going to come back out."

For everything but a jacked up pickup truck, the road was essentially a dead end. The only way out was either to turn around and leave the way you came or to risk a stalled motor by attempting a traverse of the Missouri crossing along the exit road, where the creek flowed over the road in unpredictable depths. That summer, beavers had been busily constructing the Taj Mahal of dams, backing the water up and making the Missouri crossing much too deep for a motorcycle.

"Was the bike blue by any chance?" I asked.

"Yeah, I think so. The driver had his helmet kinda tilted back on his head, and he kept looking back like you were chasing him or something." You Shoulda positioned his hands out in front of him, mimicking the driver gripping the handlebars and watching over his shoulder.

"Well, someone was looking for him, it just wasn't me. We'll go have a look around."

Kate and I continued west, peering into the tall grass and brush and down service lanes that branched off from the main road. Eventually we came to a large stand of willows where a muddy trail cut back from the road, leading through the trees to the hidden bank of the river. The place was like a siren song to drug users, meth cookers, wanted persons, and necking teenagers. If the motorcyclist was hiding anywhere at Hawkeye, it would be here.

I pulled my truck off the road and onto the muddy lane and told Kate to wait in the truck while I checked the riverbank. I got out of my truck and walked along the trail until I was hemmed in on both sides by the encroaching willows. As I walked, I checked the dense stand of trees for any signs of disturbance. The willows were so thick on all sides that the view was obscured just a few feet off the path. But then I saw it. Through a swarming haze of mosquitoes and thousands of slender willow leaves was a hint of blue plastic. I took a step into the trees for a better view. A blue crotch rocket was leaning against a tree, a white helmet hanging from the handlebars.

A hit of adrenaline pierced my gut when it occurred to me that I lacked any background information about the driver. I didn't even know what had spurred him to flee in the first place. Did he steal the bike? Have an arrest warrant? Or was it something much worse? His reason for fleeing could dictate how he would respond to my presence. The only thing I knew for the moment was that I could see his bike, but I couldn't see him. Running blindly into the trees after a target I couldn't even see through the curtain of thick brush didn't seem like the best plan. I retreated from the trees and returned to my truck to request backup.

Upon returning to my truck, I told Kate about the motorcycle and called in my location to the dispatcher. Just as I was hanging up the microphone, the motorcyclist stepped out of the trees and onto the trail between the stands of willows. He was wearing a bright red shirt and knee-length black shorts. We made quick eye contact before he ducked back into the woods. I jumped out of my truck, drew my gun, and yelled, "Stop! Police! Come out of the woods!" The only answer was the sound of snapping twigs as he retreated deeper in among the branches of the willows.

A short while later backup arrived in the form of several deputies, state troopers, Macbride's Ranger Jace Travers, and an Iowa City police officer with his K9, Luke. Police K9s are notoriously intense, and Luke was no exception. He was a deep chested, huge pawed, Czechoslovakian German shepherd—a bundle of unspent energy with sharp teeth.

As Luke began searching the willows, Chris Sullivan, another DNR seasonal officer, called to tell me that he was on his way with my johnboat.

"I heard you on the radio and thought you might need to get across the river. Your johnboat has half a tank of gas," Chris said. "Should I stop and top off the tank?"

"No," I said impatiently. "That should be plenty. Just get here as quick as you can."

Luke continued searching the woods and appeared to pick up the driver's scent several times. According to Luke, the trail led to the water's edge, increasing the chances that we'd need my johnboat.

I hopped into my truck and met Chris downstream at the nearest boat ramp. We loaded some gear, launched the boat and worked our way back upstream to pick up Luke and his handler. Kate stayed behind to assist the other officers.

When we arrived, Jace, Luke, and his partner slid down the riverbank and onto our small boat. It was Luke's first ride on the water. He panted madly, his feet skittering across the metal floor as he left slobber dripping from every surface.

The shoreline on either side of the river was steep and muddy. As we scoured the riverbank we found several foot tracks and the driver's discarded red shirt, but there were no obvious tracks on the opposite shore. After a thorough search of both banks, our passengers disembarked so Luke could search the willows a second time. But again, Luke was stumped. It was possible that the driver had made his way through one of the numerous wetlands surrounding the willows, which would make tracking difficult for the dog. Eventually, the search came to an end, and the officers trickled back to their cars to return to service.

The deputies requested a tow truck to remove the motorcycle, while Chris and I wound our way back downstream to the boat ramp. It was a disappointing end to the search. If the bike turned out not to be stolen, but the fugitive driver's property, chances were he would be tracked down eventually.

Halfway back to the boat ramp, the motor of my boat sputtered to a wheezing halt. Chris lifted the red gas tank a little too easily and tipped it upside down. We were out of gas.

"I guess half a tank wasn't quite enough." Chris smiled judiciously.

"Apparently not," I sighed. As an officer overseeing seasonals, I tried to make everything a teachable moment. Most often these moments followed one of my numerous blunders, and the main lesson almost always turned out to be, "Do as I say, not as I do, unless what I say is a bad idea." The unintentional lesson for Chris in this case was to ignore anything I might say in the future and instead top off the gas tank.

I was settling in for the slow float back to the ramp when my phone rang. "Hey, Erika, it's state radio. Can you respond to Jace's location?" the dispatcher asked.

"Well, I can but it might take a while. Why? Where is he?" I asked.

"He found the subject you were looking for about a half-mile east of where you guys were searching," she said. "Jace has the guy in the woods at his location."

"I'll do my best to get there, but I'm stuck on the river at the moment," I said. "I'm kind of out of gas."

I listened to my portable radio as the dispatcher relayed information, and I heard Jace ask for the K9 to return to Hawkeye.

"We gotta get off this river," I impatiently told Chris. "Jace has him, and we're gonna miss the good stuff."

We paddled as fast as we could using a tree branch as a push pole, but the effort only seemed to have the reverse effect of making everything move more slowly.

"Think we should try walking?" I asked Chris.

"I'm up for it."

"Let's tie up at the bank and see if we can figure out where we are. If we can get to the road easily from here, that might be our quickest option."

We inched the boat to the bank and tied up to a snag along the shore. Chris leapt out of the boat and dashed up the near vertical bank like he was Spider-Man. I struggled off after him and clambered to the top of the bank, sinking my feet and hands deep into the mud. We set out through a wall of weeds, willows, stinging nettles, and thorns. Only twenty steps into the expedition I was covered in burs. Sweat pooled under my body armor, and mosquitoes feasted on my face as though I was an all-you-can-eat buffet.

"Nope," I muttered, slapping at the bugs landing in droves on my exposed skin. "We're not doing this."

"Good," Chris said with relief. We scrambled back to the boat as if we were being shelled by enemy forces and resumed our lethargic float downstream.

"We got him," Jace said when he called me on the phone a few minutes later. His voice was bursting with excitement. "You shoulda been here!"

"I'm sorry. I can't believe I missed it. I feel bad!" It was one thing to run out of gas, but Jace and I always had each other's backs. I felt like I'd let him down.

"No big deal," Jace reassured me. "You would have enjoyed it, though. This guy looked awful! He was barefoot and shirtless—just covered in mosquito bites like I've never seen before. His mosquito bites had mosquito bites! It was great!"

"Was he wanted or what? Why did he run?" I asked.

"Apparently, he just didn't have a motorcycle license," Jace replied.

"You've gotta be kidding me! He could have killed someone!"

"Yeah. Well, those mosquito bites looked like good punishment."

Jace went on to give me the details of the takedown. They had surrounded the fugitive and shouted the dog announcement, letting the motorcyclist know that if he didn't surrender, a very enthusiastic dog was ready for a chase. Luke was at the end of his leash, salivating for action. When the driver wisely decided that he didn't want any part of being the dog's afternoon snack, he walked sheepishly out of the woods, scratching madly at the bug bites on his chest.

Chris and I continued to float downstream in silence, frustrated that we'd missed the action. As we rounded the last bend, we met another boat wending its way upstream.

"Are you out of gas?" called the gray-bearded fisherman on the other boat.

"Uh. Yeah," I had to admit.

"We'll yank you back to the ramp quick." A brown line of tobacco juice streamed from his lips into the water. We hooked his towrope to the bow of our johnboat. As we sat back for the ride, Chris spoke up. "From now on every time I go out on the river I'm taking an extra gas can."

"Good. That's exactly what I was trying to teach you." I scratched a mosquito bite on my face and leaned back in my seat, watching the trees on the shoreline pass by on our way downstream. Chris looked back at me with a sarcastic smile, silently calling my bluff.

WHEN A PARK WORKER found a blue duffle bag lying at the edge of a parking lot at Lake Macbride State Park, he initially thought nothing of it. He assumed that the bag had been forgotten by a park visitor. Usually, forgotten items were wallets and cell phones, which always spurred desperate calls to the park office in hopes that an honest person might have turned them in. Unfortunately, those calls almost always ended in disappointment. But no one had called to report a missing blue bag. It wasn't until the worker zipped open the duffel to check for some kind of identification that he realized that, in this case, no one would be calling the office to check the park's lost and found.

When the bag was discovered, Jace, Macbride's ranger, had the day off and was out of town. Jace knew I was working and called to let me know about it.

"Hey, just wanted to let you know that one of the seasonal guys found a bag this morning. It's crammed full of women's underwear and sex toys. I'm off today so I haven't had a chance to look at it. I told the seasonal to put it in the shop and leave it alone. There's a pretty good chance that it might be related to an email I got yesterday from the Department of Corrections. Apparently a sex offender by the name of Chad Felter has been hanging out at Macbride. They wanted to make me aware of him because they think he might be up to something bad."

"That's not good," I said.

"I'm pretty sure I ran into the guy a few days ago," Jace went on. "He was in a blue Jeep up in the marsh parking lot all by himself. When I pulled in he got really nervous. Looked like he was trying to stash something under the seat. I figured it was marijuana, but I didn't smell anything. Then I got the email later and realized it had probably been Felter. Anyway, I'm going to go through the bag when I get back to work. I'm guessing it's probably his."

I wrote down the license plate information and told Jace I'd keep an eye out for the car. When I got off the phone, I realized that this was one of those cases that, due to his placement on the shit magnet spectrum, always landed in his lap. And, since he was too far away to do anything about it, it was the perfect opportunity to poach off his magnetism until he returned to work.

Later that day, Ben Harper, my seasonal officer, and I pulled into Macbride to check fishermen. The blue Jeep was parked so far back in the Hillbilly Hill parking lot that we almost missed it.

"Hey that's it, isn't it?" Ben craned his head to look backward out the passenger side window. I hit the brakes, slid my truck into reverse, and pulled into the lot. There, behind some tall grass, sat the blue Jeep baking in the sun.

We got out of our truck and peered through the Jeep's windows. The interior of the vehicle was fairly clean. A laptop computer lay on the back seat, along with a tackle box and a pair of gray tennis shoes. The console compartment between the front seats was closed. Resting on top of the console lid was an unopened Twix bar, likely turning to melted mush in the summer heat.

"I'm pretty sure I've seen this car before. I think it was in the boat ramp parking lot yesterday, and maybe the day before too," Ben said. The seasonal officers lived in a house located within the state park. Driving to and from home several times each day took Ben right by the parking lot where he thought he had seen the Jeep parked.

"Well, I wonder where the hell Felter is then," I muttered.

"Not sure. Maybe he works during the day and someone picked him up here?" Ben suggested.

"Could be, but I doubt it. Why wouldn't he just drive himself? And I don't know about you, but I'd never leave an unopened Twix sitting in the sun while I was at work. I would eat it, or at least take it with me. Normal people don't leave perfectly good candy bars to melt in the car for no reason."

Ben looked at me, a smile playing at the corner of his mouth. "Are you serious? Your investigation is gonna be based on the candy bar?"

"You should know by now that I don't joke about chocolate." I smiled back. "Let's go look at the bag."

We found the duffle bag inside the dark shop where Jace had asked the park worker to leave it. I picked the bag up and moved it outside for better lighting.

"Holy shit." I winced at the weight of the bag. "If all that's in it is underwear, they must be made of cement. This is way too heavy for a bunch of clothes."

I set the bag down in the sun and put on a pair of medical gloves that were stored in a pouch on my duty belt. After pulling them on, I slid the bag's zipper open. It was nearly bursting with what appeared to be hundreds of pairs of women's and girl's underwear—slinky thongs, plain white briefs, lacy bikinis, and children's size threes plastered with colorful pictures of a smiling Elmo. They were all wadded up and stuffed in the bag together.

"Oh, my god." I recoiled at its contents. While some of the underwear appeared clean, others clearly were not. "This is disgusting. I don't want to touch this stuff even *with* gloves on." I slowly removed some of the underwear. Wedged deep into the pile of clothing was a club shaped, crudely designed dildo crafted from a large stick. One end was covered with a condom. In the duffel's side pocket were a couple pairs of women's dress shoes, a cell phone with a cracked screen, and an SD memory card. Near the bottom of the bag was a pile of photographs. I leafed through the pictures, careful to touch only the edges so as not to disturb any possible fingerprints. Judging by the clothing and hairstyles of the college-aged girls in the photographs, they appeared to have been taken in the mid-1990s. The poses were typical of college girls—beer cans clutched in hands, tight dresses, laughing faces with heavy makeup pressed cheek to cheek.

"He must have been after that one." I pointed to a smiling brunette in the photo. "She's in every picture."

"Yeah. That's just scary," Ben agreed. "I wonder if she even knows this guy is creeping on her."

I continued to search the bag, groaning with disgust at each new discovery. Finally I peered into a pocket at the long end of the bag. "No way," I said, flinching slightly.

"What is it?" Ben cautiously leaned over to look. "What the hell is that? A diaper?"

"No, it's worse," I said. "We should have just let Jace do this."

"Why? What is it?"

"Looks like a bunch of used sanitary pads. What the fuck?"

I closed the bag and called Jace to update him about the Jeep and the contents of the duffle bag. His voice sounded strained. Whether his frustration was due to the fact that he was out of town and therefore unable to be there for such gruesome discoveries or if it was because I was swiftly horning in on his investigation, I wasn't sure.

"I just can't figure out why the Jeep is still at Hillbilly Hill," I told Jace. "It doesn't make any sense. I thought about checking the woods to make sure he didn't off himself somewhere. But that doesn't make sense either—there's an uneaten Twix in the front seat of his car. If I were going to kill myself, I'd definitely eat the chocolate first." Ben smirked at the mention of the Twix.

"Yeah. Well, it probably wouldn't hurt to go look. You never know what he was thinking. I really wish I could be there to help."

"It's no big deal—we don't have anything else to do right now."

"Alright, let me know if you find anything. I'll have the car towed in the morning when I get back to work."

Back at the parking lot, Ben and I fought our way through the surrounding underbrush. The pine branches reached out and grabbed at our clothes as we pushed through them searching for Felter's body.

"Hey, come over here," Ben called to me from a nearby thicket.

"Why? What did you find?" I ducked under some branches and walked toward his voice.

"Nothing yet," he said. "But it smells like something died over here."

I stood by Ben and sucked in a whiff. I couldn't smell anything.

"Either my nose is bad or you're hallucinating."

We continued searching the woods, sniffing the air currents like dogs on point, but found nothing significant. Felter wasn't there.

As we were getting into my truck to leave, my phone buzzed with an incoming text message from Jace.

Department of Correction guys will be meeting me in the morning to look over the stuff in the bag. Meet at the south shop at 8:00 if you want.

"Of course I want to," I muttered as I sent my reply.

We will be there at 8:00.

The next morning as I drove into the park, Lake Macbride was at its pastoral best. Low-lying mist rose from the water, leaving shadowy ghosts flashing across its glassy surface. Canada geese honked and descended toward the far end of the lake with set wings and grace. I always loved working early mornings on the lake when the fog obscures signs of human life. When the view is hazy and white I can almost forget about the houses and docks that inhabit the shoreline on a spit of land between the two arms of the lake.

As I passed by the Hillbilly Hill parking lot, my thoughts returned sharply to Felter and the ugliness he brought into this place. His sickness spilled into the park like a sacrilege. The Jeep was no longer parked in the lot—either Jace had already gotten it towed or it was picked up sometime during the previous night. I turned past a stand of pine trees and onto the service road leading to the shop. Deer watched my truck indifferently from their morning beds under the trees along the roadway. Jace and Ben were standing in the parking lot, sipping coffee and talking in hushed voices.

"How was your day off?" I asked as I stepped from my truck into the damp morning air.

"It was fine. It was our wedding anniversary, so we were trying to get away for the day."

"Oh, sorry." I remembered our constant communication during the day before. "So, did you tow the Jeep this morning?"

"Nah. It was already gone when I got here," Jace said.

As we waited for the corrections officers to arrive, the sun rose behind the branches of the pine trees, scattering shadows in random geometric patterns across the pavement. The deer stood and walked in single file through the woods before crossing the driveway and disappearing behind the shop.

The Department of Corrections officers pulled up in a black Dodge Charger. They introduced themselves and took the duffle bag from Jace, as if it were a valuable treasure. Jeff, an officer with a vibrant shock of red hair and a friendly smile, said, "This looks like the perfect job for you, Seth."

Seth, the shorter of the two, appeared to be constructed entirely of muscle. His biceps bulged, straining at his shirt sleeves, and it appeared that his thighs would at any moment burst through the seams of his jeans like the Incredible Hulk.

"This is definitely Felter's," Seth said after donning protective gloves and sifting through the bag. "This is exactly the kind of stuff he always has."

"His Jeep was here yesterday, but it's gone this morning. Not sure where he went," I said.

"Oh, we know where he is," Jeff smirked. "We arrested him out here yesterday morning for skipping out on his probation check-in. He didn't go down without a fight though—tried to run, so we had to taze him. It took five of us to get him into custody."

"That explains the Twix bar." I winked at Ben. "How did you know he was out here in the first place?"

"He got out of prison two weeks ago and has had an ankle monitor on ever since. We'd been watching him, and, based on his movements, it looked like he was up to no good—probably the same stuff that he was caught doing before. Breaking into apartments and robbing them—mostly taking women's underwear and other shit like that," Seth told us. "Basically, stuff like the things in that bag. His monitor showed him moving from one apartment to another and only staying for a few minutes in each. We tried to catch him in the act, but it didn't work out."

"What was he in prison for in the first place?" I asked. "Anything besides theft?"

"Oh yeah. Sexual assault. He's had multiple victims—the youngest was just a little kid."

Back in my truck, I loaded the SD card into my computer and looked at the images. Most appeared to be photos of his teenage son playing various sports. But the last two images were photographs of a sheet of paper. They appeared to be medical records for an eighteen-year-old girl—proof that she had been vaccinated against hepatitis B, a sexually transmitted disease. I searched Facebook, hoping that I would be able to connect the name on the medical record with the image of the young woman pictured in all of the photographs in the bag, but when I found her online they didn't match. I wondered how he had obtained the vaccination record, why he would photograph it, and if she had any idea who Felter was and what he was doing with her private paperwork. I stepped out of my truck and handed the SD card to Jeff.

"Unfortunately, it looks like Felter could bail out of jail pretty soon. But he has a probation hearing in two weeks, and if we can link this bag to him, there's a good chance that he'll stay locked up for a while longer," Jeff said as he snapped off his latex gloves. "It might be enough that his monitor puts him in the same parking lot that the bag was found, but it would be better to attach him to that bag with some more solid evidence."

The next day Jace took the phone and photos to the crime lab to get them processed for fingerprints. In the meantime, we all went back to our regular summer work lives. Sweating through our shirts in the patrol boat, hounding campers for registration fees, patrolling wildlife areas, making after-park-hours drug stops, and checking fishing licenses occupied our time. But I never stopped thinking about Felter.

The results from the crime lab testing were unsurprising. Smeared and unreadable fingerprints covered the phone screen, but positive evidence was found on the four-by-six photographs. Felter's prints were etched like perfectly preserved fossils on the surface of each picture.

When Jace called with the news of the print match, I imagined Felter sitting in his truck fingering the photographs, eyeing the families picnicking and fishing on a bluebird Sunday afternoon. Kids chasing one another around the playground equipment, parents absorbed in the screens of their cellphones, kayakers paddling against the wind, and all the while, Felter would have been lurking as the others lived their charmed lives. Oblivious to the man in the blue Jeep, the visitors forgot the turmoil, worry, and drama of their daily lives. Those problems were discarded like litter as they entered through the park gates. After all, they knew that nothing bad could ever happen in an idyllic and beautiful place like Lake Macbride State Park.

—THE WILDLIFE—

"Tissue. The fresher the better. Muscle tissue is best. Organs such as the heart and liver are good if fresh. Collect about a dime-sized piece and place in a sealable plastic bag and freeze as soon as possible. Do not store tissue samples in paper bags. The more degraded the tissue is the more you want to collect—up to a golf-ball size piece."

—*Wildlife Forensic Field Manual,* Association of Midwest
Fish and Game Law Enforcement Officers

LONG BEFORE WE WERE MARRIED, Tom and I took a winter trip to the north woods of Minnesota. We spent our days hiking through pine trees dipped in white powder and along rivers banked with blue ice. We hiked until our toes tingled from the numbing cold before heading back to the hotel, where we heated homemade chili in the room's microwave.

The evening we saw the wolf we had decided to skip the chili and splurge on a supper in Grand Marais. The snow-dusted road muted the hum of the tires. We drove north in silence on Highway 61 from Lutsen, spellbound by Lake Superior's flat horizon. Suddenly, a gray streak of canine crossed the road in front of our car. It loped from the woods on our left toward the lake on our right. It was gone in a moment. A sharp intake of breath. A tap on the brakes. It was a smoky specter too large to be a coyote. And too wolfish.

"Was that a wolf?" I asked.

Tom is rarely uncertain about anything, and he wasn't ambivalent about what he'd seen that winter evening. I ask him again now, some twenty years later, whether he remembers seeing something that looked like a wolf in the dead of winter in northern Minnesota, and his response is the same as it was then. "I saw a wolf," he said matter-of-factly.

Despite the brevity of my encounter with the wolf, it somehow struck my core and wedged itself deep into my memory banks. Like the Devonian fossils my kids scoop from the creek bed in our backyard that compel us to finger the ridges of our ancient selves, the relationships we have with wildlife of all kinds collide with something equally and intrinsically profound within us.

Iowa is no longer home to animals like wolves, bison, mountain lions, and black bears. The domestication of Iowa's tallgrass prairie and woodlands brought with it a major loss of habitat and the eventual disappearance (with the exception of occasional lone strays) of these species. But still our connection with wildlife, such as it is, endures.

My daughter, Andi, catcher and hoarder of critters, is a prime example of what it means to be connected with living things. In her little patch of Iowa, she has been captivated by feeding live crickets to her prisoner, a praying mantis, and watching it strike. She has sat with her dad in the turkey blind, waiting for a tom to gobble. One morning, Andi patiently guarded a cicada-killer's nest until it emerged and alighted on her out-stretched palm. The bright red patches of milk snakes have coiled through her fingertips, and summer days have passed in which my daughter did nothing but wade through a marsh trying to land a giant bullfrog with her net. Andi has proudly collected and brought to her bedroom for further inspection more bones, feathers, and dead or decaying body parts of various wildlife than I care to think about.

Many people, when they think of Iowa wildlife species, don't think about the smaller fauna. They tend to forget about the quiet ones, like the ornate box turtle, slowly creeping through sandy prairies. Endangered animals like the common barn owl or the Higgins' eye pearlymussel slip easily from our thoughts. Wildly successful reintroduced species like the wild turkey gobbling in the spring woods and the river otter playing along the shoreline make us smile, but they aren't always in the forefront of our minds. And in spite of their fascinating lives, we seldom give a second thought to commonplace critters like largemouth bass, Canada geese, raccoons, and American robins.

Conservation officers are the sworn guardians of Iowa wildlife, no matter their size and no matter their classification as a non-game or game species. And all too often I find myself wading among their remains, hoping to solve the mysteries of their deaths.

No crime-scene tape ropes off the perimeter of my crime scenes. No rubber-necking crowds gather around victim chalk outlines. No crime-scene technicians swoop in to mark evidence while detectives puzzle over clues. No mourning family members or eager newspaper reporters solemnly look on. And, almost always, no eyewitnesses step forward to help identify the perpetrators.

My victims are found lying headless in plowed bean fields. They are lumps in the distance, an irregularity on the smooth landscape. They were left to suck in one last lungful of winter air and to exhale it back out again in a final frosted cloud. Sometimes all that's left is a pile of feathers or white bones stark against the bromegrass. Others wash up on riverbanks or lakeshores, half decomposed. Dogs drag my victim's limbs home, scattering their parts behind barns. Vultures hover and land, picking at their entrails. In my mind's eye, I watch as my victims are stuffed into coolers, dumpsters, and freezers. I watch as they are drug through leaf litter before being loaded onto a truck and driven away, their blood leaking through the crack in the tailgate. I find them adorning living room walls and on social media pages, macabre displays in a digital trophy room.

Season after season I'm called to fields, parks, yards, and woodlands to inspect the carcasses of mysteriously dead animals. I follow the putrid odor and try not to breath as I roll bloated dead deer over from side to side, searching for bullet holes, broadhead cuts, and broken bones. I sift through the remains of geese left to rot in roadside ditches, looking for evidence to identify the person responsible for the waste. I canvass neighborhoods, check social media for chatter, and ask around, but my efforts are almost always futile. My cases usually run cold before they were ever warm. And my victims are quickly forgotten.

It may take days, months, or even years to gather enough information for the pieces of a poaching case to twist and turn into the perfect alignment required by picky prosecutors. Only in moments of sheer luck, when the stars quickly align, does a case crack before my very eyes.

MY CELL PHONE RANG on a frigid morning in late February. Three inches of snow had fallen overnight, covering the icy snowpack left by an earlier storm. By morning, the sky was a cloudless cerulean. The caller was Stan Bowen, a grizzled old trapper with a salt-and-pepper beard down to his chest and a voice like a coughing tailpipe. Stan had stalked the local wildlife area since he was ten years old. His ancestral home was a farm long underwater as part of the federal impoundment floodplain.

"There's a dead deer down here on Hanging Rock Road," Stan said. "It looks like it's been poached."

I turned north onto a gravel road shimmering white with untouched snow, "I'm on my way." Another dead deer. All told it was the eleventh victim in the same ten-square-mile section in the last two years. Someone was terrorizing the neighborhood.

I'd been getting calls about late-night trespassers, gunning engines, and post-midnight rifle shots since the white-tail rut in early fall. The calls continued through late winter, when the bucks started dropping antlers. My efforts to be in the right place at the right time left me continually frustrated. I raced to the scene when I received calls of suspicious vehicles, but by the time I arrived, the vehicle would be gone as if it had disintegrated into a cloud of gravel dust. On mornings after I received such calls, when light made the evidence more apparent, I searched the area to find tire tracks crisscrossing bare fields, occasional dead deer, and empty beer cans dotting the landscape like field stones.

Hard-packed snow squeaked under my tires as I turned onto Hanging Rock Road, where Stan was waiting. The road dead-ended in a floodplain bowl. The flat, short-grass prairie field, pressed under ice and snow, was surrounded by willows, ash, and honeysuckle. The leafless branches rattled in the cold morning breeze as I stepped out of my truck and looked at the grisly mess on the road in front of me. If ever there was a wildlife crime scene deserving of police tape, this was the one.

"Not what you wanted to see first thing in the morning I bet." Stan shook my hand.

"Yeah. No kidding. This is horrible," I said.

The doe, stiff and frozen, lay on her left side on the edge of the gravel road. A six-inch gash exposed the red flesh of her neck. Frost-dotted blood drained from her mouth, and the backstrap meat had been cut and removed from the sides of her spine. The doe had apparently been pregnant. The tiny fetus had been slashed from her belly and was lying on the ground between her feet, its underdeveloped eyes bulging black against a thin membrane of skin.

My fingers ran through the doe's stiff hair, parting it, feeling for bullet holes. I scanned and finger-combed the length of her body but found no evidence that she'd been shot.

Aside from the deer, random junk lay broken and scattered all over the roadway. The wildlife area was regularly used as a dumping ground for trash of all kinds, but this appeared to be less intentional. Pieces of an old billiards table covered in blood were scattered along the length of the road.

Several 1950s-era cookbooks lay spread-eagle on the gravel, pages flipping in the breeze. Also strewn about were two spray-paint cans, six Bud Light beer cans, and several grease-stained McDonald's bags crumpled into balls. Two sets of tire tracks cutting through the snow-covered ditch traced a winding path through the adjacent field, revealing the story line of the crime like invisible ink appearing under the glow of a black light.

As I stood on the edge of the field looking out over the frozen landscape, I could envision the sickening events of the previous night. Tire tracks drew large circles in the field, plainly indicating where the doe had been chased down and run over. Where the tracks appeared to temporarily come to a stop, I found two sets of boot prints and a large plastic tub smeared with blood and deer hair. I surmised that this was the spot where the deer's neck had been slit and back straps carved out of her steaming body. I could see one of the poachers standing in the back of the truck, pulling the deer by her legs onto the truck bed and on top of the billiards table, her head resting on a cookbook. Once loaded with the illegal deer, the truck took off through the field. When it bounced over the ditch, the contents of the truck bed were jostled loose and spilled onto the road. The poachers were either spooked by something or too drunk to notice that they had lost everything.

"I have a good guess who did this," Stan said.

"Me too. Paul Wilson?"

"That'd be the one," Stan agreed shaking his head. "That kid has been causing trouble from the day he was born."

From the age of five, Paul was seated in the passenger seat of his father's rusted Ford truck, prowling the roads after dark looking for an easy kill. When Paul was eleven, his dad, drunk and without a valid driver's license, handed him the muzzleloader when they spotted a nice buck in a cornfield. Paul took aim and fired out of the passenger side window, dropping the deer instantly. Before they had a chance to get away, however, a neighbor spotted the truck, chased it down and got the license plate number.

Paul was seventeen now, a full-blooded poacher with a diverse background of crime. His latest stunt had involved stealing a John Deere tractor from one field and hiding it in another—grand theft auto Iowa-style. But to the farmer it was no joke. A missing two-hundred-thousand-dollar piece of farm equipment during harvest season might justify the formation of a posse.

Paul was rangy and crass. A scraggly goatee sprouted from his chin.

Overgrown hair hung down over his forehead and covered his eyes, like an ungroomed dog. One would swear Paul was born with a cigarette dangling from the corner of his mouth. He grew up just down the road from the crime scene in a clapboard house painted sickly yellow and reeking inside of stale cigarette smoke and booze. Paul's parents, both alcoholics, were still married, despite frequent family brawls that commonly ended with a call to the police, followed by a visit from child protective services. Paul's older brother, Tim, was a convicted felon. He, too, had a problem with alcohol. Tim was regularly arrested for getting lit and beating the piss out of his wife.

According to a sheriff's deputy, Paul had recently gotten kicked out of his parent's home and had moved in with Addie, a twenty-one-year-old woman who lived a mile away in a converted barn. Addie's barn apartment was paid for by her wealthy grandparents. The doting couple believed her to be a sweet, innocent young woman. The Addie I knew was no such thing. I'd made her acquaintance the previous fall when I caught her and Paul illegally spotlighting raccoons before the season opened.

Stan and I loaded the doe into the back of my truck, bagged the fetus, beer cans, and cookbooks and headed out in search of Paul's truck.

Paul tended to be nocturnal, sleeping off his hangovers during daylight hours. He'd wake up in time to start the night off at Boots, a line-dancing bar in a nearby small town. On chilly fall nights Boots was filled with crowds of underage kids, clad in Wrangler jeans and cowboy hats and boots, stomping to the beat of country songs.

I was at home preparing for a late-night stakeout at Boots when Stan called again.

"Hey, wanted to let you know that I just drove by Paul's parents' house. There's a white Dodge there. Older model. Looks like there might be blood on the tailgate."

"Get a plate by any chance?" I asked.

"Yep. I took a picture too—I'll text it to you."

By the time I drove to Paul's parents' place later that afternoon, the truck was gone. I ran the license plate Stan had given me through dispatch. It came back to Mitch Trower, a convicted felon who lived in a neighboring county. The dispatcher determined Mitch's parole officer to be Sue Sheldon. She gave me Sue's number, and I decided to give her a call.

"It looks like Mitch might have been involved with a deer poaching," I told Sue. "Do you know where I might be able to find him?"

Sue gave me Mitch's current address. "I'll head over there and meet you. He's subject to search at any time as part of the conditions of his parole, and that includes his truck," Sue said.

The truck, a dirty white Dodge Ram, was parked on the street outside a small ranch home in a quiet neighborhood. While Sue went into the house to talk with Mitch, I checked out the blood-speckled truck. The bed of the truck was a mess of beer cans, cookbooks, a piece of a broken billiard table, and rusted tools. In a corner, behind a spare tire, I found a plastic bag containing a bloody mound of deer backstraps.

"That meat isn't from the deer on the road," Mitch later explained. "There was more than one deer killed last night." He was seated in the passenger seat of my squad, nervously glancing out the window at his parole officer. Warm air poured from the vents and sweat began beading on Mitch's forehead.

"Who did the killing?" I asked.

"Paul. He was driving Addie's truck. Addie was hammered. She couldn't even dance, she was so bad. So, after Boots, Paul drove Addie's truck, and I just followed along with mine. They made me take that deer in my truck, but I swear I didn't kill it. When he hit one of the deer it busted out one of the headlights. I think it was on the right side. So, if you can find Addie's truck you should see the broken light," Mitch said desperately. "I'll help you out with anything you want. I can't go back to jail."

Mitch had confirmed my suspicions. If I wanted to find the truck responsible for bumper poaching, I'd have to find Addie's black pickup. I collected evidence from Mitch's truck and took his written statement.

That night I drove to Boots and parked my squad in a corner of the dark parking lot. I spotted Addie's truck parked in the lot among the crowd of other beat-up farm trucks. Music could be heard droning in a lazy beat from the front door of the dance hall. When the music came to a halt, young people spilled out the door and stood in the pool of light cast by the streetlamp. They talked in loud bursts, interspersed with laughing and teasing. Cigarettes were lit, their tips burning brightly, then tempering like fireflies in the dark. A few kids casually strolled over to parked trucks where they took turns taking pulls from bottles hidden inside paper bags.

When the next song began I waited for the crowd to flow back inside before getting out of my squad. I wove my way between the rows of parked cars and pickups until I was standing at the front of Addie's black truck.

Strands of silver-tipped deer hair protruded from the broken right headlight like grass growing from a crack in a sidewalk. Small fractures, like spiderwebs, spread across the plastic light cover, and black blood-stains were smudged along the front bumper. The pickup's bed looked like a murder scene without a body. Large sticky pools of blood interspersed with small bunches of deer hair spread in an oblong smear, and a bloody double-edged axe held down a blue plastic tarp piled near the front corner of the bed.

A small grin pulled at the corners of my mouth as I quickly took photographs. I snuck back to the safety of my truck just as Paul and his friends emerged from Boots for another smoke break. They stood in a haze of cigarette smoke near the front door, oblivious to my presence. I had enough evidence to get a search warrant, but fish and game violations are rarely viewed as important enough to wake a judge from a late-night slumber. The warrant application would have to wait for daylight.

The following afternoon five conservation officers converged on Paul's parents' house and, simultaneously, another five on Addie's. Search warrants in hand, they carefully combed through freezers, bedrooms, garages, and basements. Addie and Paul were interviewed. The resulting story contained all the drama of a hillbilly teenage soap opera: countless flimsy lies, several dead deer, adolescent love triangles, cheap-beer-fueled poaching escapades, sideways confessions, and blush-worthy cell phone photos.

When she learned that the brand-new pickup they'd purchased for their sweet granddaughter was being used as a weapon to thump deer, Addie's grandmother pursed her lips into a sharp line. Her grandfather's brow furrowed when he walked into the disgusting mess that was Addie's apartment. They were even less pleased when Addie admitted that she'd been housing Paul, the freeloading neighbor boy whom they'd been led to believe had left the state three months earlier.

According to Addie, bumper ramming deer had become somewhat of a hobby for the two of them. As often as three nights a week they'd head out to joy ride the neighboring fields to fulfill Paul's poaching addiction.

"So, it's just something you liked to do? Was it fun?" I asked.

"Yeah, I guess," Addie answered indifferently.

"What did you do with the deer that you killed?"

"Sometimes we picked them up and butchered them, but usually not," she admitted. "Usually we just left them there. Mostly we were just bored—ya know. It was just something to do."

Paul's only remorse was over getting caught. Mitch had already revealed to me that Paul not only ran deer over going forward, he also routinely slammed the gear into reverse and ran over them again, ensuring the deer were good and dead. I had no expectation that issuing citations or revoking Paul's hunting privileges would cure him of whatever dark psychological forces clogged his mind, but I tried just the same.

Paul and his friends were found guilty on several charges. I requested a ten-year court-ordered suspension of Paul's hunting privileges, which the judge quickly signed, her face wrinkled with disgust. I knew that even with a court order, chances were good that Paul would be at it again soon, that it would only be a matter of time before more wildlife would fall victim to his deadly habit.

For people like Paul, lurking in the woods unseen is easy, and the business of killing satiates some inexplicable urge, like water soothing a parched throat. But the thirst always comes back. And, when it does, a trail of more victims will lie on the forest floor, their wild lives seeping away with the spring thaw.

IN IOWA, DEER haven't always been the nuisance that many people believe them to be today. Beginning around 1857, the deer population began a steep and long decline. They gained legal protection in 1898, and eventually their numbers began to increase, thanks in large part to escapees from three deer farms located throughout the state during the years 1894 to 1937. The size of the herd grew from an estimated five to seven hundred in 1936 to today's four hundred thousand.

Whether the population is too high depends on whom you talk to. Through one ear, I listen to frustrated deer hunters complain that they "aren't seeing the numbers" that they used to, while my other ear takes in the grievances of farmers losing crops and motorists losing bumpers, both believing the numbers are "the worst" they've ever been. Either way, white-tailed deer have undoubtedly adapted well to Iowa's agricultural landscape and its lack of apex predators. Over-sized Iowa deer, stuffed to the gills from the all-you-can-eat buffet of the state's healthy crop yields, become nearly impossible temptations that poachers of all stripes can't seem to ignore.

Little research has been done to explore the dark recesses of aberrant poaching behavior. Why do some people cross over the line from healthy sporting practices to something more sinister and psychologically complex? Is a poacher born or made? Why do some people become ethical hunters, act as stewards of the land, believe in fair chase, and abide by the rules, while others swerve into deviancy, killing merely for the sake of killing? Why do seemingly normal humans reveal hunting-crazed alter egos each fall? What causes some folks to be susceptible to the sudden onset of buck fever as soon as the daylight hours shorten and golden leaves drop from the trees?

Before smartphones came along, bars, sports shows, coffee shops, workplaces, and friendships provided the venue hunters needed for bragging about their exploits. In those environs, men would reach into their shirt pockets and extract photographs of the game they had taken, like proud parents showing off their surprisingly good-looking children. Most hunters were satisfied with basking in the limelight this congenial boasting afforded. The illegal passions of others, however, were only fueled by the attention. It ignited a competitive drive for more and bigger tales to tell. The difference between these two types of personalities may be largely rooted in their education in the field as young hunters. In other words, sometimes the apple doesn't fall far from the tree.

The internet has magnified these processes. Nowhere is ego more evident and the need for immediate gratification more prevalent than within the pressurized world of social media. The platform encourages the development and enhances the addictive tendencies of its users. An increasing number of hunters and anglers today seem to be more influenced and manipulated by the screens they hold in their hands than by the lessons they may (or may not) have learned from an ethical mentor.

These days cell phone search warrant dumps are the social equivalent of an anthropological dig. The technological evidence unearthed from these devices strongly mirrors the swaggering men who lie, exaggerate, and play-act themselves as characters in their own lives. Based on the time-stamped data, GPS locations, and instant messages I've read, it is apparent to me that some hunters expend more effort recording and narrating each minute of their time in the blind than actually experiencing the hunt. Ironically, this practice of constant boasting and posting seems only to further remove the hunters from the land, the hunt, and the game they claim to respect.

In photo after photo, people kneel behind big deer made to seem bigger by extended arms, camera angles, and photo-editing software. Social media posts encourage friending and tallying likes. Some folks will do anything to attract the attention of ego-boosting professional sponsorships. The more dramatic the post, the better.

The side benefit of this technological revolution is that wildlife crimes are very often electronically preserved. Given persistence and a little luck, investigating conservation officers often get a chance to sift through the data. Devices in poachers' hands house evidence of their wrongdoing, mainly because they just can't help but save and share images of their doppelgänger lives. But with each turn of the page in a huge stack of electronic data, I find myself cringing. It's common for conservation officers to proclaim that ninety-nine percent of the people they come into contact with are good people and ethical hunters and that it is really only about one percent of the hunting population that needs some correction and guidance. Thanks to people like Cade Sinwell, I, for one, am losing faith in those numbers.

The photo posted to Cade Sinwell's Facebook timeline was taken in early November. In it, Cade is outfitted in Realtree camo. He wears a ball cap, over which is strapped a headlamp, still turned on from the search for the downed deer in front of him. The background of the photo is dark, the woods fading into the black hole of night. The flash from Cade's iPhone camera illuminates both his eyes and those of the buck that he is kneeling behind, transforming them into glowing orbs like beings possessed. The buck is lying on his left side, his head held aloft by Cade's tight grip on the antlers. The angle of the photo is perfectly aligned so as not to draw attention to the fact that Cade's arms are outstretched in front of him, giving the illusion that the antlers he's holding are twice their actual size. The text accompanying the photo reads:

What a rollercoaster of emotion in deer hunting this year. The big man above sent me a mature buck to harvest tonight. After months of Tim Garrison and I watching our target trail cam deer this one was not documented but too mature to pass on. I was watching the Iowa game on my phone. He came in hot from a rattle and grunt 20 minutes prior. It's amazing how fast a rutting buck can show up. I didn't even lock my phone, volume still on (low), and managed to pockit it, draw and take out both lungs and skim his heart. Big thanks to Marv Hartson for helping us transform our meat into jerky and burger. Thanks to Tim for allowing me to bow hunt his land. It is world class. I admit we have many larger bucks on camera and we are excited to see who else is able to harvest mature bucks out here. We all enjoy the chase and management of these deer. Congrats to everyone who harvested a deer already and good luck to those in pursuit.

The night the buck died, sheriff's deputies had been dispatched to a trespass call on 200th Street in the northeast corner of my territory. When they arrived, they found Cade Sinwell and Tim Garrison trudging through a field, dragging a dead deer by its back legs through the corn stubble. The landowner, having seen two men in his field after dark, believed they were trespassing and called the sheriff's office. Though Iowa law allows for unarmed retrieval of game on private property, most hunters make the effort to contact the landowner to avoid being the subject of either a trespass call or the business end of a shotgun. But Cade and Tim had reasons for failing to call the landowner. The first reason was that Tim was the only person with permission to hunt on Mitch Harrison's ground, where the deer was shot. Second, the deer wasn't properly tagged, which was required before it could be legally moved.

It was at this point that the confusion of the case began. The responding deputy noticed the lack of a tag on the deer's antler and asked the men about it. Tim, knowing that he was the only person allowed to hunt Harrison's ground, took credit for the deer and told the deputy he'd merely forgotten to tag it.

"I'm not a squirrel cop, so I'm not going to write you for the untagged deer, but I can guarantee if the DNR officer was here you'd be up a creek," the deputy told Tim.

Tim was an ex-military man accustomed to handling authority. "Yes, sir. I'll get it tagged right now." Tim retrieved a tag from the pickup and wrapped it around the buck's antler.

"Alright. You should be good now to drive it home. Next time it would be a good idea if you'd just check with the landowner before you go looking for a deer. Even though you technically don't need permission, it's still a nice thing to do," the deputy advised, before climbing back into his squad and closing out the call.

A month later I received a phone call from Bill Franklin. Bill's property lay just to the south of Mitch Harrison's timber paradise where Cade and Tim spent most of their time.

"I just think they're up to something," Bill told me. "I caught both Cade and Tim hanging a trail camera on my property back in October. When I confronted them, they said they thought they were on Harrison's land. But they know better than that. My property is signed every fifty feet. You can't miss the boundary."

"Have you seen them since?" I asked.

"Only on Facebook. My daughter has been keeping an eye on their posts ever since we caught them on our property. Cade has a post from November third where he's posing with a huge buck. And the weird thing is, he's been hunting every day since then. Obviously he's already used his buck tag, and I just can't imagine that he'd be hunting that hard for a doe. There are does everywhere. Makes me think he's after another buck."

"How do you know he hunts every day?"

"Because he parks his truck at a field entrance onto Harrison's property every afternoon. He usually stays until just after sunset. He's probably parked there right now."

"Alright. I'll check it out," I said.

Later that afternoon I drove past Harrison's property. The rolling wooded hills of Harrison's ground were a deep shade of red from maroon-tinted oak leaves. Every gust of wind knocked more leaves loose and sent them fluttering to the ground in a whirl of fall color. Just as Bill predicted, Cade's truck was parked in the field's drive entrance. The front end of the dark-blue truck was tucked just inside the tree line.

I hopped out of my squad and inspected Cade's truck. The thin layer of gravel dust coating the truck bed cover was wiped clean by fingers near the latch. Blood droplets spattered the tailgate. When I looked through the driver's side window, I noticed an empty bow case lying on the back seat and an open beer can in the cupholder. I climbed back into my truck and positioned it across the road in a hayfield, partially hidden by the brush that sprouted from the ditch, and waited for Cade to return.

As dusk fell, the shadows in the woods across the road slowly darkened and eventually turned black, hiding individual trees in an obsidian blur.

In contrast, the gravel road between my truck and Cade's reflected the moonlight, glowing a shade off white. I sat in my truck and monitored the opening in the timber. Eventually Cade's inky figure materialized like an apparition from the woods just west of the field drive. Clad in camouflage coveralls and carrying a compound bow, he walked toward his truck. As Cade opened the door to place his bow inside, I stepped onto the road to greet him.

"Any luck tonight?" I asked.

Cade flinched in surprise, my sudden appearance catching him off guard. He recovered quickly, smiled, and adopted a shaky tone of nonchalance. "I finally got a small buck tonight. It's been a rough season though—I've had terrible luck. And I admit I've taken a few bad shots—no excuse for those, I guess."

"That's alright. Nobody's perfect, right? I'm just out checking licenses if you don't mind digging yours out for me."

"Not at all," Cade said as he opened the glove box and began rummaging through it.

"So, where's the buck down at?"

"Oh, probably about two-hundred-fifty yards to the south." Cade pointed into the woods in front of his truck then handed me his license and tag. "I tried calling the landowner to the south to see if I could drive through his property to pick up the deer, but he hasn't called back yet."

"Who's the landowner to the south?"

"His name is Bill Franklin. I'm sure he won't mind. He knows who I am."

I asked Cade why his deer tag was in his truck and not on the deer. Once deer are taken they are required to be tagged within fifteen minutes or before they're moved, whichever occurs first. Since Cade hadn't even been carrying his tag, he clearly wouldn't have been able to tag it within fifteen minutes. It was becoming increasingly clear to me that Cade and Tim had been using the age-old poaching strategy of not tagging deer as a way of culling them for size. Given that each hunter only receives one buck tag, if they could manage to shoot a deer, drive it back to the house and butcher it without burning their tag or getting checked by an officer, they could keep hunting until they got the big one they were after.

"I know I'm supposed to carry my license and tag but I just forgot 'em in my truck. So I was going to grab it and head back out to tag him just when you walked up."

"So you haven't had much luck the rest of the season? Did you shoot anything else yet?" I asked.

"Nope. Just this little buck tonight."

I pointed to the blood on the tailgate. "Where'd that come from?"

Cade nervously shifted his weight from one foot to the other. His tone suddenly became defensive. "My buddy shot one yesterday, and I helped him load it. You can call him right now if you don't believe me," Cade said quickly.

"Which friend is that?"

"Cooper Reese. You want his number?" Cade's voice trembled.

"Nah. I don't need his number. But what about your Facebook post from earlier this month. Looks like you shot a nice buck," I said.

Cade froze momentarily. His face turned to stone masked with panic. "Tim shot that one. I didn't."

I told Cade that I'd seen the Facebook post and read his detailed account of the hunt. Everything from watching the football game on his phone to the buck's rattle and grunt. "Hunters don't pose with deer other people shot. And why would you write such an elaborate story about a deer that you didn't even kill? Not to mention that Tim didn't even post a picture of that deer on his Facebook page."

"I just wanted people to think that I shot it. And Tim was embarrassed about shooting it. That's why I took a picture with it," he said.

"Why would he be embarrassed about it? It looked like a nice deer," I said. "Do you have any pictures of it on your phone?"

Cade denied that his phone contained any pictures of the deer. He said that Tim had been watching another buck that they'd nicknamed Moose. Tim's goal was to shoot Moose, but when another decent-sized buck appeared, he'd been unable to control himself. Cade claimed that Tim had no interest in posting pictures on social media of any deer other than Moose. I got Tim's phone number from Cade and asked him to put his phone onto the hood of my truck. While Cade stood outside my truck waiting, I gave Tim a call.

"Yeah, I shot that buck," Tim said. "I just let Cade take pictures with it to help him out."

"What do you mean by 'help him out'?"

"Cade's got lots of professional sponsors, so he needs to show that he's killing big deer—it helps him make money from his sponsors. But it wasn't really a big deer—it was just a good picture," Tim explained.

I hung up with Tim and quickly called Bill Franklin, the landowner to the south and the original complainant.

"Just wanted to let you know that Cade was out here hunting, just like you said he'd be. He shot a buck on the south end of Harrison's land. Obviously he's got a problem since he bragged on Facebook about the other buck. Anyway, Cade said he left you a message asking permission to go onto your land to get the deer," I explained.

"Really? The only message I have is from Tim. He said that he shot a deer and wanted to drive up on my property to get it," Bill said. The story was becoming increasingly tangled. Bill told me that he'd meet me at his property to help with loading the deer. Cade and I drove to the entrance of Bill's land and waited for him.

When Bill arrived, we accompanied Cade onto Bill's property. Bill waited in his truck while Cade and I walked into the woods where the small buck lay on the ground. The buck was a spike, one of its tiny antlers deformed and smaller than the other. Resting on the side of the deer was another compound bow and quiver of arrows.

"Why did you have two bows with you?" I asked, remembering the bow Cade had been carrying earlier when he returned to his truck.

"Oh. That other bow was Tim's. He left it in the woods yesterday, so I told him that I'd grab it for him," Cade replied.

I'd never heard of a bowhunter forgetting his bow in the woods following a hunt. Nothing Cade told me was making any sense.

"Why would Tim call Bill about shooting a buck? Is he out here hunting with you?" I asked Cade.

He shifted uncomfortably and hesitated before answering, "No. I called Bill. I was just pretending to be Tim. I figured since Bill knows who Tim is, that it would be less confusing for him."

I looked at Cade in disbelief. "Well, you're wrong. This whole thing is confusing—and your story is becoming less believable by the second."

We field dressed the deer then pulled it through the weeds to my truck. There, I took possession of the deer, the bows, and Cade's iPhone.

"You might want to start thinking about telling the truth about that buck from November third. You know that what you told me isn't true. Based on your Facebook account, it's pretty evident that you killed that buck and that Tim took credit for it as a favor to you. You may want to rethink things. And, by the way, I'll be applying for a search warrant for your iPhone."

The data from the phone dump filled hundreds of pages. Every text, Facebook message, email, photo, and GPS location were recorded. Based on the number of messages sent each day, it wasn't clear how Cade had had time to do anything other than stare at his phone. He carried on multiple texting conversations simultaneously. Trying to sort out who he was talking to at any given moment was mind-boggling. When I was finally able to make sense of the mess of data, the results were convincingly damning.

Cade's iPhone revealed that in early October he and his friends had killed a total of six does, which they quickly took home and converted to burger. At least two of the deer were untagged and transported illegally. One had been shot with Cade's Glock handgun, which is illegal to carry and use during bow season. Another deer had been taken with the aid of a mobile transmitter. Cade and his hunting partner on this occasion texted each other multiple updates throughout the hunt, detailing the location of the deer, thereby completely eliminating the notion of a fair chase. None of the deer were reported to the DNR as was required. Finally, I found several Facebook messages from November third sent by Cade to friends and to his mother bragging about the big buck he'd just shot.

Aaron Bell, a conservation officer from a neighboring territory, and I met with Cade for an interview two weeks after the warrant was served on his iPhone. Despite the pile of evidence against him, Cade continued to deny killing the does, and he maintained that Tim had killed the deer on November third. Sticking to his lies, he seemed incapable of even recognizing the truth plainly revealed in the evidence before him.

"Okay," I said, after listening to Cade lie for the first twenty minutes of the interview. "Do you remember what happened on October twenty-fifth?"

"No."

"Let me refresh your memory. You sent a message to your mom that read, 'Tim's got one down.' Ten minutes later you sent her another message that read, 'Doe down.' Your mom wrote back and asked you if you tracked the doe down yet, and you responded, 'No. Tim's is dead by now but I'm not pushing mine.' Your mom suggested that you would have a good time drinking beer and tracking your doe. Then, about twenty minutes later she asked if you'd found her yet. You said, 'Found both. We had to shoot Tim's with my Glock lol. Mine was dead.'"

I looked at Cade and waited for him to accept the truth and fold. "I didn't say those things," he said flatly.

I stared at him in silence for a moment, unsure how to proceed. "It came from your phone, Cade. I'm not sure how you can deny physical evidence like this," I said, my blood pressure slowly rising. I showed him the message log. "See? This is *your* phone number. It says 'outgoing.' Then right here is your mom's number where it says 'incoming.'"

"It wasn't me."

"Who was it then?"

"Sometimes I let Tim use my phone."

"So you're saying that Tim was messaging your mother. And simultaneously messaging your girlfriend? Are you sure about that? How about the big buck on November third?" I asked.

"I already told you that Tim shot it. Just ask the deputies—they were there that night."

"They were there after the deer was dead. But your phone shows that you messaged about six people to announce that you killed a big buck." I was completely exasperated by Cade's insistence on lying.

Aaron asked Cade, "You understand that we have all of your messages right? We have every outgoing and incoming message. Every photo with GPS locations attached. Every phone call. Every email. Are you sure you want to stick with that story?"

"Yes. I didn't shoot that deer," Cade said. "And I didn't send those messages."

In all, I charged Cade with seven violations and filed for liquidated damages of two deer, totaling over four thousand dollars, and I filed five hunting violations against Tim. Iowa's hunting revocation system works by the accumulation of multiple offender points, with each violation assigned a preset number of points. Once a person reaches five points, hunting privileges are revoked for a year. Based on past experience, I knew that the chances of getting Cade prosecuted on all seven charges were slim. Tim failed to appear for court and was therefore automatically found guilty. He was assessed six points, resulting in suspension of his hunting, fishing, and trapping privileges for a year. Cade, on the other hand, opted to appear before the judge. He pled not guilty on all counts.

When I received notice that a trial date had been set for Cade's charges, I contacted the county attorney's office, worried that a plea deal might take place without consulting me. I explained the revocation system to the county attorney in detail, and I insisted that, if a plea deal happened, the county attorney needed to see to it that Cade maintained at least five points against his hunting privileges, ensuring a clearly needed revocation.

I firmly told the attorney that as long as Cade's privileges were suspended, I'd be happy.

The next morning, I received an email from the county attorney's office informing me that a plea deal had been reached. Cade pled guilty to two charges of failing to register a deer harvest and one count of using a mobile transmitter while deer hunting. The charges of illegally taking a deer and the associated liquidated damages were dropped. His plea deal came to a total of only four points and a fine of around three hundred dollars. Although I was very disappointed, I wasn't entirely surprised.

In a ten-minute meeting between the prosecutor and the defense attorney, two months' worth of field work, investigations, interviews, and time were flushed away. I wondered, not for the first time or for the last, if my livelihood chasing down poachers was nothing more than just that—a job. A way of making money. It was more apparent to me than ever that if crimes against wildlife were a low priority in the eyes of the people who could make the most difference then that low status would be reflected in society at large. If plea deals took the place of true prosecution in the majority of cases, Iowa's wildlife would be the ultimate victims. And as much as I tried shouting into the wind on their behalf, the voices of those I was sworn to protect would be stifled. Their voices and their well-being would be drowned out, lost in the din that howled each and every day through the halls of justice.

—THE LAW—

"Counting officers' murders and accidental deaths from traffic together, more than one of eight law enforcement fatalities occur during vehicle stops. So whether you've picked up on early indicators of suspicion or not, remember: Conducting a vehicle stop is one of your highest risk activities, not only because of the offender who may be armed and assaultive but because of the environment in which you're working."

—"Fish and Game Vehicle Stops"
(training handout, 2000)

THE OLD BOYS from my first statewide meeting had one thing right: The job isn't what it used to be. As society has changed, our role as conservation officers has evolved as well. It didn't happen suddenly. I remember sitting through classes during police academy training and wondering why, as a future conservation officer, I would need to be concerned about half the things they were teaching. But now I understand. While before our attention may have been solely focused on the care and protection of our natural resources, we now find ourselves pulled into the realm of traditional public policing. Absorbed in sneaking up on a deer spotlighter, we may trip over a meth lab. Fixated on looking for a dead hen pheasant, we may miss the person with the felony arrest warrant. What we assume to be a hunting accident may, in fact, be a murder.

Gone are the days when courtroom testimony from someone wearing a badge could be assumed to be the truth, the whole truth, and nothing but the truth. That illusion has run its course. It is understandable that the public's perceptions about the law and those charged with enforcing it would not emerge unscathed. Mistrust on both sides has taken root, grown, and begun to smother time-honored perceptions, like a weed overtaking a forest floor.

While fish and game officers have largely been spared the criticism, wrath, and distrust endured by other law enforcement agencies, the thin blue line is slowly mixing with our green one. More and more I find myself investigating cases outside the norm for conservation law enforcement officers. Wild and isolated places attract the good and the bad equally. Drug production and use, sexual assaults, thefts, and domestic fights. The graceful and the crude. The harmless and the perilous.

The societal problems customarily found in homes, neighborhoods, and urban areas have seeped into the backcountry. The gun on my hip isn't for raccoons—okay, sometimes it is—but for my protection and yours. The biggest threat I face isn't from a malicious hunter or a rabid wild animal. The threat may come when I am alone, miles away from the nearest backup, and encountering a desperate person harboring a warrant for assault, or worse. It might come from assisting in an active shooter situation or from contacting a drug user fresh from prison and desperate not to return. My body armor, with a camera attached to my chest, isn't an attempt to look militaristic, it's my way home.

THE BURST OF RADIO TRAFFIC jolted me from my daydream. It was Sunday, and I was on my way home after spending a long weekend fighting the monotony of the blazing sun and choppy water aboard a patrol boat on the Coralville Reservoir. Ben Harper, my seasonal officer, still on the water, was going to take one last north to south pass over the lake before trailering the boat for the weekend.

"C352, C179 Car 2," Ben came over the radio.

"C352, go ahead. Did I forget something on the boat again?" I sighed. I'd been looking forward to a refreshing shower and was prepared to leave anything I'd forgotten on the boat to be picked up another day.

"No. Can you start back here? I need your help." I could sense the anxiety in Ben's voice.

I turned my truck around, headed back to the ramp, and called Ben. He answered on the first ring and launched into an explanation. Shortly after dropping me off at the boat ramp, he was contacted by some pontoon boaters who were concerned about the welfare of a passenger on a red Mastercraft speedboat. The Mastercraft had been stuck in a shallow stretch of the lake, and when the driver of the pontoon attempted to provide assistance, he noticed some telltale signs that the driver of the Mastercraft was drunk. The driver was slurring his speech and had a hard time balancing in his grounded boat. A female passenger was acting strangely. She appeared to be playing a secret game of charades with the people on the pontoon boat, desperately trying to communicate to them that she wanted off the drunk driver's boat.

"Copy." I pushed a little harder on the gas pedal and told Ben that I was on my way back to the ramp.

Before I had even driven a mile in the direction of the boat ramp, Ben called again.

"I can see the Mastercraft—it's coming under Mehaffey Bridge right now," Ben said quickly. "Looks like a male driving and a female sitting in the back of the boat. Do you want me to wait for you or go ahead and stop them?"

"Better get them stopped. I'm still five minutes out. Call me when you know what's going on."

When I pulled into the boat ramp parking lot I could see the patrol boat stopped alongside the red Mastercraft. I parked the truck and watched through binoculars. Blue lights flashed on the roof of the patrol boat, and Ben, leaning over the edge of the patrol boat, was holding onto the side of the red boat. He appeared to be in the midst of a conversation with the boat's occupants. The driver was gesticulating madly at Ben, throwing his hands into the air and waving them around as though he were trying to swat at an annoying fly. I was familiar with that body language—I had been on the receiving end of it many times. The driver was not pleased, and he was letting Ben have it.

Ben pushed away from the red boat and drifted nearby, blue lights still pulsing like a disco ball atop the patrol boat. My phone rang. "I'm going to come and pick you up at the ramp." Ben's voice was shaking. I continued to watch through binoculars as Ben spoke into the phone. "This guy is plastered, and he's pissed. The woman wants off the boat. She's acting like she's scared to death of him."

"Alright. What did you tell them?" I asked.

"Just that I needed the registration paperwork and that I was going to pick you up. I told him that we'd be back to talk to them in a second." Ben steered the patrol boat in my direction. I grabbed my boat bag and hurried to meet him at the dock.

"Do you think this guy's going to fight?" I asked after climbing onto the boat.

"I don't know. He's really mad and seems pretty drunk."

"Alright. I'm calling Jace to get him started this way just in case." I dialed Jace Travers's number as we glided back toward the red boat.

When we pulled up alongside, I noticed that the driver's eyes were bloodshot and that he smelled like a brewery. The strands of his thinning gray hair were windblown, giving him a slightly deranged look. Gray hairs sprouted sparsely from his bare chest, and his Hawaiian-flowered swim trunks hung low on his hips, exposing more of his backside than I cared to see. The man towered over the woman seated at the back of the boat. Wearing shorts and a bikini top, she appeared to be in her late fifties. Despite the ninety-degree temperature, she was shivering, hugging her chest and gazing down at the floor of the boat. As soon as she lifted her head, we made eye contact. The woman picked up the bag lying next to her on the seat and stood up. "I'm just going to get on your boat, okay?"

"That's fine," I assured her. "Can I ask why you want to get off this boat?"

She shook her head slightly, almost an unconscious reaction. "It's just time for me to go home."

"What the fuck is going on?" The driver was staring at me in a rage. He took a step and stumbled forward, lurched toward the steering wheel and caught hold of it before falling. "I don't know why the fuck you stopped me in the first place."

"You don't have a capacity number displayed on your boat," Ben said. "I already explained that to you."

"What the fuck are you talking about?"

"We already went through this."

"How much have you had to drink?" I interrupted.

"Nothing," the driver said as he took a step and careened into the captain's chair.

"Nothing? Sir, I can smell the alcohol on you from here."

"Nothing," he repeated.

"Not to mention that you can barely stand up."

"I'm diabetic. Have you ever thought of that?"

"Do you think you're having some kind of a diabetic reaction?" I asked. I was certain that if he was diabetic, he was a drunk diabetic. At the same time my thoughts immediately drifted to possible lawsuits and the loss of a drunk boating charge over my refusal to provide medical attention.

"Are you saying that you think you need an ambulance?" I asked.

The driver immediately seized on the opportunity for distraction. "I suppose I should be checked. If I'm acting weird, it must be because of my diabetes."

Ben hooked a towrope between our boats so we could pull the Mastercraft to the dock. As we moved toward the dock, I radioed for an ambulance, then turned my attention to the woman now at the front of our boat. She introduced herself as Karen. She went on to tell me that Ted had been acting strange ever since he had picked her up from the marina earlier that afternoon. She wasn't sure if he was drunk or on some kind of drug, but she was certain that something wasn't right. She related that they'd almost crashed into other boats several times, and each time Ted reacted by shouting obscenities and flipping the bird to the other boaters. Karen told me that she frequented the lake on her own boat most weekends and was horrified and embarrassed by his behavior. Not only that, she was worried that she wouldn't make it off the lake alive.

Jace and two sheriff's deputies were waiting when we arrived at the dock. Jace helped Karen off our boat and escorted her to shore where she sat on the curb and called a friend for a ride. As I waited for the ambulance to arrive, I gathered Ted's information. When the EMTs arrived and began questioning their patient, I learned that Ted Hartson was a fifty-seven-year-old man with Type 2 diabetes. Ted told the EMTs that he'd eaten a sandwich two hours earlier and had had only bottled water to drink while he was on the lake.

"Are you sure about that?" I asked again. "I smell more than water on your breath."

"I only drank water!"

"After the medics check you out, I'm going to ask for consent to get a sample of your breath, blood, or urine. If you haven't had anything other than water, you shouldn't have anything to worry about. Are you going to be willing to provide a sample?"

"I ain't fucking doing anything for you," Ted slurred.

The medics continued to tend to Ted, taking his vitals and blood sugar before loading him into the ambulance. An EMT stepped out of the ambulance and rolled her eyes as she said, "His blood sugar is a little bit high, but not nearly as high as his blood alcohol level."

"Yeah, that sounds about right," I said. "But I didn't think I should risk it. He won't give me any tests anyway."

"He wants to go to the hospital, so he'll be in the ER if you need to follow up with him," she said before stepping back into the ambulance for the ride to the hospital.

With the lights off and sirens silent, the ambulance slowly pulled out of the parking lot. I made my way over to Jace and the group of deputies gathered around Karen, who was still seated on the curb. Jace saw me approaching and met me halfway.

"Long story short—she finally came clean about what happened on the boat. Turns out that Ted basically held her against her will and threatened to rape her. I think we've got a possible kidnapping charge," Jace said.

"Can't say I've ever charged anyone with kidnapping before. Are you sure?"

"Go listen to her story, then we can talk about it with the deputies."

Jace introduced me to Karen and asked her to go through her story again. Crying in earnest, lines of black makeup snaked down Karen's cheeks. She nodded her head and took a deep breath. "I might as well start at the very beginning," she said. "I met him back in January on Match. com. We went out for dinner a couple times—an hour at the most each time. Honestly, he seemed a little full of himself. Only really wanted to talk about how wonderful he was. I guess I chalked his ego up to nerves. I mean, I can't be too picky at my age." She started to choke up.

"Take your time," I encouraged. "It's not your fault."

"I hadn't heard from Ted in months until he texted me this morning. He asked if I wanted to go out on his boat this afternoon. I thought it was a little weird since I hadn't heard from him for so long, but it's such a perfect day for boating, I decided it might be nice. So I went. Biggest mistake ever."

"What happened once you got on the water?" I asked.

"We were supposed to meet at the marina at one o'clock. He was ten minutes late. He finally came flying into the parking lot in his Mercedes like he was God's gift to women." Karen rolled her eyes, recalling Ted's ego. "When he got out of his car he kind of stumbled down the dock. He just seemed off, you know? He fumbled around when he was taking the cover off the boat. At one point he even fell down into the boat. I should have gone with my gut right then and there. I mean, he was acting drunk, but I just didn't want to offend him you know?"

"How did he do driving the boat?"

"He drove like a fucking maniac. I was seriously scared that we'd get killed. I kept telling him to slow down, but he wouldn't! There were several times we almost hit other boats, and he'd get so mad that he'd yell at the other driver and give 'em the finger. By the time he started asking me to make him drinks, his temper was so horrible I was scared to tell him no."

"What was he drinking?" I asked.

"Mostly rum and Cokes. A couple wine coolers too. But he seemed to be spilling most of what I gave him."

"How was he spilling it?"

"I don't even know, but he poured half of it on the floor every time he tried to turn the boat," she recounted. "Eventually I started dumping the rum overboard when he wasn't looking. He kept asking for more even after I told him that it was all gone. That made him really angry. Eventually he told me that he wanted to go up to the northern part of the lake so we could be alone." Karen paused and took a deep breath. Her voice became shaky. "At that point, I just wanted off the boat. I wasn't comfortable. You know how it is up north. There just isn't much traffic up there. By this time, he'd already tried to kiss me twice. I told him no, which must have *really* pissed him off. Finally, I said, 'Ted—turn around. I want to go back to the marina.'" Karen's voice dissolved into sobs. She crossed her arms over her knees, buried her face in them, and shook her head side to side.

"It's okay," one of the deputies reassured her. "You're safe now. What happened when you told him to take you back to the marina?"

Karen lifted her head slightly, sucked in a breath, and said, "He told me that he wouldn't take me back. He said he was going to take me into a cove. He said, 'We're going to find a cove so we can fuck.' I'm sorry for this whole thing. I shouldn't have let this happen."

"Karen, it wasn't your fault," I said. "He did this. Not you."

Karen wiped the tears from her face with the back of her hand and struggled to regain her composure. "Thank god he got stuck. Right after I told him that I wanted to go back to the marina, he turned the boat to go further north and ended up getting stuck in the flats. He's such an idiot! I told him that he was going to get stuck if he went out of the channel, but he didn't listen. I tried to tell the people on the pontoon who came to help us that I wanted off the boat."

"They got the message. They found my seasonal officer and told him about it."

"Thank god. If they hadn't come I don't know what would've happened. I told myself that if I had to, I'd try jumping into the lake and swimming just to get away from him. But even then—where would I go?"

"Thanks for telling us what happened. I doubt this was the first time he's tried this with someone. Do you have a friend coming to get you?" I asked.

Karen nodded, "Yeah. Sharon should be here any minute."

After Sharon arrived and the two women left, I met with the deputies and Jace. We talked about possible charges. The consensus was that aside from driving drunk, Ted had every intention of forcing himself on Karen. And given that she was stuck on a boat in the middle of nowhere, she didn't have a reasonable means of getting away from him. His actions met the definition of third-degree kidnapping—a code section I never envisioned charging when I became a conservation officer.

Jace nodded in agreement. "Yeah. His intent was pretty clear. She asked him to turn around, and instead he tried taking her further away from the marina. It's good they got stuck."

"Can't hurt to charge him with third-degree kidnapping. It'll probably get dropped to false imprisonment anyway," the deputy said. The practice of plea bargaining and lowering charges to less serious offenses was rampant and often maddening. But once the charge is filed, the prosecution's decisions are out of an officer's hands. A guilty plea of any kind is a win for the prosecutor.

Jace and I drove to the hospital to interview Ted further. At the emergency room, we were directed to Ted's room. As we passed the array of desks clustered in the center of the ER bay, a nurse glanced up from her computer and said, "I hope you get him outta here. He's such a whiner."

"Fun, isn't he?" I said.

"He's an ass," she whispered. "And besides that, he faked his urine test."

"How do you fake a urine test?"

"It looked like he mixed soap and water together. I told him that I've been a nurse for thirty years and that I had never seen urine that looked like that. Of course, he denied faking it, but I'm not stupid."

"Any chance the lab will test it?" I asked.

"They will if I request it."

"That would be great. The results would make pretty good evidence for the drunk boating charge."

"I'll put in the request with the lab if you promise to get him out of here soon," she said.

Jace and I walked into Ted's room, where he was lying on a hospital bed flipping through channels on the TV. The room smelled like alcohol as it continued to seep from his pores and float through the sterile hospital air like a fog.

"What the fuck do you want?" Ted sneered.

"We came to talk to you about what happened on the boat today," I said.

"I already told you. Nothing happened other than getting stuck in shallow water."

"What happened with Karen?" Jace asked.

"Nothing."

"That's not what she said."

"Well, she's lying then. I don't even know what you're talking about."

"She said that you told her that you wanted to go into a cove and have sex with her. Is that true?" Jace asked.

"No." Ted's face contorted in feigned disgust.

"She had some pretty specific details, and she was really upset. Did you try kissing her?"

"Oh, yeah. She liked it though. But she knows we're just friends."

"Turns out she didn't like it," Jace said. "And the fact that you wouldn't take her back to the marina when she asked and instead threatened to have sex with her means that you were holding her against her will with the intent of sexual assault."

"What?"

"So, I'm letting you know that you're going to be charged with third-degree kidnapping and with boating while intoxicated."

"What?" Ted repeated. "You've got to be kidding me!"

"We're not kidding, unfortunately." Ted sat in the bed shaking his head and staring at Jace.

"Kidnapping? Seriously? You're saying I kidnapped her?" Ted's voice reached a higher octave with each word.

Jace read the Miranda warning to Ted, who sat in stunned silence. "Do you understand your rights?" Jace asked after reading the warning.

"Of course, I do," Ted snapped.

"It's our understanding that you faked your piss test," Jace said.

"What? No, I didn't. I don't know what you're talking about."

"I'm talking about when the nurse asked you to pee in a cup and instead you filled it with water and soap."

"What?"

"Why would you do that?"

"What?" Ted didn't seem capable of uttering anything beyond that single syllable. I found his poorly executed act of incredulity sickening.

When it was clear that the interview wasn't going anywhere productive, Jace and I waited in the hallway for the doctor to finish her assessment. When she finally handed over his discharge paperwork, Ted rose from the bed. Jace handcuffed him, and as he whined we escorted him to my truck for the ride to jail.

In the days and weeks that followed Ted's arrest, I received phone calls and emails from Michelle, one of Ted's four ex-wives who, thanks to Google alerts, followed his criminal history like a hawk. She lived in Arizona, maintaining her position as Ted's most devoted enemy, dedicated to getting revenge for the sexual abuse he had inflicted on their then eight-year-old daughter. According to Michelle, he'd slipped through the fingers of the court system too many times. She offered to do anything in her power to help Karen, his most recent victim, find justice. I also spoke with Claire who was in the final stages of a divorce settlement with Ted. She, too, had nothing good to say about him. The ex-wives plus Karen were members of a bleak club that none of them had wanted to join. They all laid claim to being on the receiving end of Ted's physical, mental, and sexual abuse.

Later still, working through bouts of tears, Karen wrote her victim impact statement for the court, detailing how the incident with Ted had affected her. At the end, she expressed her desire to be a positive example for her granddaughters. She wanted them to know that no one can determine what is done to their bodies but themselves. And Karen insisted her granddaughters learn that if someone like Ted tried to override their wishes he would pay dearly for that decision. Brimming with hope for justice, she expectantly mailed her paperwork to the prosecuting attorney's office.

Meanwhile, I researched Ted's criminal past. I obtained police reports detailing domestic violence, theft, drunk driving, and the loss of his medical license due to falsification of his educational records. For her part, Michelle sent a letter to the prosecutor describing Ted's past crimes and behaviors. If the justice system worked flawlessly, Ted would end up behind bars. Unfortunately, little about the system is flawless. Cogs in the wheel of justice rust. They can wear down and become imprecise, like an unbalanced tire, making for a very rough spin.

Law enforcement officers are often told to stick to the job and not to take the outcome of individual cases personally. In other words, the time spent during an investigation, the days of report writing, the hours of interviews, and the late-night phone calls with weeping victims should be set aside once the paperwork is filed and forwarded to the desk of a prosecutor.

But in real life, any particular case file, however compelling, is never the only one sitting on that prosecutor's desk. It is just one in a towering stack of many cases, each with its own details and ugliness, some more pressing and some more serious than others. Reports are read and motions are made. Emails are sent, and continuances are sometimes granted. Case law is reviewed, and defense attorneys are contacted. Once the wheels of justice finally grind one case to completion, another two are tossed on top of the teetering pile. By the time cases are triaged and time is prioritized, some cases just don't make the cut. Those end up in a slush pile to be dealt with quickly, mainly by means of plea bargains.

On the day of Ted's scheduled court appearance, Karen's family assembled in the courtroom. Her granddaughters were there, along with her sons and daughters-in-law. Michelle had travelled all the way from Arizona and was seated behind Karen. Claire, a doctor with her own busy schedule, had taken time off to come down from Minnesota and was seated next to Michelle. They all hoped for and expected due process. What they got was a plea deal. The felony third-degree kidnapping charge didn't even make the cut as false imprisonment, which would have been a serious misdemeanor. Instead, it was lowered further still to a simple misdemeanor assault. The drunk boating charge was thrown out altogether. From the prosecutor's perspective I suppose it appeared that justice had been served. A guilty plea, no matter the circumstances, can be chalked up in the win column.

When Karen called the following week to tell me about the plea bargain, she wept on the phone. "I don't understand," she cried. "I just don't know how they could do this."

"I'm sorry. I did the best I could—it's so frustrating," I said. The familiar feeling of disappointment washed over me. It wasn't the first time I felt my work on a case—a case in which I'd invested extra investigation time and thorough consideration—had gone unnoticed by the court, settled without so much as a phone call from the prosecutor. I knew it wouldn't be the last time.

"Did you know that he already has a new girlfriend?" Karen asked.

"No, I didn't know."

"Yep. He has a girlfriend. And she has a teenage daughter. I'm terrified of what he might do to that girl."

"I know. I'm so sorry," I repeated. "I hoped that it would turn out differently. I really did."

"I know you did what you could." Karen's kind reassurance didn't dispel my feeling of inadequacy.

After hanging up the phone I sat in my truck, closed my eyes, took a deep breath, and let it out in a long slow hiss through my pursed lips. I'd heard it at the police academy, and over the years I'd heard it from numerous officers with plenty of courtroom experience. "Don't take cases personally. Just do your job. Once it gets to the prosecutor's office it's out of your hands. Move on to the next case."

I've never been especially good at heeding that advice. I'd seen too many of my cases lost in the currents of paperwork that floated from one desk to the next like a leaf washed downstream in a torrent. I'd spent too many hours of my life invested in the minutiae of investigations in an effort to build a strong case, only to have it broken into shards and lost in the debris of justice not delivered. I'd lain awake too often as my restless mind swam through stories, replayed interviews, searched for the one thing that would make a case bulletproof. But in the end, there's seldom such thing as a flawless investigation or a bulletproof case, at least in the eyes of those charged with prosecuting it. A case that is plea-bargain proof is an even longer shot.

EVIDENCE OF BLATANT MISUSE of the Hawkeye Wildlife Management Area had been apparent for years. Like a battered wife who keeps returning to her abuser for more punches, the wildlife area suffered from a continuous beating.

Something like the compulsion for a thorough spring cleaning triggered the decision to finally launch a comprehensive assault on the abuse of Hawkeye. I don't know what caused the sudden urge to grab what I could and salvage it. All I knew was that I could no longer stand by and watch Hawkeye's bruises turn yellow. But perhaps what seemed like a sudden decision to put my foot down was more of a slow percolation bubbling through my veins every weekend that I was forced to play babysitter to the area's users. Too many acted as though they were entitled to treat the land any way they pleased. It was as though they didn't think of themselves as just one of many stewards of this publicly held land, but instead, as the sole proprietor.

Our shirts stuck to our backs and mosquitoes droned past our ears on the summer afternoon that the chief of the law enforcement bureau came to the Hawkeye Wildlife Area to survey and assess the problems we had been describing to him. We needed some kind of systematic enforcement plan that would lay out steps for tackling the many problems that had been plaguing Hawkeye for the last decade. Problems needed triaging, time and attention needed to be invested, and most importantly, the chief had to be on our side. Targeting Hawkeye's long-ignored issues was bound to raise the ire of a number of the area's heavy users. Generations of families had grown accustomed to using Hawkeye as a free-for-all campground. It had been the go-to party spot for high schoolers since the beginning of time. The X-rated adult entertainment at the Hill had grown to the point that advertisements for it could be found all over the internet. Without the chief's endorsement, however, our action plan would be stopped in its tracks at the first complaint from the public.

The wildlife biologist, the land manager, and I toured the area with the chief, pointing out problem spots: woods destroyed by tire tracks; piles of used mattresses and other trash; vulgar graffiti on bridges; stumps left behind by campers who chopped the trees down for firewood; parking lot posts pulled over, pushed over, or completely destroyed; and the blackened remains of bonfires left behind in parking lots.

"You're right," the chief said. "This shit has to stop."

"Do you want to check out the Hill? The damage there is pretty extensive," I said.

"Might as well look at it while I'm here," he said reluctantly. The chief was aware of the Hill's history, but he had yet to see it for himself.

The Hill went by many names, and most of them were vulgar. Starting in the sixties, the Hill had become a popular spot to sunbathe in the nude, but over the years, it had progressed to something much less innocent. The Hill had become a destination for men whose activities went well beyond sunbathing. Many an innocent hiker, birder, and mushroom hunter, some with children in tow, had wandered onto the Hill and witnessed much more than birds and plant life. The local TV news had even featured the Hill in a story when one disgruntled citizen on a walk with his son complained about their surprise experience. At the time, the sheriff had told the media that there was nothing they could do, that the laws regarding indecent exposure were too narrow to be enforced in situations like those occurring at the Hill. He believed that no laws were being broken. I, however, disagreed.

We caravanned to the north side where we pulled into the nearly full parking lot habitually occupied by Hill patrons. I gestured to the cars in the lot. "Looks like it's fairly busy. But sometimes you can't even find a place to park."

"It's definitely the busiest parking lot today." Sweat ran down the chief's face as he sighed. "Let's get this over with."

We walked single file out of the parking lot and onto a well-trodden path leading uphill into the woods. As soon as we were under the canopy of the trees it became evident just how heavily used the area was. Plastic water bottles dotted the ground. Crumpled wet wipes and wads of toilet paper were strewn about the forest floor, giving the illusion that small snow piles had somehow survived the summer heat.

Just where the trail began to climb steeply up the muddy hillside, we found patio blocks wedged into the hill, forming a convenient staircase. When we arrived at a fork in the trail I pointed to the right and whispered, "This leads up to the mowed section. Do you want to go there first?"

The chief nodded his agreement, and we turned to the right. Ahead, the trees thinned, and sunlight fell on a patch of ground carpeted with thick, short grass. It was a nicely tended lawn amidst the surrounding thicket of honeysuckle bushes and trees. As we stepped into the clearing, several heads of men sprawled nude on blankets and towels turned in our direction like startled deer. Despite their initial shock at seeing us, the men made little attempt to cover themselves as we walked through the grass, following the trail like tourists on safari.

A large man perched on a paisley blanket commented, "Beautiful day, eh?"

"Uh, yeah," the chief muttered awkwardly as we hurried to the other side of the meadow.

I began narrating like a museum docent conducting a guided tour. "So, I think this grassy area is the main meeting place. But as we move into the woods you'll see they've cut all kinds of trails and openings into the trees. Someone's obviously spent a lot of time maintaining it. There are piles of cut wood, and the quality of the paths is almost better than the state park trails."

The trails had been cleared of tripping hazards and overhanging limbs.

Used condoms hung from tree branches like nightmarish Christmas tree tinsel. Every now and then larger areas of trees were cleared out at the sides of the trail. "We call these spots hotel rooms," I said as I stepped into one of the clearings. "At least I assume they are used for something like that. There are at least twenty of them cut out in this trail system."

"And there shouldn't be a trail system at all," the chief pointed out. "According to code, wildlife areas aren't allowed to have maintained trails." As we rounded a bend we saw a completely naked man walking along as if he were out for a Sunday stroll. He turned onto a connecting path and disappeared into the trees.

"I don't really understand the procedure," I pondered aloud, trying to make sense of everything. "I mean, do they arrange to meet someone ahead of time? Or do they just show up and hope someone else is here that they'll like?"

The chief shook his head. "Got me. I've seen enough. Let's head back to the parking lot."

"That was worse than I thought it'd be," Dan, the wildlife area manager said. "We've avoided that area for so long because none of our workers feel comfortable going up there. The invasives are horrible." Invasive plant species like honeysuckle, autumn olive, and garlic mustard were constantly on the minds of land managers as the species most aggressively taking over land from native Iowa species.

"It's not right that our own employees avoid sections of the wildlife area because they don't want to see what's happening. Obviously, someone's been mowing it and maintaining the trails for a long time. If nothing else, maybe if we catch the person who's mowing, we can start to slow the traffic here a bit," I suggested.

The chief nodded in agreement, wiping the sweat from his face with his forearm. "Not only mowing, but cutting trees, littering, and trail maintenance. Let's get some cameras up and see exactly what's going on. Maybe put one on the parking lot too—see if you can catch someone unloading a mower. If we're going to target all the problems on the south side of the area, we'll need to address this place too. If we don't, we're bound to run into even more complaints."

The summer seasonal officers and I spent our nights over the next two weeks hanging cameras, checking memory cards, and becoming increasingly horrified by what we saw. The amount of traffic on the Hill and its connected trail system was staggering. On the afternoon that an undercover officer was scheduled to run parking lot surveillance it was so busy that he had to wait thirty minutes for an open parking space. When he finally managed to squeeze the undercover van into an opening, he began recording license plates and sending them to me to verify the owner information. As an added measure, he also photographed people as they returned to their cars in order to positively identify them and associate them with specific vehicles.

As I ran the license plates through dispatch, the list of owners revealed a diverse assortment. A quick internet search showed that some Hill visitors were retired cops, newspaper editors, teachers, youth sports coaches, sex offenders, drug dealers, visitors from out of state, and one of my neighbors.

Every evening we hit the trails replacing full memory cards with empty ones, refreshing batteries, and repositioning cameras. Then we'd huddle around the computer in the office checking the images and videos, our hands over our eyes and peering through the cracks between our fingers. It was like a traffic wreck that you couldn't stop looking at. I became numb to the porn as I flipped past images at lightning speed looking for something usable—something criminal amid all the nudity, contorted bodies, and blow jobs.

Eventually, working the cameras paid off. We identified the man responsible for mowing the grass, unofficially dubbing him the King of the Hill. In his mid-sixties, shirtless, and wearing Hawaiian shorts, he unloaded his lawn mower from a small pickup and lugged it up the hill. He spent the next hour cutting grass and clipping offending limbs from the trail as if he were trimming his suburban yard.

Later, after tracking him down through his license plate information, I met up with the King in his kitchen and issued him a citation for altering plant life in a wildlife area. He casually confessed that he had begun mowing the Hill after the previous caretaker died. He explained that he'd been making the hour-and-a-half drive south every week because he so enjoyed sunbathing in nature. As he spoke, his wife scowled at him from the doorway.

Near one of the larger hotel rooms our cameras caught a man who sported a chest-length white beard and thinning ponytail as he engaged in unmentionable behavior with a younger partner before jamming a water bottle into his nether regions for a quick clean. After the wash, he took a big swig from the same bottle and then tossed it into the patch of ripe wild black raspberries behind him, earning him a littering citation. This was definitely the most unusual video evidence for a simple misdemeanor that I'd ever obtained. It also taught me a lesson about berry picking on public land.

Aside from lewd behavior, the cameras caught some footage that was downright spine-tingling, made even scarier by the glow of the infrared flash. At around two o'clock one morning a parking lot camera caught four images of a ghostly figure. A skinny man appeared out of nowhere, wearing dirty cutoff jean shorts and worn leather work boots. The images showed him walking from the empty parking lot directly toward the camera, then bending down and peering into the lens. The infrared flash illuminated his freakishly blank eyes, making our next trip into the dark woods one fraught with jumpy nerves, imagined sounds, and false bravado.

Now and then, in the midst of all the bawdy behavior, a little humanity would show itself. One person quite charitably slapped at the cloud of mosquitoes on the back of his partner as he performed a marathon seventeen-minute blow job session. We were disappointed one day when, sure we'd finally come across a blatant case of prostitution, we were able to decipher that dollar bills weren't being exchanged, but rather a wad of wet wipes that, after being used, were promptly tossed into the trees. Unfortunately, the parking lot camera was unable to capture the license plate of the litterbug.

The appearance of two known drug dealers caught our attention as well as that of the drug task force. From camera footage, we watched the dealers walking the trails. The fact that they remained fully clothed further heightened my suspicion. I knew my sense of reality was becoming permanently twisted when I asked the drug task force guys, "Why would these guys go to Hawkeye and walk around with their clothes on? It doesn't make any sense!" A looping, stomach-flipping helicopter ride with an undercover drug agent later reassured me that no marijuana farms were hidden away on the Hill.

Some regulars frequented the Hill on a daily or weekly schedule. Some visitors brazenly undressed at their cars before scampering into the trees. Some waited in their cars in the parking lot, not leaving the confines of the air conditioning until others arrived. Some slapped a sunshade on the windshield and spent the entire day on the Hill. They carried in bags or backpacks. Some carried coolers. And all carried towels and water bottles.

The law concerning indecent exposure can be a tricky one to enforce. The elements of the crime require not only that a person expose himself but that he do so with the intent of sexually arousing a person, either himself or another. In addition, he must know or reasonably should know that doing so would be offensive to the viewer. Prosecution under Iowa's indecent exposure law varies significantly from one county to another. In some places, people might be convicted merely for steaming up the car windows in a public parking lot. In some counties, law enforcement officials could be considered "the offended viewer." In my territory, the offended party could not be officers performing their duties. And as long as the person suspected of indecent behavior was considerate enough to step into the woods before getting naked and engaging in sex acts, that person should all but be applauded for discretion and refinement.

Prosecution and conviction for a charge of indecent exposure would be a steep uphill battle. We decided, however, that since conviction was unlikely, it would not be the ultimate goal of our efforts. We just wanted to take back the Hill. We wanted our employees to feel comfortable working there, and we wanted scout groups or school groups to survive a trip there without trauma. In the end, our goal was to stop, or at least slow down, the orgy of activity plaguing the Hill.

The plan for the Hill operation was days in the making. I met with officers from other departments and the county attorney and continued monitoring the Hill for any sign that the users knew what we were up to. Finally, on a Saturday in mid-July, multiple conservation officers and other law enforcement officers who had volunteered, however hesitantly, to help with the Hill project congregated at Hawkeye.

Howard Lightman, a balding, middle-aged conservation officer, fit the profile perfectly to play the role of a "sunbather." Along with Officer Chad Douglas, Howard was to sit in the mowed section of the Hill to gather information. According to the plan, they'd get up every now and then and wander through the trail system, hoping to "stumble" upon someone violating a law. Attired in shorts and t-shirts, they would appear to be just a couple of average Joes, the type of person one could reasonably assume would be offended by unexpectedly encountering an instance of indecent exposure. Other officers would be scattered throughout the trees, bushes, and brush, hidden in ghillie suits and camouflage, staking out locations from which they could help the undercover officers make good trail choices. In other words, if it appeared that something nasty was about to go down, they'd call in the unsuspecting hikers, Howard or Chad, to witness the offending event.

After witnessing the illegal incident, the officers hiding in the woods or acting as hikers would text a description of the offender to an officer stationed in the parking lot. When the offender returned to his car, the parking lot officer would then call out the departing vehicle description to other officers waiting in nearby wildlife area parking lots. Once we were notified of a targeted moving vehicle, we'd make a traffic stop and begin an investigation.

As I sat in a parking lot down the road, I was pleased to see a yellow Kia turn into the Hill lot around two o'clock in the afternoon. I knew the Kia well. Since we'd begun monitoring the Hill, the Kia was frequently seen on the parking lot camera. With a little internet research, I'd learned that the owner, Dwight Knorr, was employed as a youth sports coach. Posing as a Hill newbie, I'd also chatted online with Knorr through Craigslist, asking him how to go about approaching someone on the Hill. At the end of our conversation I mentioned that I was thinking about giving the Hill a try over the weekend and that maybe I'd see him there. It didn't take long for the undercover officers to make his acquaintance.

Howard's phone lit up with a text message: "Get over to room #4." The message was from James Brady, a veteran officer, bound for retirement in three months. Brady was hidden in the honeysuckle just off the trail with a view of the clearing we'd designated as Room #4. Sweating in a ghillie suit, he was virtually invisible as he sat hunched just a few feet from the clearing. The dense leaves of the invasive plants forced him to sit close to the room. Any deeper into the brush and his view would have been blocked by foliage.

Howard responded to Brady: "On my way."

Brady was probably a little too worried about being caught and tried to control his breathing as he waited for Howard to approach. The two naked people on the ground in front of him, however, were distracted with their own actions. They weren't likely to be spooked by a little rustling of the leaves.

Howard, with his cell phone camera rolling, rounded the bend in the trail, saw the men in an extremely compromising position and let out a little gasp of horror. "Oh my," Howard blurted, acting as convincingly offended as he could. He covered his eyes for good measure. "Holy shit.

What the—?" Howard added, hurrying past the couple and continuing to walk until he was out of Brady's sight. The couple was briefly startled by Howard's outburst. They paused momentarily but showed little interest in calling a complete halt to their fun.

"They're still going at it!" Brady texted to Howard. "I'm calling in Chad."

Five minutes later, Chad strode into view. He laid it on a little thicker than Howard had. "What the hell are you guys doing? Can't you do that somewhere else? This is a public place you know! Geez!" Chad stomped off down the trail.

Brady watched as the lovers stood up, brushed the dirt from their bodies, and hustled off in opposite directions, neither bothering to get dressed. Brady quickly messaged the officer in the parking lot with the physical descriptions of the people involved. Ten minutes later, the two arrived in the parking lot.

"Get ready," the parking lot officer radioed. "You're gonna be looking for a yellow Kia on the first guy—plate comes back to Dwight Knorr. He's just getting in his car now—I'll let you know which direction he goes."

Waiting just west of the Hill's parking lot, I started my truck, poised to move in either direction.

"He's headed east," the officer said.

I peeled out of the parking lot and sped east, attempting to catch up to the Kia. Brian Floyd, another officer, was located just east of the Hill. I knew Brian would be the first to intercept the Kia.

"I've got him in sight," I said to Brian over the radio. "Go ahead and stop him when he goes past you. I'll be right behind you."

Through the haze of gravel dust, I watched as Brian's emergency lights flashed on and the vehicles came to a stop. When I pulled up behind Brian's squad, he was at the driver's door of the Kia.

"I don't know what you're talking about," Dwight said to Brian. "I didn't do anything."

"Step out of the car," Brian instructed. "You are under arrest for indecent exposure."

As Dwight stepped out onto the gravel road, his eyes darted in my direction.

"I only pulled into that parking lot to make a phone call," Dwight said to me. "This is bullshit! I didn't do anything to anybody."

"That's not what the witnesses say. You know exactly what happened," I said.

"I want my attorney."

"That's fine." I escorted him to Brian's squad for the ride into town.

Shortly after Dwight was arrested, his friend, who drove out of the parking lot and made a beeline westward, was also arrested. Both individuals were transported into town to be booked into jail. The project continued for an hour following the two arrests, but it didn't take long for word to spread and for the Hill patrons to depart.

At the project debriefing, Howard and Chad played videos of conversations they'd had on the Hill with various visitors. Howard's face turned a dark shade of purple as a video played showing a skinny guy wearing a button-down shirt asking Howard to remove some of his clothes. "I'm not comfortable with that," Howard faltered. Chad took a more direct approach when he encountered a completely naked man multitasking by pleasuring himself as he hiked. As he walked by, Chad scolded the man, "Ah, come on dude—stop that. Put on some clothes!"

"I'm never volunteering for a project of yours again," Howard said dryly as we walked back to our trucks to head home after the briefing. "That one was enough to last a whole career."

Our work over the summer started to pay off. There were a few stragglers to the Hill who hadn't watched the TV news or read the newspapers following the arrests. Whenever I'd see a car parked at the Hill, I'd take a stroll through the trail and across the grassy area that was growing longer with each visit. Any embarrassment I'd felt before was numbed by weeks of viewing trail camera pornography. Instead of quickly walking away, I began taking a direct approach. "Where are your clothes?" I'd ask random naked men along the trail or sprawled on a towel on the grass. "You realize this is a public area, right? And that any moment there might be a hiker through here, or a hunter, or a group of school kids? How about you put on some clothes." I'd return to my truck and wait the ten seconds it usually took for the person to slink back to his car and leave the Hill.

The indecent exposure arrests were predictably dismissed when they reached the county attorney's office. The reasons were many. Did the people make a reasonable effort to hide their sex acts by moving away from the roadway and into the woods? Did I lure Dwight Knorr into visiting the Hill by mentioning that I would be visiting it that weekend? Did the men have a reason to believe that they would offend a viewer, since most of the people who frequent the Hill expect to see such behavior?

It didn't matter much. We'd accomplished our objective, or at least gotten closer to accomplishing it. The arrests made the news and word got out. After more than forty years, this type of traffic at the Hill slowed significantly. One day that fall I stopped at the Hill parking lot after noticing a truck parked at the back near a stand of maple trees. I stepped out of my squad and prepared myself for the hike up the trail to the grassy clearing. Just before stepping into the trees, however, I noticed the truck's occupants standing near the tailgate. A squirrel hung upside down from the branch of a tree and a young boy stood next to an older man as he skinned it.

I approached the hunters. "How's it going today?"

"Pretty darn good," the older man said. "Been wanting to teach my grandson here how to skin a squirrel. We finally got one right up on the hill up there," he said, pointing toward the Hill and the grassy meadow where naked ghosts frolicked in the sunshine.

INVASIVE SPECIES SUFFOCATE Iowa's woodlands like hair clogging a drain. White flowers of garlic mustard cover the forest floor in a plush carpet, effectively crowding out native species. Honeysuckle and multiflora rose, once planted for habitat enhancement, had spread and now rule the timber like a gang of bullies on the playground. Walking through the underbrush in some Iowa woodlands is an exercise in slow-motion bushwhacking. You're likely to emerge on the other side with torn clothing and scratched skin. Wildlife management workers wage constant war against such species using chemical weapons and chainsaws, but progress is generally slow and hard won.

One day in late summer, David Carter, a retired US Army Corps of Engineers park ranger, struggled through the trees in the midst of his own garlic mustard battle. He was dragging a garbage bag behind him, stuffed to the gills with fresh-picked garlic mustard. An eternal land steward, even in retirement, David had spent all afternoon picking the pest from the woods in Sugar Bottom Recreation Area, a piece of public property managed by the Corps of Engineers.

As long as the weather is tolerable, people can be found at Sugar Bottom. A tangle of interconnecting mountain biking and hiking trails twist their way through the woods. Frisbee golfers toss discs on the adjacent course in everything but a blizzard, and the beach draws crowds seeking relief from the heat of summer.

David worked his way through the honeysuckle, plucking garlic mustard from the moist ground amid the bike trails. He was in a race against time because as soon as the garlic mustard flower heads dry, they spread seeds like germs from an explosive sneeze. If he missed even just a few plants they'd repopulate the woods the following spring, effectively erasing the results of his hard work. But David was thorough and quick, covering every square inch of the section he'd promised himself he would finish before heading home.

It was David's attention to detail that drew him into the small opening in the woods. As he broke through the woody barrier in search of more garlic mustard, he stumbled into a shaft of sunlight pouring down through an opening in the web of tree branches arching over him from the canopy above. The first thing that caught his eye was the wooden shack. It was cobbled together with two-by-four-inch pine boards and topped with a slanted, corrugated plastic roof. Aligned at the corners of the roof to catch the rain runoff were two blue plastic fifty-five-gallon drums. A coil of hose lay on the ground inside the shack along with wire fencing, a small saw, and plant food.

David soon realized that what he'd stumbled upon was the irrigation system for a small marijuana farm growing in the clearing. He quit picking garlic mustard and, returning home, reported his find to the Corps of Engineers.

"You interested in looking at some marijuana plants David Carter found yesterday?" Park Ranger Neal Fry asked when I stopped by the Corps office the following day.

"You've got a grow?" I asked. "Where is it?" I was surprised. Iowa isn't California—it's not easy to find a hidden place to grow marijuana on Iowa's limited public ground.

"Just fifty feet off one of the bike trails at Sugar," Neal said. "But the honeysuckle is so thick back there you can't even see it from the trail."

I was game. "Definitely. Let me call Zane with DNE first though. I'm pretty sure he'll want to be involved."

Zane White, an officer with the State Patrol's Drug and Narcotics Enforcement Division, was in charge of the county drug task force. Zane was short and muscular. Like all narcotics agents, he dressed casually in the low-slung jeans and a flat-brimmed ball cap, a style popular with the drug dealing crowd. He immediately agreed to meet me at Sugar Bottom.

Later that afternoon, Zane and I met Neal in the bike trail parking lot. We set off for the hike up the hill toward the trail system, with Neal carrying a small stepladder. He led us down a series of narrow but heavily traveled bike paths, searching for the intersecting deer trail that served as the route to the grow.

When we finally punched through the brush into the clearing, the aroma of marijuana hit me like a wall of skunk. The grow was small, only twenty-eight plants in all, but each had been tended as carefully as a baby. The plants were neatly labeled by strain—Diesel, White Rhino, Blue Dream—and each was carefully wrapped in a small wire cage to protect the valuable plant from marauding rabbits and deer.

"I don't see a great place to hang this camera," Zane said as he inspected our surroundings. The trees immediately bordering the clearing either were too small or were blocked by thick foliage.

I pointed to a medium-sized ash tree on the edge of the clearing. "That one looks like our only option. It makes me nervous though. It'll be pretty obvious."

The tree I'd pointed out was the only one in the area with a trunk large enough to support a camera. Unfortunately, it was also in the direct line of sight of anyone entering the clearing.

"Let's try it anyway," Zane said. Neal leaned the stepladder against the trunk, and Zane climbed as high as he could before wrapping straps around the tree and hanging the camera. "How's it look from down there?"

I cringed. "Like a glowing neon sign. But it'll have to do. We need to identify the guy if we ever want to catch him."

I photographed the scene to add to the evidence file, clicking away at the grow, the shed, and the equipment. After fully documenting the farm, I followed Neal back out onto the bike trail. As we walked back to the parking lot, Zane and I established a plan. I would increase my patrols of the two parking lots near the bike trails in hopes of distinguishing the marijuana grower's car from those of mountain biking enthusiasts. Zane and his team agreed to periodically check the camera's memory card and report any findings.

After two weeks of increased patrols, my spirits began to flag. I hadn't seen any suspicious vehicles, and the only photos the camera had taken were of browsing deer. But, by the end of the third week, our luck changed.

"We got him on camera," Zane told me over the phone.

"Any good shots?"

"I haven't been through all of them yet. We have over 400 pictures to go through," Zane said. "I'll put them onto a CD if you want to pick them up and take a look for yourself."

The photos confirmed that the grower had visited the clearing twice during the third week. Both times he was dressed in a gray t-shirt, a plain green baseball cap, and army fatigues and was equipped with a camouflage backpack. He was a lanky young man and wore black rimmed glasses. His reminded me of a scientist, if scientists dressed in military gear. He even tended to the plants like a scientist. The camera caught him watering his crops meticulously, repairing the wire cages, and applying chemicals with an eyedropper from a small boxed kit. Each of his visits to the grow lasted about an hour.

As I was going through the photos for the second time my phone rang. Without so much as a greeting Zane asked, "Did you see his pants?"

I wasn't sure what he was getting at. "Yeah, camo pants, right?"

"They say 'Ritter' on the back," Zane explained. "They have a name plate—he must be in the military."

I scrolled through the photos carefully until I came to one that captured the grower as he turned to leave the clearing. With his camouflage backpack strapped on, he walked away from the camera. His head was turned as if to take one last look at his farm. I zoomed in on his trousers and squinted at the name patch situated above the right back pocket. "Sure looks like 'Ritter,'" I agreed.

That night, and for several ensuing nights, I struggled to sleep. I was consumed with research, spending hours on the computer, making phone calls, and hoping for a break in the case. Surely someone with the last name of Ritter who was or had been in the military would show up somewhere. But every lead I uncovered turned out to be a dead end.

A couple weeks later, Zane and I met to check the trail camera. While Zane was up in the tree removing the SD card, I poked around in the shack looking for a clue to the identity of the grower. "Looks like he's been shopping since we were here last."

"What did you find?" Zane asked from the top of the ladder.

"He's got a new soaker hose. Hasn't even been opened." I photographed the barcode on the package. Alongside the hose, inside a plastic bag from the local Lowe's Home Improvement Store, was a three-way nozzle assembly for the hose. "I'm heading to Lowes after we leave. Maybe they can do a search on this barcode. I bet he bought the hose and nozzle at the same time."

"If you're really lucky, maybe he paid for them with a traceable credit card," Zane said.

"Hope so. But I'm never that lucky."

After scanning the barcode, the Lowe's loss prevention specialist came up with a list of dates on which that particular type of soaker hose with matching barcodes had been purchased. One date in particular jumped out at me. It was within the range of possible dates that our suspect could have visited the clearing. Zeroing in further, I was excited to see that a three-way nozzle had been purchased at the same time. The coup de grâce was that the purchase had been made using a credit card. Despite the fact that the credit card number did not match the name Ritter, I was certain that it would turn out to be our bespectacled pot grower.

I called Zane from the Lowe's parking lot. "Ritter used a credit card. But the only problem is that his name isn't Ritter. It's Hendrickson. Ryan Hendrickson."

"You sure it's him?"

"Not yet. The security guy is searching through the video right now. I'm going back inside in a few minutes to look at it. But what are the chances that someone bought the same exact soaker hose and nozzle within the time frame that our guy would have?"

"Pretty slim I'd say. Let me know if Hendrickson looks like Ritter after you see the video."

"I'll call you back when I know something," I said before hanging up. With the addition of a new name, the case was becoming more complicated. Having no solid way to connect Hendrickson with Ritter, I entertained the possibility that the marijuana grow was a two-man operation.

Maybe Ritter and Hendrickson were working together to split the profits from the sales.

I sat in Lowe's security room anxiously studying the video. But as I tried to connect the blurry image on the store's video with the clear photos from our camera, they didn't add up. As much as I wanted Hendrickson to be Ritter, he wasn't. Hendrickson was heavier set and older by a decade. I had a sinking feeling that I'd just wasted a bunch of time chasing a wild goose.

Over the next few weeks our camera snapped hundreds more pictures of Ritter. Each trip to the grow was the same. Ritter wore the same clothes every time, with the exception of the Fourth of July weekend, when he patriotically switched out his plain green hat for a blue one with an American flag stitched onto the front.

I continued to patrol the Sugar Bottom parking lots religiously, peeking inside cars and running license plate numbers. Finally, one morning I came upon a car that was distinctly out of place—a small blue Honda hatchback. The car didn't have a bike rack like the rest of the cars in the lot, and the interior was obviously too small to carry a bike. I sidled up to the car and discreetly looked through the windows. A child's car seat was strapped into the back seat, and the floor was littered with debris. I walked to the back of the car, and looking through the hatchback window, I noticed a small piece of paper lying on the floor. I leaned closer to the window and cupped my hands around my eyes to block out the sun's glare. "Holy shit," I whispered to myself. It was a receipt from Lowe's for a three-way hose nozzle.

I got Zane on the phone right away. "He's here right now!" I quickly recounted everything I'd observed about the small blue car.

"We're in the trail parking lot on the other side," Zane said. "We'll be right there." Zane and John Knight, another narcotics agent, had been sitting in an undercover car in the opposite parking lot hoping to spot the grower themselves. They drove the five miles to my parking lot in record time and pulled into a spot at the far end, out of sight of the trail.

I stayed hidden in my truck, tucked between two full-size pickups. I called Zane. "I just ran the plate. It comes back to a Maxwell Simpson out of Iowa City. The driver's license photo matches our guy."

"Okay. I think we'll wait for him to come to us. All we need right now is to identify him and see him get into the car. That should be enough to get a tracker."

GPS trackers require a search warrant. Once the warrant was secured,

Zane and his team would be able to attach the tracker to Simpson's car and watch his movements remotely. Their goal was to catch Simpson with the plants in the clearing as they matured into a harvestable size.

We waited in the parking lot for twenty minutes before Simpson walked down the hill and back to his blue Honda. His camouflage clothing, cap, and backpack matched what we had seen in the trail camera photos. He set the backpack in the back seat of the car, got into the driver's seat, and pulled out of the parking lot, apparently not noticing our vehicles. I breathed a sigh of relief.

The narcotics team obtained a GPS tracker warrant and, in the middle of the night, placed the device on the underside of Simpson's car as it sat in his driveway. From his office, Zane was able to monitor the movements of Simpson's car while we waited for the harvest season.

One afternoon in late September, about five months after starting the investigation, Zane contacted me out of the blue. I was just crossing the county line, returning from a meeting, when my phone rang. "Can you meet us at the grow?"

"Yeah. How fast? I'm just pulling into the county."

"As fast as you can. Simpson's at the grow right now, and we want to do the takedown before he gets back to the parking lot."

I stomped on the gas pedal. Fifteen minutes later I pulled into the parking lot just two minutes ahead of a caravan of five dark-blue undercover DNE vehicles.

Greg Sands, an undercover narcotics officer wearing jeans and sporting an unkempt beard and an armful of tattoos, joined Zane and me as we hurried up the trail toward the woods. My heart began to race as we stepped onto the bike path adjacent to the grow. We stood silently on the trail, listening to Simpson shuffle through the weeds, a mere fifty feet away. As we held our collective breath, his muffled cough drifted through the woods, interrupting the birdsong. I thought about the many times I'd walked my dog along the bike trail, never imagining that someone could be so close to me and yet remain so hidden. I double-checked my radio and cell phone to make sure I'd shut them off, not wanting to accidentally alert Simpson to our presence. The last thing we needed was a manhunt.

Finally, after what seemed like an eternity, Simpson pushed the branches away and stepped onto the trail in front of us. We greeted him at gunpoint.

"How are you doing, Simpson?" Zane asked.

"Fine," Simpson replied hesitantly. No doubt he was taken aback by our presence, not to mention the guns pointing his direction. Greg moved in to handcuff Simpson.

"What were you doing back there?" Zane asked as Greg clicked the cuffs into place.

"Hiking," he lied.

"Did you see anything back there?"

"No."

"Well, let's go have a look for ourselves."

Zane led Simpson back to the plot. Greg and I followed, trying to avoid getting stuck by thorny multiflora rose branches. We stepped into the clearing and threaded between the marijuana plants, which were much taller than the last time I'd seen them. Zane pointed at the trail camera hanging from the tree. "What do you suppose that is?" Zane asked Simpson.

As Simpson's gaze followed Zane's finger, his jaw visibly dropped. "That would be a camera," he muttered quietly, slowly shaking his head with ironic disbelief. We took more photographs, then led Simpson, handcuffed and depressed, back to the parking lot. As we walked down the hill Zane asked, "So, what's up with the 'Ritter' pants?"

"The what?" Simpson's brow furrowed in confusion.

"Your pants. Why do they say 'Ritter'?"

"Oh. That. I bought them used from the army surplus store."

"Yeah. That's what we thought." Zane glanced back at me and smiled.

While some of the narcotics team stayed onsite to disassemble the marijuana grow, Zane and Greg took Simpson to the police department to interview him. Simpson, a PhD student in chemistry, insisted that he'd only grown the marijuana to use for his own back pain. "I swear I wasn't going to sell any of it. I only use it in brownies for my back."

"Are we going to find anything at your house that will tell us otherwise?" Zane handed Simpson a copy of the search warrant for his home and car.

"No, the only thing I do with it is make brownies," he insisted.

When we arrived at Simpson's house, his wife answered the door. She held a baby in her arms as she read the search warrant. Her apparent lack of surprise made me wonder if she'd been expecting this moment.

One officer waited in the living room with Simpson's wife and baby while the rest of us began searching. Simpson's home was a warehouse of sorts for chemistry equipment. Beakers, test tubes, pipettes, and other glass bottles filled boxes, shelves, and closets. Chemicals, powders, and liquids of all sorts spilled from cabinets. Grow lights, seed starter trays, and other greenhouse equipment were found in the basement, along with tiny baggies, small bottles, scales, and empty pill capsules, suggesting that marijuana wasn't his only controlled substance interest. Simpson admitted that he'd experimented with making MDMA, a psychoactive drug. He insisted that he did so merely for the challenge the chemical process presented. He claimed to have never tried the final product. Later, while searching the bedrooms, one officer found a large cardboard box shoved under the baby's crib. It contained big bags of thermite, a pyrotechnic composition of metal powder and metal oxide.

"Someone make a phone call to whoever hands out the father-of-the-year awards around here," Bruce, one of the narcotics officers, announced wryly. "I think Simpson here is up for father of the year. It isn't everyone who stores thermite under the baby's crib."

"I just forgot it was there," Simpson feebly explained. "It can't ignite without a fuse anyway."

Bruce lifted one of the boxes from the pile stacked in front of him. "Oh. So that's what these magnesium strips are for right? Why do you even have thermite in the first place?"

"It's what got me into chemistry to begin with." Simpson's face lit up with excitement as he started to lecture. "It's a really impressive chemical reaction. It gets hot enough to melt steel!"

"But . . . under the baby's crib?" Bruce peered derisively over his reading glasses at Simpson, who quickly lost his enthusiasm for teaching us about chemistry.

"Like I said, I just forgot it was there. And it's not dangerous."

"Hot enough to melt steel. Under the baby's crib." Bruce muttered as he entered the thermite and magnesium strips onto the evidence seizure form.

A few days later Zane called my cell phone. "I'm emailing you a present."

"Oh yeah? What is it?" I asked.

"You'll see. Just open up the picture on the email and let me know what you think."

I hung up and logged onto my computer. As promised, there was an unopened email from Zane. I clicked on the attachment, and a photo popped open. In it, Zane was standing next to Simpson in the middle of the marijuana grow. I was right behind Zane, and Greg was just pushing his way through the brush at the edge of the clearing. Zane's right arm was outstretched, his finger pointing directly at the lens. The photo had been taken at the exact moment that Zane pointed out the camera to Simpson. Simpson's eyes were the size of dinner plates, and his lower jaw was hanging open in shock.

The trail camera had captured the precise moment when Simpson not only recognized the camera but suddenly realized that we'd been watching him all along, that the place he'd carved out, tended, and protected from the encroaching sea of honeysuckle, multiflora rose, and garlic mustard wasn't his private garden after all—that we probably had thousands of photographs of him as he lovingly tended his plants. Written on his face was the knowledge that all his potential defenses were rendered useless simply because he'd failed to look up at the one and only tree big enough to support a camera. The image summed up all his thoughts in one tiny click, and the look on his face said it all. "Oh. . . . Shit."

—THE PEOPLE—

"Staying positive is not always easy. You will deal with difficult and even down-right nasty people regularly, and you will see many frustrating and discouraging situations. It would be easy to become cynical and negative. A negative attitude is not only unprofessional, it makes good communication difficult, and it is hard on you personally because it can increase stress. It's important to stay positive."

—*Professional Communication Skills: A Training Guide for Law Enforcement and Jail Officers*, Wisconsin Department of Justice, Law Enforcement Standards Board (December 2014)

I CALL IT THE "What the Hell?" game. It typically commences as I drive down the gravel roads of the Hawkeye Wildlife Area, see a parked car, and think, "What the hell are they doing here?" If based on the limited clues I can find in or around the vehicle I can prove my guess to be correct, I win the game.

Upon seeing a vehicle at the wildlife area, I begin by asking myself:

Is the vehicle occupied? If so, by how many?
How much mud coats the exterior of the vehicle?
Is the license plate visible? If so, to whom does the vehicle belong?
Is any hunting or fishing equipment visible?
Are the occupants wearing camouflage or blaze orange clothing?

When I snoop around an occupied vehicle, a quick license plate check while approaching should tell me the owner's age, if he is valid to drive, or if he has a warrant. If time allows, a cross-check with the DNR computerized licensing system may be valuable as well, letting me to know whether the owner has a hunting license before I even approach.

One day, Jace Travers drove by a parking lot on his way to do some trail work. In passing, he noticed a lone man sitting in the driver's seat of a parked car. In the spirit of the "What the Hell?" game, Travers briefly wondered what the man was doing there. When he returned a few hours later, he saw the same car still parked in the same place with the same occupant still seated behind the wheel. Jace stopped and approached the car with a sense of dread. The occupant was dead, with a .22-caliber-sized hole in his temple.

ONE AFTERNOON I NOTICED a white truck parked in a lot at Hawkeye. Sitting at an odd angle next to a trail leading into the woods, the truck appeared to have pulled into the lot hurriedly. As I drove into the lot, I typed the license plate information into my computer and learned that the truck owner's driver's license was revoked. As I walked toward the truck to talk with the occupant, whose appearance matched that of the revoked driver, he quickly closed the door. When I asked him to roll the window down, the man's eyes widened in surprise.

"What are you up to today?" I asked, quickly peering around the inside of the car.

"Uh . . . ," the driver stuttered.

He quickly glanced at his lap and looked back at me. I followed his gaze. "Oh! Why don't you have any pants on?"

"I had to poop. Really bad."

"Ok. Where are your pants now then?"

"They're up there on the trail. I left them there."

"That's weird." I was at a loss for words. "Well, you'll need to call for a ride. Your license is revoked."

When I play the "What the Hell?" game, unoccupied vehicles often present the most challenging mysteries. A thorough examination of any available evidence is necessary to come up with a field of promising guesses.

Are the car's occupants visible in the field?
Are there tracks leading from the car?
Is there a dog box?
Are there hunting- or fishing-related decals on the windows?
   A political bumper sticker?
Is the dust, gathered from the trip over gravel roads, disturbed near
   the trunk or tailgate? Do I see any blood?

To gain further information, I pull up next to the vehicle, park, climb out of my truck, and listen for clues as to the occupants' location. Maybe I hear a gunshot, or a dog barking, or voices carrying on the wind. I cup my hands around my eyes to block glare and peek through the windows.

Do I see anything to identify the user? A piece of mail? An ID?
Is there drug paraphernalia in plain view?
How about hunting equipment? A gun case? An arrow release?
   A box of ammunition? Hunting clothing? A loading block? A bag
   of decoys?
Is there evidence of a possible hunting violation? A salt block or
   empty bag of corn? A spotlight?

How about fishing equipment? A rod and reel? A fishing regulation
booklet? A container of split shot?
Could the person be digging ginseng? Is there a shovel? Garden
blade? Plastic bags?

In general, hunters, anglers, and trappers make up the majority of the
game's subjects, and they aren't too difficult to identify. But obscure clues
that offer scant explanation set my imagination on fire.

The most intriguing games of "What the Hell?" are those I never solve.
One was an unoccupied car seen at two-thirty in the afternoon that contained only a steaming piece of pizza, one bite missing, sitting on the
dashboard; a box of cookies in the back seat; a woman's purse on the passenger side floor; and a pair of men's sandals on the driver's seat.

Another was a blue Honda Civic with a "My Labrador is smarter than
your honor student" bumper sticker pasted on the rear window. It was
parked at the end of a dead-end road, near a muddy boat ramp. A traffic ticket was crammed into the cupholder, and an old-fashioned metro-
nome strangely ticked away on the dashboard. A rear-facing car seat was
strapped into the back, a small plastic pet carrier was next to the car seat,
and a beat-up copy of Jane Austen's *Pride and Prejudice* was open on the
passenger seat.

After years of peeping into hundreds of cars and concocting life stories
based on random items I'd seen inside them, my curiosity about people
and their life circumstances has only grown. What draws some people to
wild places? And why do they bring metronomes and abandon perfectly
good pizza? Why did the person driving a small SUV completely filled with
empty white paint cans suddenly feel the need to visit a wildlife area? And
where is the person who wore the leather pants lying across the front seat
of the Ford Explorer? There seems to be no end to the possibilities.

Most people using wildlife areas are there for obvious reasons. The deer
hunters swarm to the timber in late fall, anglers spend summer nights chasing after big catfish, birders tromp through the marsh looking to spot a rare
species of shorebird, and dog walkers take in the fresh air and open spaces
with their canine companions. Other visitors, however, seem to emerge
from the fringes of society only to abscond to the periphery of the wild in
search of a place to hook up, shoot up, find themselves, kill themselves,
party, take up residence, or drink themselves into a stupor. For them, the
vast acres are less a place rich in nature to be enjoyed than a backdrop for

playing out a life scene the meaning and motivation of which are so personal as to confound the average observer.

The majority of the unsavory things that happen at a place like Hawkeye occur in the shadows, unwitnessed and unexplained. Still, I imagine that the personal truths that even these visitors pursue are the same as those we all hope to find when we visit out-of-the-way places, places where the world leaves us alone, the noise dampens, and we can find something of ourselves and acknowledge our lives for what they are, in all their glorious disarray.

IT WAS AROUND NOON on a Wednesday in mid-July when Robert Felton and Jim Kincaid drove to the Hawkeye Wildlife Area in Robert's blue Dodge pickup. Why they chose to go to Hawkeye at all, or to the Babcock boat access specifically, is still not entirely known. Interviews and a search warrant didn't yield much information either. They were an odd pair. Robert, a seventy-year-old white man who used a walker to get around, was nicknamed Einstein due not to his intelligence but to his wild head of white hair. Jim was fifty years old, black, short, and unassuming. Neither was a sportsman looking for an afternoon of fishing.

According to the police interview with Jim, the two men were drinking buddies. That day they were sharing a can of beer while driving around the backroads of the wildlife area. When they arrived at the boat access, Robert's amicable attitude toward Jim took an unexplained turn for the worse. Robert suddenly asked Jim if he could swim. When Jim told him that he couldn't, Robert inexplicably ordered him to hand over his phone and to get out of the truck and into the river. At first Jim thought Robert was joking. The joke was over, however, when Robert pulled a semiautomatic pistol from between the seats and pointed it at Jim.

"You think I won't shoot you?" Robert asked before pointing the gun out the window and firing two shots into the brush along the river's bank. When Jim, who was bent over attempting to stash his phone into his sock, didn't respond, Robert turned and began to pistol whip him. Robert cracked the butt of his gun over his drinking buddy's skull. Jim, fighting through the pain, confusion, and foggy array of stars dancing in his vision, tried to bail out of the truck. But as he reached for the door handle, Jim was stunned by the searing pain from Robert repeatedly jabbing a knife blade into his back. By the time he stumbled out of the truck, Jim was bleeding profusely, and his troubles were far from over. He shuffled across the gravel parking lot, head ringing, blood soaking his shirt. According to Jim, Robert took advantage of his disoriented state to try to run him over with the truck. When that was unsuccessful, Robert took aim and fired four shots at Jim, missing his target each time. Shortly thereafter Robert hightailed it out of the parking lot, leaving Jim to bleed out.

Jim pulled the phone from his sock and dialed 911. But having never been to Hawkeye, he had no idea where he was. The only landmarks were a boat ramp, willow trees, and parched grasshoppers winging across the gravel lot, pelting his shins as they flew out of his way. The dispatcher who took Jim's call advised him to try to make it to the main road. She encouraged him to try to find a road sign or some other means of identifying his location.

Jim was uncomfortable with his situation as a black man covered in blood in unfamiliar territory. He didn't know what kind of reaction his appearance would elicit from an unsuspecting passerby. Nonetheless, he managed to stagger the quarter mile back to the main road that transects the south side of Hawkeye, leaving behind a blood trail like a gut-shot deer.

Just as he emerged onto the road, Dan, a DNR wildlife technician on his way back to the office, noticed Jim and pulled over. Dan was shocked by the sight of the man dripping with blood and asked him what had happened. When Jim told Dan that he'd been stabbed and shot at, Dan assumed the shooter was still at large. He quickly surveyed their surroundings and kept an eye on the tree line as he took the blood-smeared phone from Jim and relayed their location to the dispatcher.

By the time law enforcement arrived, Robert was likely back at his home settling into his easy chair in front of the television. When deputies later caught up with him, Robert refused to provide a statement and offered no explanation for his actions. No empty bullet casings were found in the blood-spattered parking lot. The only thing a search warrant turned up at Robert's residence and truck was a dog-shit-infested home where it was impossible to walk across the living room without soiling your shoes. The gun, if there ever was one, was gone.

This incident, like so many others that happen in remote areas, left more questions than answers. That afternoon I stood over the blood-stained gravel looking for clues that would lend any clarity to the story. But all I saw was a parking lot strewn with litter and the river's current pushing past the boat ramp, splitting into Vs as it threaded through the willow trees along the bank. I was surrounded by the only possible eyewitnesses: red-winged blackbirds screaming at me in territorial defense, a swarm of gnats, and a flock of geese quietly picking their way through a food plot. And those witnesses, who don't concern themselves with the dramas of human existence and the mysteries that plague wild lands, weren't about to give anything up.

I WAS SCHEDULED TO LECTURE at a hunter's education class the morning I encountered Liam Foster. Driving to the office at the Hawkeye Wildlife Management Area to pick up some classroom supplies from the storage building, I spotted his truck parked along the far perimeter of a parking lot. Nose pointed into the brush, the faded red Dodge with its dents, rust spots, and a bright blue tarp strapped down over the lumpy contents of the bed caught my attention. Garbage dumping at the wildlife area had increased over the past several months. In addition to the usual bags of trash, piles of yard waste, and broken appliances, someone had been dumping books—eight pickup loads of them. I decided that if the truck was still there when I returned from retrieving my supplies, I'd check it out.

With my passenger seat freshly loaded with hunting regulation booklets and clay targets, I drove back toward the parking lot expecting the truck to be gone. But, as I came around the bend, its rusty red paint was visible through the trees. The truck was parked in the same spot, the tarp still bulging tightly over the items in the back.

I was pulling into the lot with my eyes fixed on the license plate, ready to type the digits into my computer, when I noticed movement in the cab. Just as I stepped out of my squad to chat with the person in the truck, he quickly peeled out of the parking lot and took off down the gravel road.

As the driver looked over his shoulder to back up, long blond hair spilled over his face in a tangle and a bra strap peeked out of the neckline of a black tank top. I concluded that I had been mistaken in assuming the driver was a man.

As the red pickup kicked up dust along the gravel, I followed behind waiting for a reason to make a traffic stop. The blond driver had piqued my interest with her odd behavior, but the behavior alone wasn't reason enough to pull the truck over. I checked the license plate information as I followed the billowing cloud of gravel dust. The red truck was registered to an older man, clearly not the driver I'd seen behind the wheel.

As the truck approached an intersection, it made a sudden swerve to the north onto a connecting road, and probable cause presented itself: the driver failed to use a turn signal. I flipped on my emergency lights to make a traffic stop. The truck's brake lights glowed as the driver came to a stop in front of me.

"I didn't know what you wanted back there," the driver called to me as I stepped out of my truck. The deep, gravelly voice I heard didn't align with the long blond hair, eye shadow, earrings, and bra strap. The driver's left shoulder was crudely tattooed with the image of a dagger and a skull.

"I just wanted to chat with you for a minute, but you took off before I had a chance to say anything," I explained. "I stopped you here because you didn't use a turn signal."

"I was putting on makeup, okay? I just wanted to put on my makeup without people staring at me." The blond hair, I now noticed, was a wig, a cheap one. The driver had a five o'clock shadow, his cheekbones highlighted with pink blush.

"Ok. That's not a problem. It's just that your truck caught my attention because of the tarp. We've had lots of problems with garbage dumping out here. I wanted to make sure you weren't going to litter." I pointed at his load in the back of the truck.

"I'm aware of the problem," he acknowledged. "I drive this road all the time. The place looks like shit."

"Alright. I just need to take a look at your driver's license and then I'll let you get on your way."

"Yes, ma'am," he conceded in a defeated voice. He began digging through a red purse on the floor of the pickup, eventually coming up with a driver's license identifying him as a fifty-year-old man named Liam Foster.

I walked back to my squad with the driver's license and began to enter the information into my computer. As my fingers tapped the keys, I watched as Liam's truck tires spun in the rocks with a sudden burst of acceleration. It had only taken about twenty seconds for Liam to make the decision to run. The truck fishtailed as it tore out into the middle of the road and headed west.

Liam's run caught me off guard. I'd been in pursuits before, but only one other time did it start after I'd already made a traffic stop on the vehicle. The last time that had happened, the car I was chasing came to an abrupt stop only after it drove into the side of a deputy's squad placed in the road to block the driver's path. I hoped Liam wasn't willing to go to such extremes.

My sirens wailed as our vehicles moved past a crowd of people shooting at the wildlife area's gun range. Liam's truck bobbed and weaved over the grooves in the road. The gravel roads all over the county were in terrible condition. The spring rains followed by vehicle traffic gouged the surfaces, leaving ruts that caused my truck tires to get mired in the slop, pulling my squad violently from side to side. As I gripped the jerking wheel with one hand, I used the other to radio in my position and alert the dispatcher as to the driver's name and date of birth.

"Be advised, subject is 10-99 and listed as suicidal," the dispatcher calmly relayed. Learning that Liam had active warrants for his arrest wasn't surprising. Almost everyone who runs is running from a warrant.

"10-4. What's the warrant for?" There was no telling how desperate Liam would be to escape going to jail on his warrants. The fact that he was suicidal only made things that much worse. I began to plan my response to various scenarios while Liam was likely making plans of his own. I wondered if any of them involved suicide by cop.

"Looks like he has three warrants for possession of a controlled substance and carrying weapons. Multiple units are heading your way. Can you update your location?" the dispatcher said.

"I'm west of Falcon Avenue heading toward Hanging Rock Road," I began. "Wait. Looks like he's coming to a stop on the south side of the road. . . . He's bailing!" Before reaching the intersection with Hanging Rock Road, Liam flung the door open. No longer wearing the blond wig, he lurched down the embankment and ran into the woods.

"Stop! Liam, stop right there!" I shouted as I followed him several steps into the woods. Liam continued to sprint down the hill, tripping over downed trees, his arms pinwheeling in an effort to stay upright.

"Nooo!" His voice trailed into the woods accompanied by the crashing of bushes and the snap of sticks exploding under his pounding feet.

I stopped chasing Liam and walked back to his truck. The driver's side door was hanging open. A cell phone lay on the gravel outside the truck, and the cheap blond wig lay heaped on the floorboard. Two knives were attached by nylon webbing and black electrical tape to the inside of the driver's door. One knife was especially large, with a blade at least eight inches long. When carried concealed, as it was in the door, a large knife is considered a dangerous weapon. An aggravated misdemeanor.

"Cedar Rapids, C352," I called into dispatch.

"Go ahead C352."

"I'm waiting for backup. Subject is wearing a black shirt and blue jeans. Short black hair. He ran south into the woods toward the river, but I lost sight of him. Be advised two large knives are taped to the inside of the driver's door of his truck, so I don't know if he's armed. We'll need a K9."

"10-4. Units getting close." The sound of the dispatcher's voice calmed my adrenaline-jangled nerves. I peered into the woods, trying to make out any sign of Liam's presence, half expecting to hear the pop of a gunshot at any time. Whether directed at me or at himself, it was a sound I didn't want to hear.

Backup arrived in droves. Troopers from the state patrol and county sheriff's deputies, along with Jace. More conservation officers parked their squad cars in a long line on the side of the road bordering the area known as Hanging Rock. The officers spread out along the road at possible exit points in an attempt to set up a perimeter that would keep Liam from sneaking past us.

When Bary, a Belgian Malinois police K9 trained in tracking, arrived, we set off into the woods, Bary's nose leading the way. It didn't take long, however, to find out that we needn't have waited for the dog. We had only gone fifty yards into the woods when we heard a distant cry coming from somewhere out in the water: "Help me!" With Bary tugging at his lead toward the bank of the Iowa River, we paced through the timber, stopping now and then to listen for the direction of the shouting. The river was high, its flood waters spreading throughout the edge of the timber. The woods bordered an area that had been under construction for several years, progress slowed by permitting issues, bureaucratic red tape, and construction mishaps. A dike, constructed of haphazardly placed chunks of cement, separated the marsh-in-the-making from the flooded timber where the shouting seemed to come from.

While Bary and his handler walked out into the water, two state troopers, a field training officer and his rookie, accompanied me onto the dike. The unstable footing of the cement blocks made carrying our M16 rifles a challenge. I thought it would be a miracle if one of us didn't end up in the water ourselves. Liam, although he continued alternating between calling for help and cursing at us, still wasn't visible.

The rookie trooper shouted in the direction of Liam's voice, attempting to establish a line of communication. "We want to help you, Liam, but we need to know that you don't have any weapons!"

"Aaargggh!"

The trooper tried again. "Are you hurt?"

"Freeeeezing!"

"Okay—I know you're cold. We want to help—do you have any weapons?"

"Raaaaahh! Freeeezing!" Liam's roar emerged from somewhere in the trees ahead of us.

"Are you injured aside from being cold?" the trooper shouted.

"I'm in a fucking treeeee!"

The troopers glanced over at me and smiled. The rookie tried a different tactic. "We need you to climb out of the tree and come toward my voice!"

"I'm not getting back in the fucking water. I'm freezing! Can't move!"

"We want to help you, Liam—do you promise you don't have any weapons?" the rookie asked.

I couldn't help but poke fun at the rookie's line of questioning. "Maybe make him pinky promise just to be sure." I suggested. The FTO laughed.

"I don't have any weapons. When have I ever had weapons on me?" Liam cried out in agony.

"Well, you do have a giant knife strapped to the door of your car!" the rookie yelled.

"Better not poke the bear," the FTO advised.

"Yeah, but I'm sure he's unarmed. I mean, he *did* promise," I added.

Bary was shivering from the cold water when his partner finally decided to take him back to the squad. "I think I'm gonna call for fire and rescue—we need a boat of some kind," he said as he pulled Bary back to dry land.

"Sounds good. We might be able to get my johnboat into the water here.

But we might not be able to get it back out. Fire's boat will work better," I agreed.

"Better get an ambulance en route too. He might be getting hypothermic by now," one of the troopers suggested.

The troopers and I continued talking with Liam while we waited for the firefighters to arrive with their inflatable zodiac boat. Liam swore at us, begged for our help, and cried over his discomfort, while we tried to reassure him that more help was on the way.

By the time Fire and Rescue arrived with dry suits and a boat, Liam had been clinging to a tree for three hours. The officers on shore decided to try walking into the water with dry suits to determine exactly where Liam was located before launching the boat. I watched from the dike as Jace and a deputy each squeezed into banana-yellow dry suits, pulling the hoods tightly over their heads. They stepped into the cold water and waddled slowly through it in the direction of Liam's shouting. Eventually they were able to see Liam, well out into the water and halfway up a tree, hugging it like a koala. As the cold water crept past the necklines of their suits, they realized they wouldn't be able to reach him without a boat.

The newly arrived firefighters readied the zodiac on shore, filling it with equipment and removing the outboard motor, which was too big to use in the shallow entry. Two more officers volunteered to wear dry suits, and three more climbed into the boat. Liam was now four hours into his tree hugging, and he was not pleased. "What the fuck is taking so long?" he screamed. "I can't feel my fucking arms!"

The team of officers in dry suits pushed the zodiac, with the other officers aboard, toward Liam. When the water was too deep for the dry-suited officers, those in the boat pushed and pulled their way through the maze of trees to the one Liam was clinging to. Liam, resembling a pissed-off, wet cat, dropped into the boat when the officers pried him loose from the tree. They wrapped him in a blanket and everyone in the boat was slowly pushed back to shore by those in dry suits.

When they arrived back on dry land, a trooper and I led Liam, shivering and wet, to the open doors of a waiting ambulance. The trooper asked Liam if he had planned on hurting himself, or if he was merely trying to get away because of the warrants.

"No, I wasn't going to hurt myself. I was supposed to see my son tomorrow. I haven't seen him since Thanksgiving, and I just wanted to see him."

Liam gazed pathetically at his feet as we walked, shaking his head back and forth. "Running obviously wasn't a smart move."

Liam stripped out of his wet clothes in the ambulance and was transported to the hospital to be assessed by an emergency room doctor. It didn't take long for the doctor to determine that Liam wasn't hypothermic, and he was discharged back into our custody.

After the events of the day, from my first encounter with the wig-clad man, to the pursuit and eventual rescue, the ride to jail with Liam in my passenger seat was a bit awkward. We rode in silence for several minutes until Liam finally looked at me and softly said, "I'm sorry I made you drive so dangerous."

I shrugged. "It's alright."

"No, it's not. It was stupid."

We rode in silence the rest of the way to the jail. He shuffled into the booking room wearing baby blue hospital scrubs. As he placed his hands on the pale green wall to allow the jailer to pat him down, I turned and left. I was ready to go home.

The following day, indoors at the impound lot, a drug K9 sniffed the air around Liam's truck. The dog alerted on the vehicle, quickly sitting and looking at his handler for approval.

"Positive," the handler announced. "It's all yours."

Later, search warrant in hand, Conservation Officer Cole Parker and I meticulously searched Liam's truck. We sifted through four suitcases that were full of skimpy women's clothing, six wigs, multiple fake boobs, binders full of porn, and several sex toys. In the front pocket of his purse, I found four syringes containing methamphetamine. Cole came up with a couple tooter straws with drug residue lining the insides. The knife blade measured ten inches, meeting the concealed dangerous weapon definition.

"I feel kind of bad for the guy," I told Cole as we loaded Liam's possessions back into his truck. "I just wonder whether his problems with gender identity caused his problem with drugs, or if it was the other way around."

"No way to know," he replied. "But he'll start using again as soon as he gets out. That much is guaranteed. Meth is nasty stuff."

We bagged the evidence, labeled it, and after securing it into the evidence locker, returned to our trucks for the drive home.

The next day would be full of report writing. Reports were the punishment exacted on every officer who manages to get involved in anything exciting.

A month later, a mushroom hunter, searching for morels in the woods near Hanging Rock, happened upon a brown purse and a large jar. They were stashed in the cracks of the cement block dike, the same dike the trooper and I had stood on as we shouted back and forth with Liam. The purse, fake leather and cheap looking, contained baggies of crystal meth, and the jar held hundreds of used syringes. My thoughts immediately returned to Liam.

I hadn't noticed Liam carrying a purse or a jar the day he fled from me, but they had to be his. Liam must have grabbed them before bailing in his desperate escape. In my mind's eye, I imagined him driving, desperately stuffing the jar into the purse. I pictured him pulling over to the side of the road and exploding out of the truck, clutching the now apparent purse under his arm and sprinting away. I could see his face as he heard and then ignored my shouted commands to stop. I envisioned the thicket of trees and the watery underbrush as he fled toward the riverbank. And I imagined Liam as he stashed his mistakes and his addictions deep into the dike's crevice. I felt his panicked heartbeat as he thought of his son and plunged into the cold waves. I could once again hear his lonely voice: "Help me!"

FOR YEARS, the enforcement of restricted camping locations at Hawkeye had slid to the wayside, resulting in a wildlife area that resembled a state park campground without rules, fees, or latrines. When it came to camping time restrictions, the law was vague and peppered with loopholes big enough to drive an RV through. Most campers were savvy enough to figure out that, after the ten days were up, they need only vacate or alter their campsite location for twenty-four hours before moving right back to resume their stay.

One Friday afternoon the wildlife area staff alerted me to a group that had been camping along the river road for more than ten days. For years, this particular grassy spot, shaded by hickory trees along the riverbank, had been a popular place for both parties and camping. Catfish lurked just off the bank, in the deep holes of the river, making the location an appealing place to throw in a line late at night.

"They've been there for more than ten days," Dan Waits, the wildlife area manager told me over the phone. "And there's junk all over the place. Looks like they don't plan on leaving anytime soon."

"Okay, as long as you've recorded the first date you saw them and are sure they never left, Nate and I will go have a chat with them," I said. Nate, one of my summer seasonal officers, was always ready for excitement, but based on his slow drawl and "Ah shucks" personality, you'd never know it. He had a talent for engaging complete strangers in long sessions of small talk so that, by the time they'd finish talking, you'd think they were the best of friends. At least, that's what the stranger would think.

I turned my truck toward the south side of the wildlife area. It was three o'clock in the afternoon, but given the long daylight of midsummer, our shift was nowhere near finished. Friday nights in the summer were party nights, and any hope of getting home early was wishful thinking. Gravel dust hung heavy in the air as pickup trucks rumbled along the potholed road, transforming it from a wildlife area into its nighttime party alter ego, featuring booze, bonfires, drugs, and the occasional angler.

I turned west onto the border road and drove toward the camping spot Dan had described. Busch Light beer cans littered the ditches, and tire tracks zigzagged off the road and through the muddy fields, where they taunted me with their donut circles and deep ruts. Off-roading trucks left these footprints like an elusive Sasquatch that I was perpetually too late to catch. Gunshots popped and echoed from the rifle range across the river, and white sulphur butterflies flitted over my truck, dancing their way to the coneflowers in the restored prairie to my left.

When we arrived at the camp, I understood why Dan believed the occupants were there to stay. Vehicles, trailers, campers, tents, and a small hunting blind were spread across the length of the bank. Beer cans littered the ground like aluminum diamonds, glittering when their silver surfaces caught the sunlight. Plastic bags containing canned food and other supplies were scattered about haphazardly. Garments hung from makeshift clotheslines strung between trees. Smoke drifted in a thin line from a campfire ring constructed with a tire rim and wafted over the faces of the five people who sat in chairs nearby. A tan Buick sedan wearing a spare tire, a rusty black pickup, and a green SUV were parked on the scorched grass near an empty flatbed trailer.

"You wanna hop out and talk with them for a second while I run these plates?" I asked Nate.

Nate yawned. "Sure. I'll see what they're up to." Nate always seemed on the verge of falling asleep. He climbed out of the truck and ambled slowly over to the campfire. I jotted down the plate numbers and called them in to dispatch.

"The female registered owner of the Buick is 99," the dispatcher said, indicating that a woman named Sue Arnold had a warrant for her arrest.

"Where is the warrant from?"

"Looks like it's federal out of Linn County with nationwide pickup."

"Really?" I asked, peering at a woman, presumably Sue, through my windshield. Sue, sitting on a chair in front of the fire, looked far from threatening. She appeared to be in her late sixties with stringy gray hair piled onto the top of her head in a messy bun, a cigarette dangling from her lips. She wore shorts, sandals, and a low-cut tank top without a bra, her tattooed cleavage swinging freely.

"I'll verify it for you," the dispatcher said.

I stepped out of my truck and walked toward the gathering. Nate was immersed in a conversation with Sue. When he glanced over his shoulder at me, his face betrayed a look of amusement. It wasn't the first time he had sent his "What the fuck" look my way.

"Well, Sue says they're just on a little vacation," Nate said by way of introduction.

"Alright. So, how long have you been here, you think?" I asked the group.

Sue looked at the middle-aged man seated next to her. "When did we come here, Dennis? Maybe a couple weeks ago?" Dennis squinted as he pondered the question. A look of confused concentration formed a worry line in the center of his forehead that reached toward his thinning gray hair. His brown t-shirt was stained with a week's worth of campfire smoke and ketchup.

He took a sip of beer before mumbling, "Yeah, I s'pose it's been a couple weeks. Problem with that?"

"Yeah, I'm afraid so. You can't stay for more than ten days at a time, and I know you've been here longer than that. Do you folks have some driver's licenses I could take a look at?"

Dennis looked at an old woman sitting across from him. The woman looked to be at least eighty years old. She sat in her chair and gazed vacantly into the distance without acknowledging our presence. An old man next to her coughed up a loogie and spit it into the fire.

"Those are my parents," Sue said, indicating the old couple with a nod of her head. "I don't think they have their licenses with them." The old folks sat motionless in their chairs, staring blankly toward the river as it pushed downstream.

Sue nodded toward a green tent, set back from the campfire. "My license is in my purse inside the tent."

"Okay, if you don't mind grabbing it, I'd like to take a peek." I stepped over a pile of empty beer cans and followed her to the tent. Outside the front flap of the tent, on top of a pile of sleeping bags, lay a small brown dog. For a moment it appeared to be dead. Flies buzzed around its half-closed eyes, which were covered in a green, crusty secretion. The dog looked like a skeleton. Its rib cage was visible and didn't appear to be moving.

"Is your dog alright?" I asked, looking for signs of life.

"Oh, she's just fine. Aren't you pooky, baby? She's just getting a little old." Sue picked up the dog, rousing it from its deathbed.

"It looks like there's something wrong with her eyes."

"Yeah. She has some kind of infection, I think." Sue planted a kiss on the dog's short snout. "My purse is in here somewhere. It just might take me a minute to find it."

I held the door of the tent open as Sue climbed inside and began tossing things out of the door onto the ground next to my feet. The dog lumbered with a sideways slow-motion gait toward the campfire as though the infection had compromised its balance.

As I stood waiting for Sue, I noticed an empty bird cage on the ground next to the tent. "What's the cage for?"

"Oh, that's just for my pigeon, Betty. She's around here somewhere. She never goes too far from her mommy." I glanced around the campsite and noticed a white pigeon walking around near the flatbed trailer.

"So you have two birds here?" I asked.

"No. Just Betty. Oh, I mean she thinks I'm her mommy," Sue clarified. "Ah, here it is." Sue stepped from the tent clutching her purse and rummaged through it looking for her driver's license.

"Thanks. I'm just going to check something, and I'll be right back," I said and walked back to my truck with her license in hand. I called the dispatcher back and asked about the status of Sue's warrant.

"Yep. It's a valid warrant. From what I can tell this lady was supposed to appear in trial and didn't show up. No bond."

"Sounds good. It's going to be a little while, though. I've got to find a sober driver and figure out what to do about all their camping stuff," I said, "like her pigeon."

"Her what?" the dispatcher asked.

"Never mind. Long story."

I returned to the campfire and told Sue that she had an active arrest warrant.

Sue's face screwed up in confusion. She began talking at a clip. "I thought that was all taken care of. I talked to Tim, the federal marshal, and he gave me a subpoena to testify in federal court. But I told him that I couldn't be there that day."

"What do you mean, you couldn't be there?" I asked.

"I mean I told them that I wasn't available to go to court that day. I left a voicemail that I couldn't be there until the twenty-eighth."

"Why couldn't you be there?"

"Well, because I was going to be here." Sue spoke as if the answer should have been obvious to me.

"Yeah. Well, I don't think camping at Hawkeye is probably a valid reason for not appearing in court."

"Oh. I see," she said slowly.

"What's the trial for?"

"He didn't really explain all that. I'm not exactly sure."

"You're a witness in a federal trial but you don't know what the trial is about?"

"Not really. I don't really know," she said. "But if I have to go to jail, I'm going to need to take my bag. It has all my medication in it." Sue opened her purse and began pulling out prescription bottles and tossing them onto the grass into a growing pile. "This one is for my cancer. Then there's this one for the seizures from the cancer. And I take this one for my heart. And I need this one for the sores I get on my foot. Sometimes I take this one for anxiety and depression. It helps calm my nerves," she explained, glancing at me. The pile of pill bottles collapsed and spread out onto the dirt.

"Okay, you can pack all that back into your purse," I instructed. "I don't know anything about your court situation other than you have a warrant. So, I'm going to have to take you in to jail to get it all sorted out." I turned back to the group. "The rest of you will need to pack up all your stuff and leave. You've been camping here too long. Who's going to be responsible for cleaning everything up?"

Dennis slowly stood up from the lawn chair. "I'll take care of it," he said. Dennis handed his driver's license to Nate, then began walking toward the black pickup. Sue's parents sat motionless by the fire as though they hadn't heard any of the conversation. Sue began digging through her purse again and handed me a pile of paperwork. "That's for my car," she said. "It had been reported stolen. But then they stopped me the other night and said that the car was stolen, and I said, 'No,' and then what happened was that they didn't take it off the stolen list because it had been recovered. So, that was another thing."

"You mean the car was stolen from you?"

"Yes, and the person that stole it wiped out my checking account and stole my jewelry. They hawked it in a pawn shop and didn't tell me. And like I said, I talked to the marshal, and he told me to meet him at the gas station in West Liberty and then he give me these papers to testify in federal court."

I sensed the conversation was beginning to spiral again, so I asked, "In federal court for what?"

"Against somebody. It wasn't all explained exactly. He said it was about a conversation we had about a month ago for an hour and a half."

I sometimes wondered how some people survived in the world on their own. "You have no idea why you were going to testify in federal court?"

"I kind of do, but there is so much that has been going on that—" she began.

"She's not supposed to talk about it," Dennis interrupted.

"Ah, gotcha," I said, relinquishing any effort at understanding Sue's confusing story. "Well, we need to get going to jail. I assume you aren't going to try anything bad if I handcuff you in the front, right?"

"Ha," Sue chuckled. "The worst thing I'll do is talk your ear off."

I clicked the handcuffs around Sue's wrists and started to guide her toward my truck when she noticed her bird. Betty, her white feathers contrasting against the shadowed grass, was still pecking and bobbing her way around the empty trailer.

"Can I put Betty away before we go? She'll only come to me," Sue begged.

"Alright," I said, assuming she would only need to call for Betty. Instead, Sue spent the next fifteen minutes crawling around the trailer, hands cuffed together and cooing to the bird. She pleaded with Betty to come to her like a good baby, but Betty, apparently enjoying her spell of freedom, was having none of it. The white bird repeatedly ducked and darted away from Sue, escaping to the opposite side of the trailer in a never-ending game of tag. I glanced at Nate who was watching the wild pigeon chase play out with obvious pleasure.

"Do you need some help?" I asked.

"No," Sue said. "Like I said, she only comes to me."

Eventually, Betty, tired of the chase, allowed Sue to cup her feathered body in her handcuffed hands and return her to the cage. An image of Sue's cage awaiting her at the county jail flashed through my mind, and I felt a rush of pity for her. Her life, at some point, had begun to unspool like a tangled wad of fishing line. It appeared that she was caught in a web of poor finances, troubling friendships, health problems, and a strange and an unexplainable plight with the law. I knew from experience, however, that her situation wasn't unique. I encountered the same story week after week as I patrolled my territory. The only thing that changed was the cast of characters and the bit parts they played in the production of their own lives. Those ensnared in chaotic lives sometimes seek refuge in wild places.

Finally, it appeared as though Sue was ready to leave. "Okay, let's get going," I said.

"Dennis," Sue called over her shoulder, "do you mind taking care of Fanny until I get back?"

"Alright," Dennis answered in his apathetic monotone. "I'll watch her, I guess."

"Who's Fanny?" I asked.

"Oh. She's my tarantula," Sue said nonchalantly. "She's in her cage in the tent."

Nate's smile widened as we climbed into the truck.

Later that afternoon, Nate and I returned to Sue's campsite to make sure Dennis had picked up all their belongings. The tents, clotheslines, beer cans, and vehicles were gone. Overall, it was better than I imagined it would be—except for the five-gallon bucket. The white bucket sat alone on the patch of ground where the hunting blind had been situated earlier. Distracted by the pigeon, the half-dead dog, and the tarantula, I'd forgotten to ask why they had set up the blind in the first place. I walked toward the bucket, already knowing enough to dread what I'd find inside. And sure enough, the container was half-full of human excrement and used toilet paper. The hunting blind had been the outhouse.

"Let's go pay Dennis a visit," I said. "He forgot the shit can."

"I'd say that the rest of the two weeks' worth of shit went directly into the river," Nate speculated.

"Sounds about right."

Dennis lived in a small house accessed by a long grassy lane surrounded by hay fields. His black truck was parked under a tree fifty yards from the house. A fleece blanket depicting a bald eagle flying over a mountain covered the front window. Pieces of cardboard covered the rest of the windows. Were it not for the truck, the place would have seemed to be abandoned. Patchy, peeling paint covered the house's weathered siding. Lacking a front porch, cinder blocks had been stacked as makeshift steps leading to the door.

"Is it just me, or do you have a bad feeling about this?" I asked Nate.

"I don't have warm fuzzies," Nate said, his face straight. "That Dennis dude was weird. Did you hear how he talked?"

"Yeah. And now I'm a little scared to get out of the truck." I imagined Dennis stepping out of the house with a rifle. "Nobody would ever find us back here."

"Yeah. And all for a shit bucket," Nate said bluntly.

"Alright," I said "You stay here in case you need to use the radio to call for help. I'll go knock."

"Okay," Nate replied all too quickly.

I parked behind the black truck and slowly approached the front door. I stepped onto the first set of cinder blocks and almost lost my balance as they wobbled under my weight. I knocked three times and then tactically stepped back down off the blocks to wait. No answer. I glanced back at Nate and shrugged. He shrugged back. Just as I stepped back up onto the cinder block and raised my fist to knock again, Dennis opened the door.

"Sorry," Dennis said, "my mom is watching TV, and I wasn't sure if someone was knocking or not."

"It's okay. Do you mind stepping out here for a minute?" I heard the truck door close and Nate's footsteps approaching from behind me. Dennis came outside and walked to a nearby lawn chair.

"The reason we're here is because you didn't completely clear out the campsite," I said.

"What do you mean?" he asked. "I took all my stuff."

"What about the bucket?"

"That's not mine. I mean I've been driving it back here to dump it every couple of days, just to be nice, but it's not mine."

"You said that you would take responsibility for the campsite," I reminded him. "And besides, the hunting-blind bathroom was yours right?"

"Yeah, the blind is mine, but Sue and her parents put the bucket in there, I didn't," he said. "The bucket definitely wasn't mine."

"Well, I'm going to issue a citation, and you'll need to go back and pick up the bucket. Just make sure it doesn't get dumped into the river."

Dennis sighed resignedly and nodded his head. "Alright. I'll pick it up."

I went back to my truck to write out the citation while Nate sat down in a lawn chair near Dennis and began chatting with him about the nearby garden. Every once in a while I glanced up from my paperwork to check on Nate. He was doing what he did best, distracting people from impending tickets with inane conversation. Nate had leaned back in his lawn chair and began chuckling about something when a gray and black cat strolled over and began twisting through Nate's legs in a figure eight. It rubbed its neck against his shins with a look of pure pleasure.

By the time I finished writing the ticket, the cat was curled up in Nate's lap purring under his constant petting. Dennis was proudly giving Nate advice about the best way to stop deer from eating his sweetcorn and the best time to plant tomatoes. Nate's banter and constant questions had the effect of stroking Dennis's ego just as his stroking had lulled the cat into falling asleep on his lap.

I walked back to Nate and Dennis, attempting to maintain the light-hearted mood Nate had so carefully cultured. "Thanks for your cooperation with this," I said before explaining the details of the citation. I found myself in the familiar position of commiserating with the person I was citing, so I tried to reassure him. "I understand where you're coming from when you say it isn't your bucket. It's too bad they left you with it when they knew you were responsible for the campsite."

Dennis nodded his head and grumbled over his apparent bad luck in meeting Sue and her family in the first place. "I just met them a couple weeks ago. I was camped in that spot first, and then they showed up and set up camp right next to me. Just thought I'd be nice ya know, so I let 'em stay without complaining about it." Dennis's head tipped upward with an air of nobility. "And now her parents are gonna be camping out in my yard here until we get Sue bailed out of jail."

"Well, that's nice of you to let them stay," I said.

Nate, anxious to change the subject and return to the truck, said, "Well, it was really nice talking to you. And your cat sure is friendly, too."

"Yeah," Dennis turned to Nate. "My mother lives with me here. She finally kicked the cats all out of the house when we figured out that they're covered in fleas. Now the damn fleas are all over the house."

Nate leapt from his chair in a move faster than any I'd seen him make all summer. The cat, rudely awakened, launched from his lap and scurried beneath the house.

"Ha!" Nate said nervously as he began speed walking toward the truck. "We'll see you later then."

As we drove back down the grassy lane, I handed Nate a bottle of hand sanitizer. "I think we'll take a little break so you can hit the shower."

Nate scratched the back of his neck. Then he scratched his legs. And his arms. "Yeah. Good idea." He was quiet the whole ride back, concentrating on each new itch with intensity.

— BECOMING —

"You can't assume anything, even what seems most logical. A supposedly simple case of drunk driving made the front page of a paper in Australia. The report stated that the offender's eyes were bloodshot. 'Both of them?' asked the defense attorney. Looking at the now clear-eyed defendant, the officer said firmly, 'Yes both of them,' whereupon the defendant removed his clear artificial eye and rolled it on the table. Case dismissed."

—Larry S. Miller and John T. Whitehead,
Report Writing for Criminal Justice Professionals, Fourth Edition

I'M IN THE HOMESTRETCH of my career. Twelve years left if I'm lucky. Things are different now than they were that sweltering July day when a badge was pinned onto my chest. Where I completely lacked confidence, I've now found some. Where I was once single, childless, and adventurous, I'm now married with two children and lean toward cautiousness. My duty belt is bigger, my stamina shorter. The older I get, the more I tend to think about the big picture and whether I've accomplished the goals of a conservation law enforcement officer as Jordan Fisher Smith described them: to protect the land from the people, the people from the land, and the people from each other. My answer is that over the last twenty years I've not been perfect, but I've gotten the hang of a few things and learned some valuable lessons.

Nobody warned me as a new officer how difficult it would be to make the best use of officer discretion. The decision whether to cite someone for a violation isn't always as easy as it may seem. To some, the world is a black-and-white place—a violation either calls for a citation or it isn't a violation. But from my perspective things aren't so simple. It took me time to learn that, in the name of educating the public, it's sometimes best to look further than minor violations or honest mistakes. Issuing citations or making arrests isn't always the answer to gaining compliance, although sometimes it's the only answer. Parsing out when it's best to lecture and warn, when to put pen to paper (or in my case, fingers to keyboard) to scratch out a ticket, or when to cuff and take to jail has been a craft that came with a learning curve. In the end, I'm guided by a rule of thumb: I'd rather go home regretting not issuing a ticket than regretting issuing one.

This job has taught me that almost everyone has a story to tell and that almost everyone is struggling with something that they probably won't divulge to me. It's my job to listen to the stories, to consider what people aren't telling me, and to determine not only what is true but why it is true.

My son once asked me which superhero I would be if I could choose just one. I would be Wonder Woman. It would be great to look presentable in a patriotic bikini, but what I really want is Wonder Woman's weapon of choice: the golden lasso of truth. My tendency to believe the stories people tell me has not always served me well as a law enforcement officer. It's in my nature to want to believe that, in general, humankind is both good and honest. But after twenty years of being on the receiving end of countless lies and witnessing people shirk responsibility for their mistakes, I'm less trusting than I used to be. My job would be much easier if only I could sling that lasso of truth around every storyteller I encounter. Instead, I strive to be a sympathetic listener and to maintain an open mind, while simultaneously preserving a skeptical distance and a prudent perspective.

My skin has gotten thicker during the course of my career. I've been called many things worse than "sir." There have been times I was yelled at and berated for merely doing my job. I've been spit on, threatened, and ridiculed. Some have filed complaints against me. Others have harassed me. One person even followed me home to give me a piece of his mind and to then threateningly remind me that he knew where I lived. My skin has gotten thicker, but it isn't impervious. I'm still working on that.

Finally, I've come to the conclusion that, despite my general lack of confidence in most matters, my years of experience as a learner in this career have given me the ability to occasionally shift into the role of a teacher.

After the boating accident that decapitated the young girl on the reservoir years ago, I became an aggressive enforcer of our state's boating while intoxicated laws. Now I'm part of a team that teaches our new officers, as well as those of other agencies, how to detect, test, and arrest drunk drivers. I don't ever again want to see a youngster fall victim to one on my watch.

Given my nerdy tendencies, I also train our department in report writing. Though it is often viewed as one of the most despised duties of a law enforcement officer, writing good narrative reports is also one of the most invaluable skills an officer can possess. A report can make or break a case. Recruits and seasonal officers are forced to spend the day with me learning about things like writing in complete sentences and how to use the past tense and active voice. The officers must practice how to make a narrative report objective, concise, and understandable, skills that don't come easily for many.

My teaching doesn't always focus on the technical. Sometimes it means doing something as simple as taking the time to ignore my introverted tendencies and chat with someone about the flock of migrating pelicans flashing in the sky, twisting in their mysterious loops overhead. Or pointing out to an angler fishing from the bank nearby a snake sliding through the water with a half-swallowed bluegill. Or sitting down and really listening to the questions and concerns of a wildlife area user.

During most spring and fall semesters, I volunteer to lead an after-school program I initiated for elementary-school-aged kids that I call "Wild Things." The thrust of the program is simply to get kids outdoors. When I am with the Wild Things I can forget my uniform and ticket book at home and once again see our natural world through the eyes of a kid. I, too, immerse myself in nature and experience once again what it means to be a child of this earth.

Finally, every year I'm presented with the challenge of guiding my seasonal officers through the craziness of a summer on the water. For many, it is their first time experiencing a job in the law enforcement field. Therefore, it's their first time deciphering when to write a ticket and when to give a warning. It's their first time seeing the gore of a horrific accident. It's their first time trying to focus on the job at hand while getting berated by an angry or intoxicated person. And it is their first time getting called to the stand to swear to tell the truth, the whole truth, and nothing but the truth.

Each season as the summer draws to a close and some of the seasonal officers move on to full-time employment, I share the same sense of satisfaction that I imagine a veteran teacher does when she watches her former students find their way in the real world. Witnessing the seasonal officers as they fledge the nest is a satisfying experience, and I admit to feeling proud of their work. When I send recommendation letters off to their potential future employers, I feel that maybe, just maybe, I've been an adequate teacher. And an adequate conservation officer.

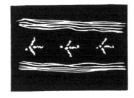

"WHAT DO YOU THINK made this track?" I asked, pointing to the ground. The spring temperatures had finally begun to warm, but snow was still visible in shady patches along the edge of the woods where we walked.

The group of kids huddled near me, their legs already muddy from trudging along the thawing trail. They peered at the ground where I pointed. There, imprinted in a patch of snow, was a series of tracks. Each stride had three long toes pointing forward, and one short one behind. The tracks appeared in a line for a short distance, flanked by two drag marks, one along each side of the foot tracks. The kids and I followed the line through the snow until the tracks veered off from the straight path and began what appeared to be a back-and-forth pacing pattern.

"Looks like mini T. rex tracks," a young red-headed boy said. This answer brought a barrage of comments, some affirming his observation and the cold hard truth of extinction from the rest.

"Actually, the animal that made this track is related to dinosaurs. But look at these strange marks to the side of the tracks. What do you think made those?" I asked.

Suddenly, I noticed a spark of recognition in the eyes of a little girl. "They look like feather marks!" she shouted.

"That's right! Can you think of a bird that goes like this in the springtime?" With arms akimbo, squatting low to the ground, I acted out my best imitation of a tom turkey in strut, the tips of my wings dragging along the ground, accompanied by a poor rendition of a gobble. The kids erupted in giggles. When they finally recognized my charade as a wild turkey, I asked if they knew what happened among turkeys every spring.

"They get married!" the first boy said triumphantly.

"Close enough," I laughed. "Let's keep hiking."

We continued down the trail and through the woods to the edge of the reservoir. There they spent the rest of the afternoon skipping rocks and exploring the shoreline.

"Where are we going next week?" a girl asked as I watched the kids play.

"Haven't decided yet," I said, "but it will be somewhere cool."

Once a week the Wild Things and I pile into a big van and head out to explore nearby wild areas. For a couple of hours, these kids build forts, explore, catch grasshoppers, creek-stomp, pretend, climb trees, and chase frogs. They generally act like kids are supposed to act when they are set free in nature, free from screens and free from parental rules. They are allowed to get dirty and wet.

Childhood isn't what it used to be. Today it's organized almost down to the minute, removing any sense of personal control children might have over their own time and lives. Rarely are kids allowed to stray beyond a parent's sight, preventing them from imagining themselves as sentries to their own personal Edens, as I did when I was young. For a large percentage of children today, natural areas are no longer viewed as safe places for unstructured free play. As a result, some kids (and adults) feel a level of discomfort when they arrive in a wild place with no plan or purpose.

It doesn't matter to me whether the kids who participate in Wild Things someday become hunters or anglers duly paying their license fees. My hope is that the girl who arrived on the first day afraid to get her feet wet will leave on the last day loving the way the sand of a creek bed feels between her toes. I want the boy who obediently looked at me the first day waiting for precise instructions about how to fill his free time in the woods to spend the last day immersed in his own imagination as he stomps through the trees like a great grizzly bear. Mostly, I want the children to know what it feels like to be connected to a place. Because if our children can appreciate how amazing it is to reach down and pluck a three-hundred-million-year-old fossil from this remnant of an ancient sea, then I know there is still hope.

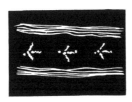

THE BODY OF THE drowned fisherman floated to the surface on the afternoon of the third day. He was found twenty feet from shore, caught up in the submerged and tangled branches of a fallen oak tree. Conservation Officer Cole Parker and I stood on shore and watched as Park Ranger Jace Travers knelt at the front of a boat, leaned over the edge, and pushed at the body with a paddle as he struggled to free it from the tree's grasp. With one final jab, the body floated free, hovering on the surface of the water like a raft, tilting like a rolling log. As the body rotated, a pistol, still holstered at the hip, appeared above the waterline. Despite the rough trip through the churning waters of the low head dam, the holster had held the gun tightly. Jace removed the gun from the holster and secured it in his boat before hooking a carabiner and rope through the belt loop of the dead man's Levi's. The officers working with Jace were unable to load the bloated body into the boat, so they decided instead to pull it to a nearby boat ramp.

Cole and I drove to the ramp and waited for the boat pulling the body to arrive. As we stood on the riverbank, waiting, we didn't talk. With Cole, I didn't need to talk. I'd known him since he worked as a seasonal patrol officer on the Coralville Reservoir ten years before. He'd been there, his first weekend on the job, the day the twelve-year-old girl had been killed. Despite that rocky start, Cole returned for duty the following two summers. Later, he was hired as a police officer for a city in my territory and then as a full-time conservation officer.

Cole's appearance hasn't changed in the last decade. His jet-black hair, combined with his skin's tendency to tan to a rich brown in the summer sun, had always led boaters to mistakenly assume he was of Hispanic descent. Now thirty-two years of age, his thin build hasn't changed either. It's always been maddening to me that he can eat like a horse without gaining an ounce.

When I was Cole's overseeing officer I took the time to listen to his softly spoken words. I quickly learned that, though quiet, he was sharp and had a gift of empathy that ran deeper than most. While I may have started out as Cole's teacher, by the time he was hired as a conservation officer, rife with his experience as a cop, we'd ended up equal colleagues and friends.

The boat pulling the body approached shore, and Jace tossed the end of the rope to Cole. Together, we reeled the dead fisherman in to shore. He floated facedown, his white t-shirt stained brown with dirty river water, his thin gray hair plastered wet against the back of his head.

Cole and I unfolded the black plastic body bag and laid it on the ground. We tugged at the body, gripping the wet clothing with gloved hands, until it was aligned next to the bag. With the body still face down on the rocky shoreline, Cole unhooked the carabiner from the belt loop, and we began to roll the fisherman onto his back. I held my breath in anticipation of the stench and the sight of the man's face.

A body that has been exposed to warm river water for three Iowa summer days becomes almost unrecognizable. Besides the gases that bloat the body cavity and allow it to float, human skin turns white and sloughs off the body in sheets. I tried to force myself to look away from the fisherman's face as Cole grabbed the man's sleeve to roll him over, but despite my self-orders, I couldn't look away.

Once he was in the body bag, it became evident that rigor mortis was holding the fisherman's right arm outstretched and bent in front of him, as if he were blocking a punch. It was going to make zipping the bag a problem. I tugged down on the top zipper, holding my breath, and tried to force it over his bent arm. On the other end, a park ranger simultaneously pulled on the bottom zipper, trying to work it over the man's bent knees. Finally, after failing to budge the zipper past the arm, Cole reached over, gripped the white puffy skin of the man's forearm, and forced it down. Cole's hand slipped slightly on the pasty skin, almost causing him to lose his balance and pitch himself over the body, but he managed to stop the fall. Finally, the zipper could move freely.

We lifted the closed body bag and moved it further up on shore to await the arrival of the medical examiner. While Cole and I stood next to his truck, talking quietly about our plans for the rest of the day, iridescent green blowflies homed in on the surface of the black bag. Soon, flies covered the bag in droves, eager to carry out their role in nature's decomposition process. The bag frustrated the insects' attempts to lay their eggs in the perfect substrate.

The medical examiner and the rescue crew arrived. They picked up the body bag, sending the flies buzzing in a flurry, and loaded it into the back of the ambulance to take the necessary photographs in relative privacy.

Cole and I bid each other goodbye and headed off in different directions for the remainder of the day. But ten minutes later, I called him on the phone.

"That was bad, wasn't it?" I asked, hoping that I wasn't alone in my unease with handling the body, given its state of decomposition.

"Yeah. That was bad," he agreed.

"I'm glad you got his arm into the bag. You saved me from having to touch it."

"I didn't want to touch it, either, but it was the only way to get it zipped."

"Well, thanks anyway."

We changed the subject and spoke for a few more minutes before hanging up. As I continued on toward home I thought about the accident I'd witnessed years before with young Cole at my side. The sight of that young girl had been worse—it had haunted me for weeks.

The following day I wrote an incident report about the recovery of the drowned fisherman's body. The sterile words describing the incident flowed from my fingertips onto the computer screen. The tedium of the police report washed the gruesome scene clean, as though wiping the event itself with an antiseptic cloth. I finished the report with the same sentence I've been lucky enough to use in hundreds of reports over the last twenty years: "At 1415 hrs I returned to service."